JOSÉPHINE:

Napoléon's Incomparable Empress

JOSÉPHINE:
Napoléon's Incomparable Empress

E L E A N O R   P .   D E L O R M E

With a foreword by Bernard Chevallier

HARRY N. ABRAMS, INC., PUBLISHERS

ACKNOWLEDGMENTS

The present volume represents a condensation of a much longer account of Joséphine's life and times. Its aim was to present a full and copiously illustrated picture of her improbable life, replete with the military campaigns that so largely determined it. In the interests of practicality, however, it has been radically pruned to a manageable length. This daunting task was assumed by my matchless editor at Abrams, Barbara Burn, to whom I shall ever be indebted and who deserves a decoration—even the *ruban rouge*. Nor would it have ever come to fruition without my astute Boston editor, Charles Pearson DeLorme, who has contributed so much toward shaping it and whose eagle eye, *mots justes*, and felicitous turns of phrase have enhanced it immeasurably.

I am also grateful to the book's designer Joel Avirom and his staff for its elegant appearance. A special note of gratitude to Bernard Chevallier for his excellent preface, his perennial hospitality at Malmaison, his encouragement for this enterprise, and his unparalleled expertise in any and everything that pertains to Joséphine.

Our profound thanks to His Majesty the King of Sweden, Carl XVI Gustaf, for lending an indispensable image, and to Leif and Elisabeth Alsheimer who made it possible. In Paris, my dear friends Jacques and Arline Blumenthal made an invaluable contribution; and I also thank Diane Baude and Claire Poirion.

Plaudits to the gifted artist James Steinmayer for his exquisite watercolors. For their generous help in procuring or lending images, I gratefully acknowledge the assistance of Alan Salz, Richard L. Feigen, Jeff Bailey, Peter Mitchell, Philip Mansel, Angela Brown Fischer, and Peter Harrington, Curator of the Ann S. K. Brown Military Collection; as well as Colombe de Meurin of Photos12 in Paris.

At Wellesley College, thanks go to my revered colleague Professor Eugene Cox, who bravely plowed through the unabridged version for historical accuracy, although any errors that may appear are, of course, my own. I am also grateful to Jeanne Hablanian, Judith Black, Jarlath Waldron, and James C. Turbert for valued photographic assistance. And for their delightful company through many hours of travel, thanks to Nancy Keith, Brooks Lobkowicz, and Barbara Glauber.

In memoriam, my father, my valued friend Ann S. K. Brown, and my mentors, Howard C. Rice and Jean Feray, Inspecteur Principal des Monuments Historiques de la France.

On a personal note, a salute to my patient husband, Dr. Thomas DeLorme, and our three sons, who have had to live for so many years under the gigantic shadow cast by "the Little Corporal." It is to them, and to my *frère français*, Roger Prigent, that this book is lovingly dedicated.

Editor: Barbara Burn
Designer: Joel Avirom
Design Assistants: Jason Snyder and Meghan Day Healey
Production Coordinator: Maria Pia Gramaglia

Library of Congress Cataloging-in-Publication Data

DeLorme, Eleanor P.
 Joséphine : Napoléon's incomparable empress / Eleanor P. DeLorme ; foreword by Bernard Chevallier.
   p. cm.
Includes bibliographical references and index.
 ISBN 0-8109-1229-5
 1. Josephine, Empress, consort of Napoleon I, Emperor of the French, 1763-1814. 2. Empresses—France—Biography. 3. Napoleon I, Emperor of the French, 1769-1821—Relations with women. 4. France—History—Consulate and Empire, 1799-1815. I. Title.
DC216.1 .D45 2002
944.05′092—dc21

2002005143

Harry N. Abrams, Inc.
100 Fifth Avenue
New York, N.Y. 10011
www.abramsbooks.com

Abrams is a subsidiary of

LA MARTINIÈRE
GROUPE

PAGE I: *Antoine Gros (1771–1835), Empress Joséphine (Musée Masséna, Nice). Joséphine was Gros's first patroness, and in 1809 he executed several portraits of her. Here she wears a dress made from a cashmere shawl with a border of pines along the hem, with another shawl wound around her waist and draped over her shoulder. Beside her stands a bust of Eugène, and on the table sits a vase of hortensias (hydrangeas), named for her daughter.*

PAGE II: *Jacques-Louis David (1748–1825), The Coronation (detail) (Musée du Louvre). For this significant commission, the Neoclassicist David arranged his figures as a frieze across the picture plane. Dominating the center, Joséphine and Napoléon are united by the color of their splendid costumes and by their gestures. Hortense, who holds the hand of her son Napoléon-Charles, is the fourth woman from the left, and Eugène, who rests his hand on his saber, can be seen in profile at the far right.*

CONTENTS

PREFACE

$\mathcal{A}$s a true friend of our country, Eleanor DeLorme cheerfully confides: "I suffer from a serious malady: I was born in love with France." In her passion she does not fail to include her deep respect for the exceptional figure of Empress Joséphine, the subject of this biography. Until now, it has never been sufficiently emphasized that Joséphine was a woman of the eighteenth century; there was a difference of only eight years between her age and that of Marie-Antoinette, and Joséphine had already lived half her life at the time the Bastille was stormed in 1789. She occupied the forefront of the international scene for only eighteen years, but she left an indelible mark on history—as the wife of General Bonaparte from 1796 to 1799, as wife of the first consul until 1804, and as empress of the French and queen of Italy until 1809. The hour of her retreat began in December of that year, and until her death in 1814 she would be called Her Majesty Empress Joséphine, to distinguish her from Marie-Louise of Austria, the new empress of the French and queen of Italy.

Having been born into the aristocratic milieu of the ancien régime, Joséphine obtained an education that enabled her to slip with disconcerting ease into the role of empress and to leave behind, forgotten, the somewhat troubling past of the widow Beauharnais. Even before she was able to avail herself of the considerable financial means attached to her position, Joséphine revealed a true passion for the arts and natural sciences. Following in the footsteps of Marie-Antoinette, she dedicated herself to playing the role of patron, and she managed to stamp the imprint of her own sensibilities on her epoch, not only on the Neoclassical interior design that we refer to as "Empire," but also in the area of collecting. Although she was interested primarily in the old masters at first, she soon became a dedicated supporter of contemporary painting as she collected (and commissioned) the works of living

Pierre Paul Prud'hon, Empress Joséphine (Musée du Louvre). Although this painting was begun in 1805, after Joséphine became empress, Prud'hon chose not to present her in court costume, as Gérard did, but seated upon a rock formation in her garden, wearing a filmy gown of scandalously expensive material sprinkled with gold paillettes. No jewelry interrupts the graceful lines of her shapely arms, but three gilt chains mark the high waist and reappear as gleaming bands in her dark hair. The trees are silhouetted against a velvety twilight, appropriate to her pensive mood.

artists. Joséphine developed a taste for what is today known as "troubadour painting," a style inspired by the Gothic period and the Renaissance in France. Joséphine's gallery at her château at Malmaison is an impressive survey of French cultural history, prefiguring by thirty years the historical galleries of Louis-Philippe at Versailles. Significantly, Joséphine made her important purchases not just to support the arts, but because she truly loved painting, of which she had a deep understanding, having learned to evaluate a canvas and to recognize the qualities of a master.

Botany, however, was arguably the greatest of Joséphine's passions. At first her interest in natural history involved the acquisition of rare species of animals and birds, such as black swans, of which no other examples existed in Europe. Joséphine quickly expanded her curiosity into an unrestrained quest for new botanical specimens. She possessed a high degree of the methodical scientific spirit that characterizes the true botanist; she knew from memory the scientific names of all the plants in her hothouses and could describe their origins and special characteristics. This was not simply affectation on her part, for everyone admired her expertise, even renowned scientists of the time.

It is in her beloved residence at Malmaison that Joséphine gave concrete expression to her passions, making it a veritable museum of natural history as well as of art. Her premature death resulted in a dispersal of her collections, but the château is now a national museum designed to evoke the exceptional domain that was admired by all her contemporaries. With each painting purchased, each piece of tableware found, each piece of furniture put back into its original place, the atmosphere of the apartments is gradually being restored. Visitors to Malmaison today enjoy the experience of being received in a private house rather than visiting a museum, and this remains the most beautiful homage that one may offer to honor the memory of the empress.

It gives me great pleasure that the sequel to this book, already in the planning stages, will cover in great depth Joséphine's patronage of the arts, a subject that can only be touched on in a biography. Eleanor DeLorme's perseverance in bringing together authors from several countries to treat the various fields in which they are specialists will eventually provide us with an essential work that explores the various artistic passions of one of the most extraordinary women in history.

Bernard Chevallier
Director, Musée National de Malmaison
Conservateur Général du Patrimoine

Andrea Appiani (1754–1817), Joséphine (private collection). Appiani was the official painter in Italy to Prince Eugène and Napoléon, and he came to Paris for the coronation in 1804. Appiani portrays Joséphine wearing one of her superb cameo ensembles, perhaps from the exemplary collection she formed in Italy. A particularly fine example is the cameo and pearl tiara inherited by Joséphine's granddaughter, Queen Josephine of Sweden, and worn today by the Queen of Sweden at the Nobel Prize ceremony.

TOP LEFT: *Georges Rouget (1783–1869),*
Alexandre de Beauharnais *(Château de Versailles).*
Joséphine's first husband and the father of her two children is
depicted here as commander of the Army of the Rhine. His
assignment ended tragically, however, for he failed to take the
necessary measures to relieve Mainz, which fell to the
Prussians in late July 1793. Imprisoned the following
March, he was executed on July 24, 1794. Despite their
unhappy marriage, Joséphine instilled in Eugène and
Hortense a respect for their aristocratic father's memory.

LEFT: *Andrea Appiani (1754–1817), Prince Eugène de*
Beauharnais as Viceroy of Italy *(Château de Malmaison).*
Joséphine's son, Eugène de Beauharnais, was named by his
doting stepfather to the position of viceroy of Italy in 1805
and was charged with presiding over the country's
administrative affairs in Napoléon's absence. Appiani,
who first met Bonaparte in Milan in 1796 and became
his official painter, has portrayed Eugène in a green court
costume almost identical to that of his stepfather in
Appiani's official portrait of Napoléon as first king of Italy.
In addition to the ribbon and badge of the Iron Crown,
Eugène also wears the necklace and medallion of the Légion
d'Honneur as a mark of the emperor's favor.

OPPOSITE: *Jacques-Louis David (1748–1825),*
Napoléon in His Study *(National Gallery of Art, Samuel*
H. Kress Collection, Washington, D.C.).
This astonishing portrait was commissioned by
Lord Alexander Douglas (1767–1852), an admirer
of Napoléon who owned other works of art related to
the emperor. David depicts the tireless statesman who
has spent the night working on the Civil Code (the clock
has just chimed 4 A.M.) and now prepares to buckle on his
sword to review troops in the Tuileries courtyard below.

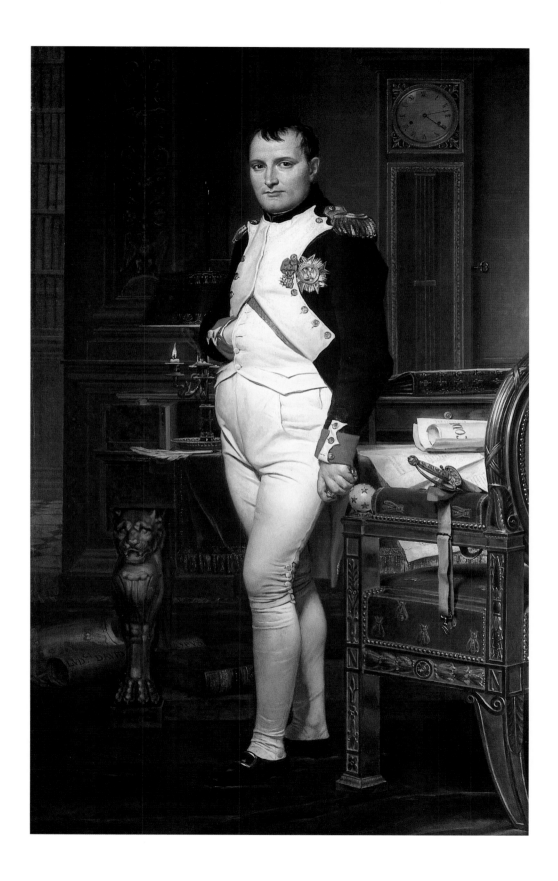

TOP LEFT: *François Gérard (1770–1837),* Hortense as a Child *(Musée Calvet). Hortense appears to be four or five in Gérard's delightful portrait, and it is a prime example of Joséphine's early patronage of this most sought-after portraitist of his day. It had to have been painted just before June 1788, when Joséphine took Hortense to Martinique, or just after their return to France in late October 1790. The sailors made little shoes for Hortense during the long voyage, and she charmed them with her dancing.*

LEFT: *Anne-Louis Girodet-Trioson (1767–1824),* Queen Hortense *(Rijksmuseum, Amsterdam). Artist, composer, musician, and major collector of troubadour paintings, Hortense was also appreciated as a social luminary who brightened the imperial court. The Dutch were so proud of their queen that this engaging portrait, painted by Girodet in 1813, was recently purchased for the Rijksmuseum.*

OPPOSITE: *François Gérard (1770–1837),* Hortense de Beauharnais and Her Son Napoléon-Charles *(Château de Versailles). The queen of Holland is seated upon a gilt Empire canapé, her arms encircling her beloved oldest son, who died in 1807 at the age of five. No doubt Hortense chose his costume for the painting, the one he wore at his grandmother's coronation. Gérard's portrait of Hortense standing beside her son, executed for Napoléon's gallery of family portraits at Saint-Cloud, was confiscated by Marshal Blücher after Waterloo.*

OPPOSITE: *Hippolyte Lecomte (1781–1857), Detail of Joséphine at Lake Garda (Château de Versailles). Lecomte, a painter and lithographer, exhibited at the Salons from 1804 to 1847. Here he depicts one of Joséphine's narrow escapes from death, when her carriage was fired upon by the Austrians in Italy. Andoche Junot was escorting her party, and he quickly pushed Joséphine and her maid into a ditch, drawing the enemy fire upon himself.*

ABOVE: *François-Guillaume Ménageot (1744—1816), The Marriage of Eugène de Beauharnais and Auguste-Amélie of Bavaria (Château de Versailles). This civil ceremony takes place in the Grand Gallery of the Residenz, and part of its renowned art collection hangs on the walls. At the left on a dais sit Napoléon and Joséphine, with King Maximilian I and Queen Caroline seated to their left. Standing opposite them, holding hands, are Auguste and Eugène. Among the many dignitaries present are the future prince primate of the Confederation of the Rhine, Prince Dalberg, with Bessières, Junot, Duroc, Talleyrand, and Napoléon's chief of staff, Marshal Berthier.*

*Georges Rouget (1783–1869),
Proclamation of the Empire at Saint-
Cloud (Versailles). Rouget, a pupil of
David, was particularly drawn to court
subjects, and this view depicts Joséphine
beside a boyish Bonaparte, who stands
before a fauteuil (armchair) probably
made by Joséphine's cabinetmakers, the
Jacobs. Also typical of Joséphine's taste
is the famous Sèvres vase commissioned
by Louis XVI on the pedestal at the
right, for she was particularly fond of
bronzes and porcelain that had been
made for the fallen monarchy.*

Joséphine's State Bedroom. *After Joséphine's divorce, the architect Louis Berthault redesigned her formal bedroom as a tent. It is hung with crimson wool embroidered in gold with cornucopia and swan motifs to match her state bed. The washstand is of the period but was not Joséphine's, and the dressing table originally stood on the other side of the room. In this room hung a series of Redouté's priceless botanical watercolors on vellum. (Watercolor by James Steinmeyer)*

RIGHT: The Council Chamber at Malmaison *as it looks today.*
Percier and Fontaine created it in ten days, probably inspired by
Joséphine's tented bedroom at her house on rue de la Victoire in Paris.
The room's principal feature is a series of eight trompe-l'oeil panels
copied from Phrygian, Parthian, Greek, Roman, and Gallic trophies,
according to the Englishman James Forbes, who visited Malmaison
in 1803. The present furniture is of the period but not original to
the room. (Watercolor by James Steinmeyer)

OVERLEAF, TOP LEFT: *Jacques Barraband (c.1767/8–1809),*
Parakeet (private collection, France). Barraband was so universally
admired for his depictions of rare birds that Napoléon commissioned
a series of his sumptuous watercolors as diplomatic gifts. This extremely
rare species is native to Bura Island in Indonesia. Joséphine appreciated
Barraband's work, which may have come to her attention through his
decorations for Sèvres porcelain.

OVERLEAF, BOTTOM LEFT: *Pierre-Joseph Redouté (1759–1840),*
Lilies (private collection). Joséphine's patronage made possible
Redouté's impressive career as a botanical illustrator. He began as a
painter-decorator working with his brother, Antoine-Ferdinand, but
when he noted the resounding success of flower paintings by Gérard
van Spaendonck at the Salons, Redouté turned toward this genre.
His delicate watercolors on vellum for Joséphine are unrivaled for their
scientific precision and artistic merit and were highly prized by collectors.

OVERLEAF, RIGHT: *Auguste Garneray (1785–1824),* Visit to the
Conservatory *(Malmaison). Joséphine, escorted by a hussar at right,*
is leading visitors through her conservatory. They are entering the
section with its glass roof raised high enough to accommodate tropical
trees, which provide a luxuriant backdrop for her exotic plants. Her
extraordinary collection was scientifically catalogued and studied by
prominent scholars and was universally admired.

INTRODUCTION

*T*he momentous day dawned cold and bleak, but it hardly mattered. By early morning on December 2, 1804, an immense crowd was already beginning to gather in the courtyard of the Tuileries to catch a glimpse of Empress Joséphine as she left the palace for her inauguration at the cathedral of Notre Dame. When she appeared on the steps, the courtiers were impressed by her grace, the seeming ease with which she wore her sumptuous gown of white satin sprinkled with diamonds and the superb diadem of pearls and diamonds, set off by a full parure of precious stones surrounded by more diamonds. At ten o'clock, salvos from cannons announced that the cortège was ready to depart, led by the dashing cavalryman Joachim Murat and escorted by squadrons of horsemen of the Imperial Guard and Mamelukes. It was to the counterpoint of a military escort that Joséphine would henceforward make her entrances and exits. On her travels through the countryside and to foreign capitals, the panoply and glitter of the resplendent uniforms and prancing horses were a fitting accompaniment to her regal bearing.

In December 1799—with the proclamation of the Consulate—Joséphine was thrust into the forefront of the political scene, and she would soon win the respect and admiration of the populace. When the Empire was proclaimed in May 1804, she became a public personage, surrounded by a court more brilliant than that of any French queen; she was constantly on parade, always exposed to the insatiable curiosity of the mobs. During her five years as empress, she conducted herself in such a way as to gain the enduring love of the French people, who appreciated her warm personality, her benevolent concern, her natural grace, and the fact that she seemed to have been born for the role she played so well.

François Gérard (1770–1837), Joséphine as Empress (Fontainebleau). In Gérard's state portrait, the empress sits on a throne chair, wearing one of her emerald and pearl parures. Over her shoulder and the arm of the chair is thrown the heavy, ermine-lined mantle embroidered with huge gold bees that she wore at her coronation; her crown rests on a cushion beside her. Joséphine's hair, worn high off the neck, and her low-cut gowns with short sleeves effectively set off the jewels of her great parures.

During her years of retreat from the court after her divorce, from 1810 until her death in May 1814, Joséphine made her personal château, Malmaison, into one of the best-known showplaces in Europe. Although a deposed empress, she was continually visited by the most prominent individuals in European society, from Czar Alexander I to the eminent botanist Baron von Humboldt. Everyone, it seems, was attracted to Joséphine. The final paradox of her extraordinary life is the fact that some of the very people who came to pay court to the woman Napoléon loved had been among his most avowed enemies.

The aim of the present study is twofold: to tell Joséphine's story, which reads like a Flaubert novel, and then to demonstrate her influence upon and patronage of the arts. Born on an island in the West Indies, where sorcery abounded, she was told as a young girl—in the often-repeated but well-founded story—that she would become "something more than a queen," a highly improbable prediction that was, of course, fulfilled when she became empress of France. At sixteen, she was taken to Paris to become the bride of an aristocratic French officer, Alexandre de Beauharnais, and although unhappily married, she was solidly ensconced from 1780 onward in the circles of Parisian nobility frequented by her husband and his protectors, the powerful de La Rochefoucauld family. From her unhappy union with Alexandre were born two unusually gifted children, Eugène and Hortense, who themselves played major roles in that remarkable period and who were loved by their stepfather, Napoléon, as if they had been his own. In 1794 Alexandre lost his life to the guillotine and Joséphine was imprisoned, awaiting the blade herself, but she was miraculously spared at the last minute by the fall of Robespierre.

In the autumn of 1795, she met the twenty-five-year-old General Bonaparte, whose reputation was in the ascendant for having suppressed a royalist insurrection in October. Ironically, he was a protégé of the affluent Director Paul Barras, whose mistress Joséphine had become, and Bonaparte fell under the spell of her mysteriously seductive personality. Moreover, she was the former vicomtesse de Beauharnais, who was at ease in the most exalted society in Paris, and in the convent for distressed gentlewomen at Pentémont, where Joséphine lived after her separation from Alexandre, she had honed her manners to perfection. An unusually attractive woman of aristocratic bearing and education, she was immensely appealing to the young Bonaparte, although her character—like that of most people—displayed not only its lights, but also its shadows. Socially unsophisticated as he was, Bonaparte thought that the well-bred Mme. de Beauharnais must have had money as well as breeding and charm, but he mistook taste for wealth.

Although Joséphine could not have imagined the unparalleled destiny awaiting Bonaparte, she did know that Barras and his associates expected great things of him. Besides, she was drawn by his unique charisma, a trait remarked upon by everyone who met him, including the members of Joséphine's own salon. On March 9, 1796, she and Bonaparte were married, and hand in hand they stepped upon the stage of history. There followed his spectacular military campaigns, his expedition to Egypt, the coup d'état that brought him to supreme power, and in May 1804 the imperial title. Thus, when Bonaparte made the astonishing leap from a general of the Revolution to emperor of France, beside him stood an empress who already knew the rules. It was she—as Napoléon himself avowed—who served as catalyst for the successful amalgamation of émigrés from the ancien régime with his own "aristocracy of merit."

The love affair of Napoléon and Joséphine is one of the most renowned and tragic in history. His adoration of her was so intense that it verged upon madness, according to his aide-de-camp Auguste Marmont, who was with Bonaparte during the first Italian campaign, and it is manifested in his love letters to her, which are among the most passionate in existence. But Joséphine did not really fall in love with Bonaparte until it was too late, and this caused both of them immeasurable suffering. "He might have been a better man," wrote Joséphine's lady-in-waiting, Claire de Rémusat, "if he had been better loved."[1]

In exploring Joséphine's relationship to the genius she married, we hope to reveal her as a more complex person than many of her biographers have depicted. Her unfailing sense of style and her savoir faire are universally admitted, and they significantly compensated for the emperor's rude outbursts, which alienated people who could have been immensely useful to him. "He would have turned all heads if only he had had a little 'French courtesy,'" wrote the comte de Caulaincourt.[2] Joséphine invariably stepped in on such occasions, and tactfully smoothed things over with an abundance of "French courtesy."

Even after her divorce, deprived of all political power, she received the greatest names in Europe at Malmaison, which became yet another court, "where dignity, grace, wit, talents and good conversation made a seat of exile into a place of enchantment, and a queen without a crown into a woman surrounded by real friends."[3] Joséphine's social finesse alone, however, would not have been enough to entice the élite of Europe. There was her native intelligence as well, a trait that her biographers rarely acknowledged (except for Bernard Chevallier). Professor Knapton, for example, called her "a relatively simple person,"[4] which seems unlikely, given the fact that Joséphine was always the emperor's "first confidante," according to Caulaincourt. Napoléon's valet Constant confirmed this as well, recording in his journal that his master would talk with his wife for hours on end. Had she not a fine mind, Joséphine would have made a strange confidante indeed for his unparalleled intellect. These gifts—coupled with her sympathetic, receptive nature—eminently qualified Joséphine to be the ideal companion for the man who was engaged in reshaping the map of Europe.

It was no doubt these aspects of her personality that caused Napoléon to spend so much time with her, for he was a notoriously impatient man, who could spare no more than twenty minutes at the dinner table. Time was what he valued most, and he was fond of saying that it was the most precious thing he had: territory could somehow be recovered, but time—once lost—was gone forever. After Joséphine's departure, we do not find Napoléon talking at length (if at all) with her successor, Marie-Louise, and his comments on their relationship leave little doubt that it was almost exclusively physical.

Not only did Joséphine provide companionship and a sounding board for his ideas, but she was also indispensable in other ways. For example, he depended upon her to carry out the unusually painful duty that followed almost inevitably upon a campaign—to inform officers' wives when their husbands had been killed. As Bernard Chevallier has pointed out, "the trait that best characterized Joséphine was her elegance: the moral elegance shown by the mastery of herself, the elegance of heart shown by the goodness of her soul, the elegance of manner and sensibility shown by her sure sense of taste, and a permanent quest for refinement."[5] It was these qualities that made her an ideal partner for her husband and enabled her to bring a touch of humanity to a society wracked by the horrors of war and its aftermath.

There was yet another, somehow indefinable facet of her personality that engendered an affirmative public response to her physical presence, and accounts in the newspapers bear this out. When the emperor had to be away for a protracted absence, anxiety began to mount in the capital, but when Joséphine reappeared in Paris (from a foreign capital where she had been holding court), public morale was instantly boosted, the accustomed fêtes were staged, and official receptions resumed at the Tuileries. To be sure, public pageantry was the administration's way of diverting the attention of the populace from political or military reversals, but the fact remains that Joséphine's presence among the people is well documented as a stabilizing, reassuring authority during times of public stress.

She also proves to have been a woman of remarkable resilience during her brief fifty-one years (he had only fifty-two). Even after she had escaped the guillotine, she came close to death on several other occasions, in Italy and in Paris. Her constant anxiety over the safety of Napoléon and her son, Eugène, when they were on campaign took its toll, but it also equipped her to sympathize in a special way with other women whose men were on the battlefield. She also bore ponderous responsibilities in her official capacity—receptions and public ceremonies that occurred with monotonous regularity; long and dangerous voyages under difficult conditions; diplomatic relationships that had to be conducted discreetly. All of these demanded a mastery of the complex political picture, a memory for names and special interests, a confident bearing, and a prudent sidestepping of any faux pas that might compromise her husband's policy or position.

Beyond all of this lay Joséphine's most formidable challenge—to keep the interest and love of Napoléon. At first, she made little effort and remained curiously, and maddeningly, unresponsive to his impassioned love, but her attitude changed dramatically upon Bonaparte's return from Egypt. Belatedly, she realized what kind of man she had married, and in spite of the heartbreak that her infidelities caused him, he loved her to the end. He even acknowledged that, in her own inimitable way, Joséphine had given him some sort of security and that his star began to descend from the moment that he divorced his "incomparable Joséphine." Mme. de Chastenay spoke of the general gloom at the Tuileries when they were awaiting the official news of the divorce and how they could hardly believe it would take place. "The idea of good fortune and happiness was superstitiously associated with the influence that Joséphine exercised upon her imperial spouse. The career of Bonaparte seemed to be attached to that of this woman so essentially amiable and good, who never made for him anything but friends."[6]

Joséphine did more than hold her own on a vast international stage and retain the love of the man with the longest bibliography in history. It might even be claimed that just as he rebuilt the structure of government, she helped to rebuild the edifice of the arts. Whereas Napoléon used art both to serve the Empire and as a branch of statecraft, Joséphine's interest was personal, and she became a major patron in her own right. In fact, she either discovered or sponsored the painters, sculptors, and architects who defined the new style (many of whom became members of her immediate entourage), and her informed encouragement of the leading artistic personalities of her day contributed immeasurably toward making the Consulate-Empire era so artistically innovative. Joséphine's own collection of art in several media, which was displayed in the gallery of her château, was singular, so that Malmaison "became a cult center for pilgrims seeking beauty," according to art historian Christopher Johns.

It was not, however, always a case of art for art's sake, because the painting, sculpture, architecture, and elaborate fêtes of the Empire played a major role in helping to establish the authority and authenticity of the Napoleonic régime. As historian Eugene Cox has pointed out, "the overthrow of the Bourbon monarchy had created a pressing need on the part of the successive revolutionary regimes to establish their legitimacy. Since popular sovereignty now replaced divine-right sovereignty as the legal basis for government, 'public opinion' now had to be wooed and won in a way that was never necessary before."[7] This was why the painter Jacques-Louis David had become the "pageant-master of the Republic," designing and staging public fêtes that united the prestige of Neoclassical art with "symbols of revolutionary religion."[8] It did not matter that this so-called religion was simply a form of neo-paganism; it still purported to encourage high ideals in an effort to raise the level of public morality.

The arts were immensely effective, too, in helping to create the Napoleonic myth. There was not only David, but also Baron Gros, Jean-Baptiste Isabey, Horace Vernet, Canova, and a host of others who made significant contributions to the legend (inadvertently or not), as we shall see. Joséphine clearly understood that artistic endeavors furthered other objectives as well. Although she certainly brought some of the major figures into the service of the Empire, we cannot claim that she actually "influenced pictorial style," as Gary Tinterow put it, "nor was she able to tell artists what or how to paint. . . . Certainly her patronage was an incentive to others to patronize the same artists, but . . . the state-run bureaucracy that commissioned paintings and distributed honors was immensely more powerful than she."[9] Numerous canvases by modern artists were to be found in Joséphine's gallery, for she was a major patron of contemporary art, and her old master paintings made Malmaison one of the noteworthy collections in Europe. Her paintings, vases, sculpture, and objets d'art were either purchased by her, acquired as gifts, or confiscated as spoils of war during military campaigns.[10] As intrinsically important as her collection may have been, it was the personal manner in which Joséphine displayed it at Malmaison that impressed the numerous visitors who came to see it.

Joséphine also knew how to present herself. As a woman of the ancien régime, she understood that clothing is an art form that helps define the person. Like Marie-Antoinette before her, Joséphine was a cynosure of fashionable taste, and with her "exquisite figure" (according to Napoléon's valet Constant), supple carriage, and graceful gestures, she proved to be an exemplary mannequin. When the Empire was proclaimed, a ceremonial robe with mantle and train was adopted to express the formal grandeur of the new court and became the model worn by ladies at official functions. Her wardrobe displayed an interesting variety and even imagination, although it was not particularly innovative. It was the way she carried it off that aroused the admiration of those around her and served to exploit her essential femininity as the perfect foil for Napoléon's powerful personality. Her fashionable costumes and spectacular jewelry were not mere feminine indulgences but contributed immeasurably to the grandeur of official occasions, and proclaimed as graphically as her smart military escort or her dignified ladies-of-honor the power and prestige of her husband's régime.

Joséphine also knew how to create inviting environments wherever she lived. Even in her first modest Paris house on the rue Chantereine—and with limited means—she invented a decor that was both tasteful and stylish. When she and Napoléon moved into the Tuileries, she drew upon the reserves of the old Garde Meuble (royal warehouse) and helped to turn the palace that had been built for Catherine de Médicis into a home for the consular family and a sumptuous seat of government. She also had her own ideas about the interiors of such royal châteaux as Fontainebleau, Compiègne, and Saint-Cloud, and those that Percier and Fontaine designed for her and the first consul at Malmaison are still recognized as the epitome of the new style. It is a singular fact that the men who played the most significant roles in Joséphine's life were military figures, which accounts for the militant decor of the rooms in which she lived, from her first house in Paris to the bedroom in which she died at Malmaison.

Finally, there were Joséphine's far-reaching horticultural enterprises at Malmaison. Her renowned landscape gardens were enhanced by the pavilions and tents she liked so much, put up for theatrical performances, concerts, cold collations, princely visits, or as a summer retreat for the emperor. The crowning feature, however, was Joséphine's great conservatory with its comprehensive plant collections, considered unique in Europe at that time, and a model for those that followed. Out of this passion for flowers and exotic plant specimens grew Joséphine's patronage of the superior flower painter P.J. Redouté, whose works for her—*Le Jardin de la Malmaison* and *Les Liliacées*—are among the most important monuments of botanical illustration ever published.

Empress Joséphine held a unique place in history, and she made singular contributions to her age. The time in which she lived was unrivaled for sheer drama, splendor, glory, tragedy, and heroism, and it was peopled with larger-than-life characters, all of them known to Joséphine. She shared their dramas, their sorrows, and their most intense joys, so that her life became, in Bernard Chevallier's words, "a résumé of the passions of her times."[11] Towering above them all was the colossal figure of the man who loved her, and it was to the counterpoint of the events which chronicled his unprecedented career that Joséphine's brief life was played out.

The age of Napoléon and Joséphine has ever since appealed to the imaginations of novelists, biographers, musicians, artists, dramatists, filmmakers, and poets. But for all the brilliance, splendor, and glory, there was the dark side that Joséphine knew only too well. As wife of the commander-in-chief, mother of an officer, and friend to so many whose lives were imperiled with each new campaign, she could identify with the millions of anxious, grieving families, not only in her own circle, but throughout France.

Alfred de Musset eloquently distilled the essence of the age in his *Confessions d'un Enfant du Siècle*: "Uneasy mothers gave birth to a nervous, pale, ardent generation. Conceived between two battles, brought up and schooled to the rolling of drums, thousands of children gazed at each other darkly and flexed their puny muscles. From time to time, their blood-smeared fathers appeared, lifted them up on their gold-braided chests, then put them down again, and rode away on their horses. . . . Never had there been . . . such a nation of desperate mothers; never was there such silence about those who spoke of death.

"And yet, there was never such joy, such life, such fanfares of war in all hearts. . . . There was no more old age . . . there were no more old men. There were [only] corpses or demi-gods."[12]

1

Bird of the Islands

The islands of the Caribbean Antilles had attracted French colonists as early as the 1730s for their luxuriant vegetation, balmy weather, and easy life. Frenchmen aspiring to replenish the family coffers found the islands particularly attractive because they offered the opportunity to become part of a planter aristocracy that cultivated sugar cane, coffee, indigo, tobacco, cacao, and cotton. For those involved in maritime commerce, there was the abominable traffic in bois d'ebène, a terrible euphemism for slaves brought from Africa and an aspect of the darker side of life in Martinique, along with dueling, witchcraft, and gambling. Frenchmen who had enriched themselves in the islands would often return after a few years to France, where they would cut grand figures in the salons of its capital.

The island chosen by Joséphine's ancestors was Martinique, and it was here she was born in June 1763, as Marie-Josèphe-Rose de Tascher de la Pagerie. She was known as "Marie-Rose" or "Rose" until well after the birth of her two children, but we shall call her by the name that Napoléon wanted her to assume, "Joséphine." Although Martinique had been captured by the English in 1762, it was restored to France in March 1763, just before Joséphine's birth. By a strange coincidence, her future husband, Napoleone Buonaparte (as he was then called), was also born on an island—Corsica—in 1769, a year after that island also became French.

Joséphine's parents were Créoles, a term used for Europeans born in the colonies. Her father, Joseph-Gaspard de Tascher de la Pagerie, was born in Martinique, his own father having

Anonymous artist, View of Martinique, *19th century. This somewhat naive nineteenth-century painting of Martinique shows the tropical world of Joséphine's childhood. Volcanic eruptions were a constant threat, and terrible hurricanes often swept the tiny island; Joséphine's house was all but destroyed when she was only three. Yet she never forgot Martinique's vibrant flora, suggested in this landscape by the palm and banana trees surrounding the little house on a promontory overlooking the sea.*

come to the island in 1726. The family was descended from the ancient country gentry of the Loire Valley who had made fortuitous marriages, endowed abbeys, and gone on crusades. Not very ambitious and fairly incompetent in the management of his business affairs, Joseph-Gaspard nevertheless made a propitious marriage to the daughter of one of Martinique's oldest families, Rose-Claire des Vergers de Sannois. Her parents numbered among the plantation elite and apparently supported their daughter's marriage to a man with distinguished antecedents.

Joséphine's early surroundings were an important factor in the formation of her personality, accounting for many of her artistic and aesthetic choices, as well as her open-handed hospitality. She never forgot the physical beauty of Martinique and wanted to re-create it after moving to France, where she eventually acquired her own country house. The flora and fauna intrigued the little girl, for there were lush breadfruit trees, mangoes, tamarinds, banana palms, oranges, tropical flowers, and brilliantly plumaged birds in this land of volcanic mountains, waterfalls, and forested ravines. The family's spacious wooden house, situated between the sea and the village of Trois-Islets, was surrounded by a curtain of trees and fronted with a parterre of flowers. But the island was sometimes swept by hurricanes, and in August 1766, when Joséphine was only three, the house was destroyed by a fierce cyclone, leaving only the sugar refinery, where the family took refuge and which Joseph-Gaspard gradually enlarged to accommodate his large family.

Although Joséphine's father had made a prosperous beginning, it was short-lived, for he soon succumbed to the local temptations—rum, gambling, and sexual dalliances. Five children offered his wife some consolation, but her husband's infidelities seem to have destroyed her spirit. She was a woman of keen intelligence but surrendered completely to the indolent island life and never risked a sea voyage to visit her daughter in France, even after she became empress. Joséphine was her oldest child and was left largely to her own devices, with little or no direction. She was cared for by her nurse, Marion, who called her "Yeyette" and sang her Créole songs accompanied by a guitar. Joséphine developed a special, enduring affection for Marion and must have spoken often of her old nurse to Napoléon, for in 1807 he was to grant Marion a pension as an expression of gratitude for the care she had given to his "much-loved wife . . . in her infancy."[1]

Marion apparently loved Joséphine, but she deferred to her as a daughter of the house, so the little girl grew up without discipline. These early years marked Joséphine's personality, for she was indulged not only by Marion but also by the other women working in her mother's household, and the lurid, superstitious, and stimulating stories they told must have appealed to her innately sensuous temperament. Everything in Joséphine's environment conspired to make her the coquette she became at an early age: the warm moonlit nights, the seductive climate, the lush foliage, the heavy, lingering fragrance of flowers and rain-soaked wood. Joséphine became a child of nature, intimately connected to an environment virtually untouched by civilization. Certainly, the sensations inspired by her early surroundings left an indelible imprint and may help explain the moral laxity that later allowed her to become the mistress of Paul Barras and to engage in an extra-marital affair that would torment Napoléon.

Yet there was a redeeming aspect to Joséphine's childhood on this island in the Antilles. Her keen interest in the complex beauty of its flora and fauna was to become an enduring fascination, so much so that she herself would be known later in life as "Bird of the Islands." She became such a recognized connoisseur that even scholars at the Museum of Natural History in Paris honored her contributions to the field. The conservatory she created at Malmaison, which housed rare specimens from around the globe, was a model of its type, visited by illustrious scientists such as Baron von Humboldt, whose colleague, Aimé Bonpland, served as Joséphine's botanist. As we have seen, her patronage of the most famous botanical illustrator of all time—Pierre-Joseph Redouté—was decisive for his career; his watercolors on vellum for Joséphine, such as *Les Liliacées*, a collection of plants in the lily family, would alone certify his position in art history.

Although highly intelligent, Joséphine did not pursue the intellectual life growing up, but she was a quick study, and it is an astonishing fact that this indulged child of the islands would acquire, in a remarkably brief time, the savoir-faire needed to meet the formidable challenges looming in France. Joséphine was baptized in the small church at Trois-Islets and attended Mass with her parents, but she seems to have had no formal religious training until she was sent at the age of ten to be educated at Fort-Royal by the Dames de la Providence, who ran a simple school where they taught good manners, dancing, music, and the difficult art of *révérence de cour* (appropriate behavior at court). Later on, through observation and association, Joséphine would master the complex etiquette governing French society, when she was called upon to preside at the foremost court in Europe.

A decided advantage was her unusual physical presence, for she captivated Europeans with her Créole languor and mesmerizing voice and eyes. She also knew how to put people of all backgrounds and temperaments at ease, and her innate kindness to people in need—such as émigrés returning from exile to France or women who had lost their husbands in battle—became legendary. Joséphine's appearance, even as a young girl, must have been striking, for she is said to have consulted with her cousin, Aimée, an aged sorceress named Eliama, who was impressed by Joséphine's beauty and predicted that she would become something "more than a queen" and that Aimée would become a queen. Not only would Joséphine be crowned empress of France, but her cousin was captured by Turks on her way to France and sold to the Bey of Algiers, Selim III, becoming the mother of Mahmoud II.[2]

A curious meeting occurred when Joséphine was only fourteen, still living with her parents in Martinique and already compellingly attractive to men. She met a young Englishman (or Scot) about her own age who was frequently received by her family. After she left Martinique for France in 1779, they never saw each other again, although she apparently haunted his thoughts for the rest of his life. Decades later, the Englishman (whose name has never been recorded) found himself in Paris and managed to contact the empress, who asked him to come to Malmaison. When he arrived she was already mortally ill, and she died the next morning. As he was leaving the château, he met an attendant of Joséphine's daughter, Hortense, and told her his reason for coming. He said he could never forget the young girl he had first met at her mother's house in Martinique, for she was admired by all who knew her. "Her elegant form was already developed, and her charming face expressed everything that would [distinguish] her heart and spirit."[3] So infatuated had he been that he could never bring himself to marry another woman. Such stories seem to belong to the realm of fiction rather than fact, but they contribute as much to the legend of Joséphine as do the works of Beethoven, Tolstoy, Goethe, Heine, and Stendhal to that of Napoléon.

The mysterious Englishman was not the only one to leave a description of Joséphine as a girl. A French officer stationed in Martinique—Captain Montgaillard of the Auxerrois regiment—also recalled her appearance in 1777: "Mlle. de la Pagerie . . . was noted for her charm, by an expression . . . against which it was difficult to defend oneself . . . of a voluptuousness . . . an indefinable grace in her manner; it caressed, it went straight to the heart, it spoke especially to the senses. Her form was that of the nymphs; her entire person bore the imprint of a vivacity, a softness, an abandon which belongs only to Créoles . . . in their manners, the accent of their voices, and even in their silence."[4]

Joséphine's considerable charms would beguile Bonaparte, but they apparently had no effect upon the man who became her first husband. Early in 1778, when she was not yet fifteen, plans for her marriage were already under way. As the daughter of a member of the island aristocracy, she would make a suitable bride for a young French aristocrat, and Joseph-Gaspard hoped thereby to consolidate the family fortunes. The proposed bridegroom was Alexandre de Beauharnais, a young military officer whose family had once lived in Martinique, where he was born in 1760. His father, François, had gone there in 1757 as governor and lieutenant general of the Windward Islands of America although he was recalled to France in 1761 because he had allowed Guadeloupe to fall to the English. Alexandre, too young to go back to France with his parents, was left with Joséphine's family until he was five years old. In Martinique, François, now the marquis de Beauharnais, had fallen in love with Joséphine's aunt, who was married to Alexis Renaudin. After returning to France, Alexandre's parents separated, and his mother died in 1767, at which time the boy was given to the care of Mme. Renaudin, who was separated from M. Renaudin and living openly with François de Beauharnais. It was "Tante" Renaudin who engineered the marriage of Alexandre and her niece Joséphine, partly to strengthen her position with the marquis (whom she ultimately married) and partly because Alexandre was heir to a large fortune that would greatly bolster the diminished assets of Joséphine's own family.

Young Alexandre de Beauharnais was sent to the College de Pléssis in France and placed under the care of a tutor, the mathematician M. Patricol, a disciple of Rousseau and the Encyclopedists. Patricol took Alexandre and his brother to Heidelberg to perfect their German, and when they returned to France, he was offered the position of tutor in the household of the duc de La Rochefoucauld, head of one of France's most distinguished families. Alexandre accompanied his tutor to the château La Roche Guyon on the Seine, thereby entering the circle of wealth and privilege. Until his death, Alexandre de Beauharnais remained an aristocrat to the tips of his fingers, and at the de La Rochefoucauld establishment, he was given the dancing lessons considered essential for a young man of his position. In fact, Mme. de la Tour du Pin noted in her memoirs that Alexandre de Beauharnais was the finest dancer in Paris.[5]

At the instigation of his sister, Joséphine's father set forth his daughter's best points in a letter to the marquis: "She has a splendid skin, fine eyes, exquisite arms, and is consumed with desire to see Paris. She possesses an excellent character and a very charming face, and is, moreover, very well-developed for her age."[6] There were complications, however, as revealed in the letters that passed back and forth across the Atlantic for almost two years. Since Joséphine was only two-and-a-half years younger than Alexandre, the marquis thought them too close in age, so Joséphine's younger sister Catherine-Désirée was chosen instead. But Catherine died suddenly of a fever, and since the youngest sister was merely eleven-and-a-half, Joséphine was the only remaining possibility. Mme. Renaudin realized that she had to act quickly, so she wrote a rather surprising letter to her brother: "Arrive with one of your daughters or with two. Whatever you do will be agreeable to us." Joséphine's aunt could not afford to leave anything to chance, so she persuaded the marquis de Beauharnais to send an authorization to Martinique publishing the wedding banns, with a blank space left for the bride's name to be inserted later.

But what did the prospective bridegroom think? All he had was the description of Joséphine from her father, who assured Alexandre that she could easily pass for eighteen since she was so well formed for her age and that she had a decided proclivity for music. Nothing is known of what Joséphine herself said or thought, but she apparently accepted the time-honored eighteenth-century manner of arranged marriages between people of her class.

In August 1779, everything was finally in place for Joséphine's departure for France. Her mother would not leave the islands, even for her daughter's wedding, so the bride-to-be was escorted by her ailing, impecunious father and the servant Euphemia, who was always suspected of being another Joseph-Gaspard offspring. The unlikely trio sailed on the *Ile-de-France*, escorted by a frigate because of wartime conditions. It was a long, tempestuous, miserably arduous crossing, and the seasick Joseph-Gaspard remained in his bunk much of the way, but on October 12, 1779, the exhausted company finally arrived in Brest.

Mme. Renaudin and Alexandre de Beauharnais set out from Paris to meet them, and on October 28 Joséphine and her future husband beheld each other for the first time. Joséphine's initial impression of Alexandre is unknown, and his letters to his father about his fiancée were guarded, for he spoke only of the "honesty and sweetness" of her character.[7] Aunt Renaudin again assured Joséphine that Alexandre was bringing to the marriage more than his title, as he would receive a substantial income and owned valuable property. What her aunt omitted to mention was that Alexandre had already embarked on the amorous adventures typical of a liberal young officer and that marriage would not significantly alter his life style, reason enough for Mme. Renaudin and her marquis to promote matrimony. Toward that end she even provided Joséphine with a dowry, a trousseau, and a furnished house at Noisy-le-Grand, outside Paris.

With this auspicious beginning, the marriage of Marie-Josèphe-Rose de Tascher de la Pagerie to the "haut et puissant seigneur Alexandre François Marie, Vicomte de Beauharnais" was celebrated in the parish church of Noisy-le-Grand on December 13, 1779. The bride must have felt lonely indeed on that dreary December day, with her mother far away at Trois-Islets and her father still too sick from the sea voyage to attend. He was represented by a distant cousin, Maurice-Charles-Marie de Tascher, who was given legal power to represent both of her parents. Mme. Renaudin, the efficient sister of the ineffectual Joseph-Gaspard, must also have been there, however, to make sure that everything went off as planned.

Although the newlyweds had received the house in Noisy-le-Grand as a wedding present, Joséphine seems to have spent little time there, and for reasons not altogether clear, most of the first two years of her wedded life were lived in the Paris town house owned by the de Beauharnais family and situated in a quarter of the city near the somber old Cour des Miracles. She found herself in an increasingly strained relationship with her husband, who apparently preferred the company of the duc de La Rochefoucauld and his friends at the château of La Roche-Guyon to that of his young wife. So Joséphine was left behind in the family town house, which looked out upon stone walls and dark, narrow streets. For the unhappy young bride, the claustrophobic Hôtel de Beauharnais was a far remove—both physically and psychologically—from the verdant foliage and the balmy air of her beloved Martinique.

2
Caged Bird

The marriage of sixteen-year-old Marie-Josèphe-Rose de Tascher de la Pagerie to the urbane nineteen-year-old vicomte de Beauharnais appeared to be doomed from the start. Joséphine was a disappointment to her demanding husband; in his circle, for example, ladies were expected to play the harp, not the guitar, although he apparently urged her to take lessons from the celebrated teacher François Petrini.[1] Alexandre thought her somewhat childish, too, for she was delighted with the jewels he had given her—a pair of girandole earrings, a pair of bracelets, and a watch and chain garnished with diamonds—which she kept in her pockets and naively showed to friends. He was also dismayed by the mediocrity of his bride's education, for he wanted a witty, well-read wife who would be able to conduct a salon like that of his famous aunt, the prolific writer Fanny de Beauharnais. Alexandre wrote to Joséphine from Roche-Guyon in May 1780: "I am delighted [that you want to be] taught. . . . By persisting . . . the knowledge you will acquire will lift you above the others and . . . make you an accomplished lady."[2] By November Alexandre was writing to Mme. Renaudin of his pleasure with the progress his wife was making, and he reported that now she should not be afraid to write to anyone—meaning, of course, people like the de La Rochefoucaulds, in whose great house he was then a guest.

He was also indulging in those light encounters common to attractive young officers of noble birth who had to leave their wives to join regiments. As time progressed, Alexandre's letters indicate that he was not as kind and patient with his inexperienced wife as a newly married man might have been. At least she pleased him in one way: on September 3, 1781, Joséphine gave birth to their first child, a son whom they named Eugène-Rose. The boy would be a delight to both parents and an enduring satisfaction to his future stepfather, Napoléon Bonaparte.

In spite of Alexandre's pleasure in his son, he often left Joséphine alone even when he was in Paris, and he regularly succumbed to the temptations of the capital, although Joséphine remained completely faithful to him. A year later, he went without her to Martinique, although he was accompanied by his mistress, Laure de Longpré, a distant relative of Joséphine's. Alexandre wrote his wife a long letter on January 30, 1783, with news of her family and her sister's illness, adding that the portrait of Joséphine he took to them had been highly appreciated. By early summer, his letters were growing colder, for he complained that he had not heard from her for three months, a complaint that Bonaparte would constantly make in later years. It may be that she remained silent in this case because she had learned about Alexandre's traveling companion, or perhaps it was simply a carelessness instilled in her from childhood.

By July 8, Alexandre's mounting fury at Joséphine's negligence exploded in an appalling letter, written under the influence of Laure de Longpré, accusing Joséphine of immoral behavior in Martinique before their marriage and of adultery afterward; he even questioned the paternity of the daughter born to her on April 10, 1783. Nevertheless, he gave the child the name Hortense-Eugénie, supposedly (with an adjustment of gender) after Caesar's rival, the orator Quintus Hortensius, in the true spirit of Neoclassicism. Alexandre's accusations were irresponsible and unfounded—even outrageous in view of his own conduct—but the consequences for Joséphine were grave, for they could lead to banishment from society and retirement to a convent, a time-honored convention under such circumstances in the ancien régime. Back in Trois-Islets, Joséphine's mother was infuriated by Alexandre's cruelty to her "Yeyette," and she sent her daughter Christian consolation drawn from the Psalms: "Goodbye, my dear daughter, do not forget to have recourse to God. He never abandons those who are His own. Early or late, He will overcome your enemies."[3]

Alexandre returned to Paris on October 26, and despite the efforts of the marquis de Beauharnais to patch up the marriage, Alexandre remained adamant that he and Joséphine must separate—the real reason being his unwillingness to relinquish Laure de Longpré. So on November 27, 1783, the twenty-year-old vicomtesse de Beauharnais was ordered to leave her husband's house for the convent of Pentémont, where the abbess bore the distinguished name of Marie-Catherine de Béthisy de Mezières. It was not a convent in the usual sense but a retreat for ladies "of the first distinction" in delicate circumstances, a sort of graduate school in gentility.

Joséphine began her long battle for a redress of grievances against Alexandre on December 8, 1783, when the king's counselor, Louis Joron, came to meet with her at Pentémont. She asserted her complete innocence of adultery, to which any number of people could attest, but she remained in the convent until the judge ordered Alexandre to provide a livelihood for her and their two children. This was to be a protracted struggle, and Joséphine at this time wrote to a friend explaining the indebtedness she incurred without her husband's support. "M. de Beauharnais must know that I have nothing and need everything, but since money is not my God, this is not what concerns me the most." What concerned her the most, unquestionably, was the fate of her children.

On February 4, 1785, Alexandre took Eugène away from her, an act that caused both Joséphine and her four-year-old son immense suffering. Perhaps no child was ever subjected to such domestic instability as Eugène de Beauharnais, for he had six homes before he was five, and six more before he was thirteen. In view of this troubled childhood, it is remarkable that he matured into so distinguished and serious a young man and that he became the buttress upon which his mother, sister, and the emperor himself depended. Joséphine and Alexandre were legally separated in March, and the terms of the agreement called for him to send her a regular income. Eugène would be allowed to stay with his mother until he was five, and Hortense could remain with Joséphine until her own marriage. Alexandre even had to repudiate his totally unfounded charges against his wife, and Joséphine emerged victorious from the struggle.

This was a pivotal period in Joséphine's life, for life at Pentémont marked the beginning of her moral and social evolution. In the middle of this aristocratic society, where she was known as "the little American," the gaps in Joséphine's education continued to be filled, and she perfected a way of thinking and a manner of life that were entirely new to her. Aided by her unfailing feminine instincts, she acquired social poise and unerring taste and tact and became proficient in the good manners that were to become so conspicuous a part of her bearing—all of them qualities she would pass on to her two children. Eugène would become a paragon of princes and Napoléon's viceroy of Italy, while Hortense would become the queen of Holland, a confidante to her stepfather the emperor, and the mother of Napoléon III. An extraordinary testament to the character of both Joséphine and her children is that the memoirs of Eugène and Hortense never mention their parents' separation; indeed they stress the respectful, dignified manner in which Joséphine always spoke of her first husband.

Joséphine remained at Pentémont until July 1785. She could not return to their house on rue Saint-Charles; it was now leased and Alexandre had sold the contents. The house at Noisy, acquired at her marriage, was too expensive to maintain and was sold, so she rented a small house at Fontainebleau, where she and the children were joined by Aunt Renaudin and the marquis de Beauharnais, who were now living in reduced circumstances. At the end of December 1785, the astonishingly durable husband of Mme. Renaudin finally died, and she was at last free to marry the marquis de Beauharnais. In 1787 the couple would purchase a house on rue de France in Fontainebleau, where Joséphine and her children continued to stay with them, off and on, until 1790.

Eugène, however, did not remain with his mother, for Alexandre—exercising his legal right—asked that his son be sent to him on his fifth birthday, and Joséphine sadly let him go. Alexandre enrolled Eugène in a boarding school on rue de Seine headed by a M. Verdière, who would be his tutor at the famous Collège d'Harcourt, where Eugène would be sent in January 1787. His nurse, Euphemia, who had accompanied Joséphine from Martinique and whom Eugène and Hortense called "Mimi," remained with the little boy and sent his mother regular reports, which she found immensely comforting.

The years at Fontainebleau were happy ones for Joséphine, and she never forgot them, for the château was used by the royal family for their annual fall sojourn. The little town was animated by the royal hunts in the nearby forest, and she sometimes followed them on horseback. Here Joséphine met the comte de Montmiron, hereditary governor of the château, in whose company were the vicomte and vicomtesse de Béthisy, whose aunt Joséphine knew as the abbess of Pentémont. Yet Joséphine missed the excitement of life in Paris and was chronically constrained by financial difficulties.

In October 1787 Joséphine met someone with connections in the world of international high finance, the banker Denis de Rougemont, who would lend her a helping hand. The family was captivated by her appealing personality and invited her and four-year-old Hortense to stay with them in Paris. This invitation could not have come at a better time, for Joséphine had barely a sou to her name, but they were happy to have her stay. M. de Rougemont recorded in his journal: "We lodged her in a beautiful apartment over our own . . . my carriage was available when she needed it, and I often accompanied her to the Opéra. . . . We always had many guests. . . which seemed to please Mme. de Beauharnais: her society was very agreeable to us. [She had] a charming face, one of those gracious, supple Créole figures, a voice that went straight to the heart. . . . She combined a fine sense of humor and education with much tact and knowledge of the world. We had the happiness to keep this amiable person with us, hoping to distract her and console her for the chagrin of her situation until the following spring."[4]

In June 1788, Joséphine suddenly decided to take five-year-old Hortense to Martinique, accompanied by Euphemia. Although many of her biographers, including Frédéric Masson, considered this trip somewhat mysterious, Hortense later explained in her memoirs that Joséphine simply wanted to see her family again. "The brilliance of my mother's social position could not make her forget her birthplace or her family."[5] Joséphine knew from Alexandre that her father had not been well and that her sister Manette was seriously ill. Another reason for the voyage may have been Joséphine's financial woes. The revenue from her dowry was far from sufficient, especially since her father's pension had been reduced in 1786, and in the society she now frequented, the vicomtesse de Beauharnais was expected to maintain a certain standard of living. On November 25, 1785, she had implored a fiscal agent to reduce the rent on the tiny apartment she kept at Pentémont, and she succeeded in having it moderated by a few francs.

Joséphine was no longer the diffident sixteen-year-old her father had brought from the wilds of Martinique. Masson, whose devotion to Napoléon left little room for a fair estimate of Joséphine, nevertheless described her as "a supple, delicate being, infinitely gracious, rare, desirable, and voluptuous,"[6] although Masson never considered her to be worthy of Napoléon. She remained at the family house in Trois-Islets for more than two years, often going to Fort-Royal to visit her uncle, Baron Robert de Tascher de la Pagerie, at whose dinner table invariably sat marine officers bearing news from France.

Meanwhile, civil unrest was coming to a head in Paris. On July 12, 1789, an impassioned young writer named Camille Desmoulins mounted a table in the Palais Royal gardens and launched a diatribe against tyranny that inflamed the populace. Two days later they stormed the Bastille, and the Revolution began. This upheaval in France was inevitably felt throughout the colonies, and by May the following year Martinique was among the islands of the French West Indies where the dominant planter aristocracy was threatened by riots and demands for political rights by the native population. During the late summer of 1790, while Joséphine and Hortense were staying in Fort-Royal as guests of the governor, M. de Damas, at the governor's mansion, the insurgents seized the fortress, threatening all whites with destruction. When Joséphine's uncle went to talk with the insurrectionists, he was seized as a hostage and imprisoned. When she heard that the natives were going to begin bombarding the following day, Joséphine frantically threw herself upon the mercies of the captain of a frigate that happened to be in port, and he agreed to take her and Hortense back to France.

Without even taking the time to say good-bye to her family or to return to Trois-Islets for sufficient clothing, Joséphine raced across the square toward the harbor with Hortense in her arms to board the French vessel *Sensible* with cannon fire bursting around them. As the frigate moved out of the harbor that day in early September 1790, the insurgents fired upon it. But her troubles were not yet over, for when the ship reached Gibraltar, it ran aground and the passengers barely escaped being shipwrecked. As frightening as the voyage had been for Joséphine and seven-year-old Hortense, this paled by comparison to the horrors awaiting them on French soil.

The two years Joséphine spent in Martinique had been critical ones in France as a new world order began ousting the old. The Assembly had retracted the privileges of the nobility in August 1789 and abolished inherited titles in June 1790. But Alexandre de Beauharnais, no longer a vicomte, had taken on a new role. In May 1789, now an outspoken liberal, he appeared as a deputy at the meeting of the Estates General that Louis XVI had called in hopes of averting national bankruptcy. The following year, on July 14, his nine-year-old son, Eugène, watched proudly as his father rode in the procession at the exciting celebration of the Fête de la Fédération on the Champ de Mars, which marked the first anniversary of the taking of the Bastille. A contingent of Americans was there as well, and it was the first time the American flag ever appeared at a public French ceremony, borne proudly onto the field by the American naval hero John Paul Jones, Tom Paine, and James Swan of Boston. An integral part of the ceremony was a republican "mass," officiated by the bishop of Autun, who would figure prominently in Joséphine's future as the shrewd, cynical Talleyrand. He would become a guest in her salon and, as minister of foreign affairs, would accompany her when she held court in foreign capitals while her future husband was in the field.

As he rose to national prominence, Alexandre naturally allied himself with his old friends the duc de La Rochefoucauld, the duc d'Aiguillon, and the marquis de Lafayette, who had returned in triumph from America. These liberal gentlemen, now stripped of their titles, were among those who would ironically help to effect the downfall of the ancien régime. While Joséphine was in Martinique, Alexandre became president of the Constituent Assembly, over which he was presiding in

June 1791, when the royal family fled to Varennes. Eugène recalled in his memoirs that he, Hortense, and his mother were at Fontainebleau at that time and—in the absence of a royal government—he believed his father was now considered to be the most important person in France. As unlikely as this seems, it has been claimed by several biographers that Alexandre's prominence attracted so much attention to Joséphine and her children that the populace of Fontainebleau went so far as to point to Eugène in the street and shout: "Voilà le Dauphin!"

After returning to Paris from Martinique, Joséphine moved into a town house on rue des Mathurins that belonged to her brother-in-law, François de Beauharnais (a royalist unlike his republican brother), although by October 1791 she was living in a house on rue St.-Dominique, off the boulevard Saint-Germain. She was no longer simply Mme. de Beauharnais, but the wife of the president of the Constituent Assembly and (after the death of Mirabeau) president of the Jacobins. With so many factions competing for control of the government (none of which lasted long), it was a tenuous position at best, but with Alexandre in such a prominent position, Joséphine was also assumed to carry some political weight by association. Although they had separated, she was linked to Alexandre by name, their children, and their occasional meetings in the salons of what remained of the *grand monde.* In fact, Joséphine was now welcomed on her own merits into the society of such leading figures as Armand de Caulaincourt, General Lafayette, and other former members of the nobility. Joséphine also became attached to Charlotte Robespierre, sister of the "Incorruptible," as Maximilien Robespierre was called, and gave Charlotte her portrait in miniature, a customary token of friendship.

A favorite Paris rendezvous of the Constituents was the magnificent Hôtel de Salm on the rue de Lille, the town house so admired by Thomas Jefferson, today the home of the Musée de la Légion d'Honneur. It was then the town house of the former prince de Salm, a German *grand seigneur* who had rallied to the Revolution. Joséphine was often a guest there, and the prince's sister, Amalia de Hohenzollern-Sigmaringen, became one of her closest friends. Residing there at the moment was the beautiful young Pole, Princess Lubomirska, who would die on the scaffold in April 1794. Joséphine also met the marquise de Montesson (morganatic wife of the duc d'Orléans), an aristocrat with the loftiest social standards who would reintroduce liveries and culottes after the Terror subsided. These people would befriend Joséphine in her own hour of trial, and in turn they would have occasion to be grateful to her for intervening on their behalf when she became empress. Alexandre was now more attentive to her when they chanced to meet, and with her newfound self-assurance, Joséphine began to feel at home in the realm of politics.

The momentary pleasures of Joséphine's life, however, were soon to be interrupted by an alarming chain of events. In April 1792, the Legislative Assembly voted to declare war against Austria and Hungary, and during the summer the armies of their Prussian ally under the duke of Brunswick moved in the direction of Paris. The ominous quiet that had settled momentarily over the capital was suddenly shattered at dawn on the terrible morning of August 10, 1792, when the mob

Jean Duplessis-Bertaux (1747–1819). Taking the Tuileries (Château de Versailles). On August 10, 1792, an irate mob stormed the Tuileries Palace, residence of the monarchy at the time. The old royal palace was left in such a ruinous state that a monumental restoration was required to make it habitable. Bonaparte and Joséphine moved there early in 1800, and it became their official Paris residence. This masterpiece created by Philibert Delorme for Catherine de Médicis was gutted by fire in the Commune uprising of 1871.

attacked the Tuileries Palace, where the royal family was residing, and invaded it while chanting "La Carmagnole" and hacking to pieces many of the chevaliers of Saint-Louis and the Swiss Guards who were trying to guard the palace. This savage butchery sounded the death knell of the monarchy and precipitated one of the most terrible episodes of the Revolution—the September massacres.

For Joséphine, and indeed all of France, it was a frightening time. In September the government put up posters reading, "The country is in danger," and volunteers presented themselves to the army at the rate of some eighteen hundred a day. As for Joséphine, she was learning to deal with adversity, and her encouraging letters to Hortense symbolized the independent person she was becoming as she fought to survive and to preserve her children. Even her signature indicated a growing confidence. Although she kept the name "Rose" (and even her familiar "Yeyette") until October 1779, by 1790 she had become "Citizeness Beauharnais," to which she sometimes appended "wife of a marshal," which lent a more authoritative note to her correspondence. There survives a drawing of her appearance at this time executed by an artist who would become the leading painter of Paris life during Joséphine's day—Louis-Léopold Boilly—and who was already sketching Joséphine

Louis-Leopold Boilly (1761–1845).
Citizeness Beauharnais (Malmaison).
Boilly's sketch of Joséphine is dated 1793, the
year that Louis XVI and Marie-Antoinette
were executed. The fall of the monarchy
placed Joséphine and others of royalist
sympathies in grave danger, so she was
prudently called "Citizeness Beauharnais,"
thereby eliminating the incriminating particle.

during the Terror. With Alexandre away in the army, she had to make decisions as best she could concerning her children's safety and her own, but her greatest trials were yet to come.

By the end of the year 1792, Joséphine became so concerned about the safety of her children that she decided to send them out of the country with other aristocrats fleeing for their lives. Both children were sent to the country home of Joséphine's friends the prince de Salm and his sister, fifty miles from Calais, but when they tried to take Eugène and Hortense across the channel to England, Alexandre stopped them. He was now serving with the armies of the Republic in the Third Corps, and he did not want his children to become émigrés. Hortense wrote later in her memoirs that the prince and princess personally brought them back to Paris, and in spite of her fears, Joséphine was relieved to see them again.

When her house on rue St. Dominique was sequestered, she found herself homeless, so she rented one with an old friend from Martinique in the suburban village of Croissy west of Paris. The National Convention had decreed that children learn trades, so Hortense acquired the skills of a dressmaker, and Eugène went off to the country as apprentice to a cabinetmaker, a choice greatly lamented by their governess, Mlle. de Lannoy, who did not consider furniture-making a proper pursuit for the son of a former vicomte. Eugène did not long remain a cabinetmaker's apprentice, however, for his father sent him to the National School at Strasbourg, capital of the Alsace-Lorraine provinces and a fortress of primary importance on the Rhine. Now eleven, Eugène entered the world he loved and in which he would feel at home for the rest of his life, with plenty of horses to ride, marching troops, and bugle calls. The headquarters of his father were also nearby, some forty miles away at the foot of the Vosges.

The so-called First Terror had begun late in the fall of 1792, precipitated largely by the war scare that made the arrest of suspects seem urgent and the execution of would-be traitors necessary. The Terror was striking down the highest in the land, and among its victims were Alexandre's protector, the duc de La Rochefoucauld and his old friend Charles de Rohan-Chabot. Yet Alexandre continued to climb in his military career, having been promoted to the rank of general in September 1792, when he was named commander-in-chief of the Army of the Rhine. But the war soon took a turn for the worse: General Dumouriez had deserted in April to the Austrians, and his successor, General Custine, in spite of his effort to renew the defense, was recalled to Paris. He was sent to the guillotine by radical Jacobins, who had overthrown the moderate republican leadership in the Convention, determined to bring a successful end to the war and to rid themselves of all who stood in their path.

It was in this climate that Alexandre took up his command, but even so he apparently had "neither the strength nor moral courage" for such a position, for when the key post of Mainz was besieged by the Austrians and Prussians (the loss of which could open the way for an invasion), Alexandre made no serious effort to relieve it. So the city capitulated on July 23, 1793; on August 3 Alexandre submitted his resignation to the Representatives of the People, as well as to the Convention, and it was accepted on August 21. Without authorization, he left for Strasbourg, and it was a "serious [matter]," wrote Frédéric Masson, "to leave one's post in face of the enemy, at the moment when [General] Custine was being tried and Dillon arrested, the suspicion of treason attaching, as it were, to all the generals."[7] In Paris Alexandre's enemies, who had already reproached him for his aristocratic origins, accused him of defection and conveniently remembered that he had served under his friend General Custine. But Alexandre had his defenders, who were (perhaps significantly) all friends of Joséphine: Pierre Réal at the Commune and Bertrand Barère and Jean Tallien at the Convention.

With the fall of Mainz fell Alexandre's reputation, although he kept professing his republican faith and denouncing his brother's decision to emigrate. "In [Alexandre's] role as an assistant to the demolition of the nation," the vicomte de Vögüé would later write, "one could say that the first husband of Joséphine worked harder than any of his accomplices to prepare the enterprises and fortune of the second!"[8]

In September 1793, the chilling Law of Suspects was enacted by the Convention, and Alexandre, as a former nobleman, returned to the town of La Ferté-Beauharnais near Blois in order to obtain his civil certificate. Joséphine was still living at Croissy, whose mayor, Jean Chanorier, was an interesting figure, a philanthropist who had endowed his community with a school, established a farm of merino sheep, planted mulberry trees, and installed a silk-spinning factory. His enterprises intrigued

Dominique-Vivant Denon (1747–1825), Self-Portrait (Musée Denon, Chalon-sur-Saône). Vivant Denon was among the most sophisticated members of Joséphine's circle. A novelist and eminent engraver under the monarchy, he had counted among his friends Voltaire, Tiepolo's son, and the portrait painter Elisabeth Vigée-Lebrun. At Lady Hamilton's house, Denon sketched her famous poses (the "attitudes") that fatally attracted Lord Nelson.

Joséphine, and she remembered Chanorier's experiment years later when she was planning her own model farm with a flock of merino sheep and her extensive greenhouse at Malmaison. Furthermore, she met the illustrious Vergennes family at Chanorier's house, notably Claire de Vergennes (whose father was the nephew of Louis XVI's minister and would be guillotined the following year). The aristocratic Claire, as Claire de Rémusat, would become Joséphine's lady-in-waiting and confidante later on.

In the midst of the Terror—December 11, 1793—there arrived in Paris a man Joséphine had known since the days of Aunt Fanny de Beauharnais' salon, Dominique-Vivant Denon. This intriguing writer-engraver had just been expelled from Italy, where he had been a vivacious addition to the circle of Lord and Lady Hamilton, Elisabeth Vigée-Lebrun, and Countess Albrizzi. It was a critical moment in the Revolution, and the name of Denon (who had left in 1777) erroneously appeared on the list of émigrés. Fortunately, it was the moment when his friend the painter Jacques-Louis David, the darling of the Jacobins, managed to save Denon, whose name was later stricken from the list.

Denon would shortly become a key figure in Joséphine's life and advisor in her art collecting. As for David, although he supposedly "remained loyal to the principles of the Revolution for the rest of his life,"[9] this preeminent Frenchman would soon be eager to serve Joséphine's court. No longer would he depict citizens in simple republican dress, but rather a bejeweled Joséphine in sumptuous imperial regalia. It is remarkable that these two figures from this dismal period of Joséphine's life—Denon and David—would shortly assume major roles in the new régime: Denon as director of the National Museum, David as first painter.

Louis-Leopold Boilly (1761–1845). The Arrest (Musée Carnavalet). After the promulgation of the terrible Law of Suspects, arrests occurred daily, and Joséphine and her husband, Alexandre de Beauharnais, were victims along with many other members of the aristocracy. In Boilly's vivid image, an arrested man is embraced by his wife and regarded anxiously by his son at left, while the mob hurls invectives and insults and a little dog slinks away from the gruesome scene. A pitiless light cast upon the central group highlights the man's tragic plight.

Toward the end of 1793, the former General de Beauharnais became a suspect. Alexandre had fallen into disfavor because he had failed to relieve Mainz, and his older brother, François, a fiercely committed royalist, was now active among the émigrés who were threatening France with invasion. Joséphine's position, too, became increasingly compromised, because of her association with François's wife, Marie-Françoise de Beauharnais (Aunt Fanny's daughter), although she was in fact separated from her husband at this time.

Early in March 1794, a closed carriage arrived to take Alexandre de Beauharnais to prison, first the Luxembourg, then to the sinister Carmelites convent, site of one of the bloodiest September massacres. As might have been expected, his sister-in-law, Marie-Françoise, had already been arrested, on November 3, 1793, and imprisoned at Sainte-Pélagie. Typically, Joséphine had valiantly defended Marie-Françoise, assuring the officials that hers was a "good republican household," which was of course absurd. She did the same for Alexandre, and in spite of the shabby way he had treated her, risked her own security by imprudently soliciting for her husband's release, thereby arousing the suspicions of the revolutionists.

A few weeks after Alexandre de Beauharnais's arrest, an anonymous letter was sent to the Committee of Public Safety denouncing those who frequented the household of Mme. Hosten, so M. de Vergennes was immediately taken, and on the black Monday morning of April 21, 1794, Eugène and Hortense discovered that their mother had been carried away during the night. She had not wanted to awaken them and instructed their governess to let them sleep, for she could not bear to see them cry. As she hastily gathered herself together to leave, she threw a few garments— makeup, hairbrush, and perhaps a book or two to please Alexandre—into a small cloth bag, on which her pet dog, a pug named Fortuné, tugged, trying to hold her back.

Joséphine was taken to join her husband in the dreaded Carmelites convent. The walls were still spattered with blood from the September massacres, which had claimed the lives of more than two thousand prisoners in Paris alone. The mobs had found their way into the convent, where they murdered 115 members of the clergy in cold blood. In this spring of 1794, Joséphine found herself in this filthy, damp, rat-infested hole, where the incarcerated were detained until their execution. In the fetid air hung the sickly smell of death, and from time to time the tumbrils of the Revolutionary Tribunal would arrive to cart away those whose names were read from the list of the condemned.

It seems that Joséphine and Alexandre came to some sort of reconciliation in prison, or at least the appearance of a reunion, perhaps for the sake of their children. Eugène was now twelve-and-a-half and Hortense eleven, and although they were forbidden entrance to the Carmelites, they were permitted to receive notes from both parents. They would arrive at the door with the tiny, barking Fortuné at their heels. The pug was allowed inside, and on hearing Joséphine's name ran through the corridors to find her, returning to the children with a twist of paper around his collar on which would be written a note from their mother.

There was an interesting roster of names in the old convent. One was the prince de Salm, whose sister—Joséphine's friend who had tried to whisk Joséphine's children out of France in 1792—bravely invited the de Beauharnais children to her house each Sunday. The prince de Salm would be among the condemned, but his sister miraculously escaped death. Joséphine never forgot those who were kind to her during those desperate days, and she later warmly received the princess at the Tuileries. Bonaparte eventually gave the hand of his niece in marriage to the princess's son, and it was a sign of the times that a scion of the exalted house of Hohenzollern would be united with a Bonaparte from Corsica.

Another who took an interest in Joséphine's children came from a different stratum of society. She was the gorgeous Spaniard with black hair and eyes, Mme. de Fontenay, née Thérèse Cabarrus, who had herself just been released from prison, thanks to the intervention of the powerful Jean-Lambert Tallien, whom Thérèse would shortly marry. Among Joséphine's other companions in the Carmélites was a lovely twenty-three-old blonde, Delphine de Sabran, who would later become a favorite of Chateaubriand. She had been a widow for two months following the execution of her much-older husband, General Armand de Custine, and everyone pitied her for having been widowed so young. It was said that Alexandre became infatuated with Delphine and gave her a ring when he knew that his end was near, a memento that (according to her brother) Delphine kept forever.

Citizenness Beauharnais could hardly blame her husband for his attentions to Delphine, for Joséphine herself became attracted to another inmate whose cell was near her own: General Lazare Hoche, who had served under Alexandre on the Rhine. Joséphine shared a cell with the duchesse d'Aiguillon and two other women, and legend has it that she and Hoche communicated by means of mirrors, but there is no proof whatsoever that any intimate relationship between the two existed. Hoche remained only a short time in the Carmelites in any case, for he was taken on May 16 to the Conciergerie, the last stop before the guillotine. By some curious chance he was forgotten, was released when Robespierre fell, and later re-emerged briefly in Joséphine's life.

One morning the jailer entered Joséphine's cell to take her straw mat for another prisoner, and when the duchesse d'Aiguillon vigorously protested, the man turned upon her with an atrocious smile, saying that Mme. de Beauharnais would no longer be needing it. Shaken as she was, Joséphine seems to have done all she could to try to alleviate the suffering of the others, for an English woman imprisoned with her, a Mrs. Elliott, recorded in her journal that the person she especially remembered from that appalling time was the Citizenness Beauharnais: "C'est une des femmes les plus accomplies et les plus spirituelles que j'aie rencontrées.'" (one of the most accomplished and wittiest women I ever met).[10]

During those terrifying days of their mother's imprisonment, neither Hortense nor Eugène ever mentioned the word "guillotine," although they knew that the public accuser, Fouquier-Tinville, had erected one on the Place de la Révolution. The children could see a crowd gathering at a certain time each day where the horrible instrument loomed dark against the sky, and they knew innocent people were being killed. One day a woman appeared at their door, bearing a note written in their mother's hand, and she took them to the bottom of a garden opposite a large building. It was an eerie spectacle they witnessed, for the woman pointed to a window in which their parents appeared, side by side, as if in a picture frame. When a sentinel arrived, the children were hustled away, and Hortense recorded that this was the last time she and Eugène ever saw their father.

On July 23, Alexandre was summoned to the Revolutionary Tribunal, leaving Joséphine and Delphine in the Carmelites. It was said that the latter, sobbing bitterly, manifested the greater sorrow, and it was Joséphine who consoled Delphine. Alexandre was executed the same day, along with forty-eight others, including Joséphine's good friend, the prince de Salm. It was all the work of the mighty Committee of Public Safety, of which Maximilien Robespierre was a powerful member.

When Joséphine heard of her husband's death, she purportedly cut off her hair in anticipation of her own. The children tried desperately, by means of petitions to the Convention, to obtain their mother's release, apparently helped by a man in whom Joséphine placed her confidence, her business consultant, Etiènne Calmelet. Alas, his efforts proved to be ineffectual, and it now seemed certain that nothing could save the widow Beauharnais.

What happened next appeared to Joséphine and her family to be nothing less than a miracle. As she languished in that ghastly prison awaiting her end, there occurred an interesting turn of fate. The war was now going in France's favor, and a power struggle set off a chain of events that led to Robespierre's ruin. When he and his cronies fell, the people went wild with joy, a more moderate political stance was taken, and Joséphine—for the first time—saw a ray of hope.

Finally, on August 6, 1794, an official order signed by Jean Tallien declared that Citizeness Beauharnais was to be freed from prison on the grounds that no incriminating evidence could be found against her. She was not unknown to Tallien, for the previous year Joséphine had written to him asking for the release of the old marquis de Moulins's niece; she had also appealed to Tallien at the time of Alexandre's arrest, but without success. So it was apparently through the intercession of Thérèse de Fontenay that Joséphine was finally freed, and she never forgot it. Even after she became wife of the first consul and then empress, Joséphine's loyalty to Thérèse Tallien never wavered, in spite of the emperor's disapproval. Eugène said later that he would always be grateful to Jean Tallien for his efforts on his mother's behalf and that he was happy to "have been in a position to give him [Tallien] repeated proofs of what I felt."[11]

Why could no incriminating evidence against Joséphine be found? The explanation is bizarre, but generally accepted: a mysterious actor named Delperch de la Bussière reputedly made a practice of entering the prisons, removing dossiers of selected prisoners, and destroying them in the evening—by eating them. When no evidence could be found against the prisoners, the trials were postponed and the prisoners eventually freed. Whatever the truth may be, Joséphine's dossier was never found, although Alexandre's reposes in the Archives Nationales. At least two of Joséphine's biographers record that she paid a good sum for tickets to a performance staged at the Porte Saint-Martin Theatre in April 1803 to benefit this strange actor and that she sent him a purse with a note of grateful remembrance.[12]

When Joséphine heard of her release on August 6, she evidently fainted, and although she was finally free, it would be absurd to claim that she emerged unscathed from the Carmelites. Like others who had lived daily with the specter of death hovering over them, awaiting the inevitable, Joséphine would never again be the same, nor would she ever refer to this unspeakable experience that had so deeply traumatized her. When she stumbled out of the convent, Joséphine was a woman in mourning and a mother in anguish. She had lost almost everything—her husband, her means of living, her rank in society—and was so profoundly shaken that she could not even imagine how she would support herself and her family. As she struggled to get her bearings that warm August day in the summer of 1794, she must have gazed with wonder upon the flowers blooming in the Luxembourg gardens before she resolutely set off to embrace her children.

3

In Full Plumage

When she was released from the prison of the Carmelites in August 1794, Joséphine was all but destitute, so she appealed to her widowed mother in Martinique for funds, which, although meager, helped her survive, as did a loan from Aunt Renaudin, who was now living at Fontainebleau. Inflation made matters worse. When people gave dinner parties, guests had to bring their own bread, and the joy that had greeted the end of the Terror soon gave way to a period of severe shortages. The apartments where Josephine's children had been living as virtual orphans had been sealed, and it would be months before she could get permission to reclaim her belongings from the Committee of Public Safety. So in September she moved with the children into a close friend's apartment on rue de l'Université, that of the widowed Mme. de Krény, whom Joséphine called her *chère petite*.

Ultimately, it was Mme. de Krény who benefitted most from the arrangement, for her tenant—the widowed niece of Aunt Fanny de Beauharnais—was a woman with connections who would soon become the leading light of a strange new order. Vivant Denon had returned to France, and it was doubtlessly through Joséphine that this gifted impresario was introduced to Mme. de Krény, who became his mistress. If the painter David had saved Denon's life, Joséphine provided the key to his brilliant career; three years later she would insist that Bonaparte appoint Denon to head his team of artists in Egypt,[1] an unprecedented expedition that would serve as the springboard for Denon's eventual unchallenged position as director of the arts of France.

Once she had found a place to live, her children's education became Joséphine's priority. Help came unexpectedly for Eugène, when General Hoche took the boy under his wing as an orderly. Eugène remained almost a year with this general, who had fought valiantly against the Austrians in 1793, and Eugène always believed he had been recommended to Hoche by his father just before his execution. Eugène was thus launched upon his military career when he was barely thirteen, and although his schooling was difficult, it helped form his stalwart character, for Hoche spared Eugène

Anonymous artist, Madame Jeanne-Louise Campan *(location unknown). Madame Campan (1752–1822), like Joséphine herself, was a link with the former régime. Essentially part of the royal family at Versailles, she served as reader to Louis XV's daughters and was so attached to Marie-Antoinette that she dedicated her memoirs to the late queen. Her boarding school at Saint-Germain-en-Laye became the most sought-after establishment for the elite of Consular and Empire society.*

neither fatigue nor danger. Later, while serving his stepfather, Napoléon, it was Eugène who would volunteer for the most dangerous and demanding missions.

By the summer of 1795, things were going better for Joséphine as her children inherited Alexandre's property in Santo Domingo. Madame Campan, formerly first lady of the chamber to Marie-Antoinette, had been ruined by the Revolution, so she opened a seminary at Saint-Germain, where she agreed to take Hortense at half-price. Madame Campan's school was remarkable in that she taught religion, morality, manners, physical fitness, languages, grammar, history, and the arts, specifically theater, music, painting, and drawing, in which Hortense won first prize. Isabey himself was the drawing teacher, and many of the finest artists of the time were invited to examine the pupils' work. Over a period of twenty years, Madame Campan molded young women from every level of society into cultivated ladies who set the tone for all Europe.

Eugène by this time was in boarding school (the College Irlandais), and Joséphine rented a house at 6, rue Chantereine (later renamed rue de la Victoire), belonging to Julie Carreau, estranged wife of the celebrated actor Talma, who would later form part of Joséphine's inner circle. Joséphine managed to reclaim Alexandre's silver and furniture, as well as a carriage and pair of horses, and gradually—through wit and shrewd calculation—Joséphine began to build a new life for herself

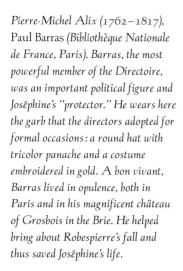

Pierre-Michel Alix (1762–1817), Paul Barras (Bibliothèque Nationale de France, Paris). Barras, the most powerful member of the Directoire, was an important political figure and Joséphine's "protector." He wears here the garb that the directors adopted for formal occasions: a round hat with tricolor panache and a costume embroidered in gold. A bon vivant, Barras lived in opulence, both in Paris and in his magnificent château of Grosbois in the Brie. He helped bring about Robespierre's fall and thus saved Joséphine's life.

and her children. Impoverished though she was, she managed to present herself as a woman of the world, endowed with the qualities she needed to succeed in that cynical society: good looks, unusual charm, esprit, intelligence, exquisite taste, remarkable social instincts, and unremitting determination. We have a picture of her at this time from the pen of Claire de Rémusat: "Her figure was perfect, her limbs flexible and delicate, her movements easy and elegant. La Fontaine's line could never have been more aptly applied than to her: 'Et la grace, plus belle encore que la beauté' (her grace is more beautiful than her beauty)."[2]

By September 1795 the government had become more stable, as a Directoire of five members with executive power was established, headquartered in the Luxembourg Palace. The most prominent of these directors was the former vicomte Paul Barras, who had amassed a fortune from his political position and lived in such unabashed luxury that the pamphleteers called him the "Sultan of the Luxembourg." Barras was typical of those who were spending money like water, offering the finest food and wine to their friends, dancing the night away in a kind of furious saturnalia. "What Paris loves most (after money)," wrote Sébastien Mercier, "is dancing. . . . Everyone dances; it is a kind of universal furor."[3] They danced everywhere—at the pleasure garden of Ruggieri, the seminary of Saint-Sulpice, even at the old prison of the Carmelites, Joséphine's former netherworld.

Philibert-Louis Debucourt (1755–1832), The Orange, *or* The Modern Judgment of Paris *(Musée Carnavalet). Debucourt's engraving depicts the manners and modes of the day. His modern Paris, seated in a Directoire chair, judges the three Graces who are ogled by his friends at left. The physiognomy of the beauty at the center strongly suggests Joséphine's; the blonde on her right must be Juliette Récamier, although the circumspect hooded figure at her left could hardly stand for the brazen Thérèse Tallien.*

Those on the highest rung of the social ladder danced at splendid eighteenth-century town houses, where Joséphine was invited to magnificent soirées, for she was, after all, a former vicomtesse.

Installed at the heart of Directoire society was its queen, Thérèse Tallien, who "smilingly directed the choir of scandals of France."[4] Her salon was the gathering place for the affluent in the worlds of government, military, business, and even art. Thérèse was the dark-eyed Spanish beauty who had taken Hortense and Eugène under her wing during their mother's incarceration; she was now married to Jean Tallien, who is credited with obtaining Joséphine's release. Joséphine and Thérèse now became virtually inseparable. They even dressed to complement one another: as they were deciding upon costumes for one of the balls at the Hôtel Thélusson, Joséphine penned a hasty note to her friend, telling her to put on a peach-colored underskirt like her own and reporting that she would be tying up her hair in a red handkerchief *à la Créole.*[5] Soon the salons of Paris were chattering about Joséphine's and Thérèse's new coiffures, as well as the blonde wigs they often donned to conceal their dark hair.

It was at Thérèse Tallien's house that Joséphine met one of the most conspicuous men in Paris, the powerful banker Julien Ouvrard, who had unscrupulously profited by his country's instability. Another was Paul Barras who, as Joséphine well knew, stood at the center of political power. How she could justify becoming his mistress is hard to say, but he had been a vicomte under the ancien régime and, besides, she was still trying to find the means to establish a home for herself and her children. In any case, Joséphine was soon enhancing Barras's salon at the Luxembourg, assuming for the first time a role she learned to play with consummate skill—official hostess presiding over the establishment of the head of government. She became an exemplar of women who were now beginning to resume their significant place in society, for as Janssens expressed it, women's influence had "yesterday been eclipsed by the austerity of Robespierre, but now they were restored to their eternal role, charming and impulsive."[6] Each of these adjectives applies to Joséphine and helps explain why both men and women were inevitably drawn to her. Joséphine could also be described as a *merveilleuse*, one of the fashionable ladies of the day who dressed rather eccentrically in quasi-classical costumes consisting of tulle or gauze dresses, worn with sandals, ankle bracelets, and Greco-Roman hairdos beneath outlandish hats. Their male counterparts were the *incroyables*, dandies who affected ill-fitting and unkempt coats and breeches.

Nothing contributed more to Joséphine's image as a leading *merveilleuse* than her alluring dresses *à l'athéniènne*, secured beneath the bosom with belts adorned with cameos and accompanied by overskirts with classical borders and stylish diadems capping her curls. From now on, Joséphine's clothing would always attract attention, and the political acumen she was quickly acquiring led her to appreciate the public-relations value of gowns that evoked the supposedly virtuous life of Greece or Republican Rome, further identifying France with the prestigious classical tradition.

Joséphine's apparent stability was suddenly jeopardized when a riot of royalist inspiration broke out in October 1795, threatening the government. It was Barras's duty to suppress it, so he called upon a young general whose resourcefulness he had noted during the siege of Toulon in 1793—Napoléon Bonaparte—and his quick action restored peace to the capital. It was during this disturbed autumn of 1795 that General Bonaparte stepped into the relatively secure world that Joséphine had crafted for herself, and he would shake it to its very foundations.

Joséphine was now proving to be not only a guide for the fashionably dressed, but a resourceful decorator even with limited means. Her small rented house, nicely appointed with marble mantelpieces and mahogany doors, provided an agreeable backdrop for the decor she achieved over the next few years. The entrance hall was painted with military trophies. In the dining room stood a proper mahogany table with saber-legged chairs covered in black horsehair, side tables for serving, and a Sheffield plate tea service of Neoclassical design. The mantel of her green and white *petit salon* was crowned with a pair of "Etruscan" Wedgwood vases, which echoed the stucco bas-reliefs depicting scenes from Roman history, and a white marble bust of Socrates.

Indispensable to all her houses were musical instruments, and in the salon stood her patrician harp and a pianoforte. Both Eugène and Hortense (later an accomplished composer) loved music as much as their mother did, and it always remained an integral part of their lives. So faithfully did Joséphine support the composer Gasparo Spontini that his famous lyrical tragedy, *La Vestale*, would never have been staged without her sponsorship.

Joséphine's bedroom, once occupied by Mme. Talma, was now decorated in an up-to-date "Roman and Etruscan style," an austere backdrop for the patriotic red and blue silk that Joséphine suspended like a tent from the ceiling. This innovation, the tent motif, would become Joséphine's special trademark. She also put up an awning as shelter for her porte cochère, and later a vestibule on the garden side suggesting a tent. Her unusual artistic sensibility would enable her to bring the fabled team of Percier and Fontaine into her service, the pair who created the famous tentlike Council Chamber at Malmaison where Napoléon would hold his conferences.

Joséphine could run her small domain with a manservant, who also prepared the meals, a coachman-gardener, a maid, and her indispensable governess, faithful Mlle. de Lannoy, who sometimes performed tasks usually assigned to servants. This small house and garden on rue Chantereine gave the impression of an establishment owned by a respectable, well-bred family, and that was Joséphine's intention. The house always held a special significance for them, for it was the first real home they had known since her release from prison. Furthermore, it allowed her to keep her life in Luxembourg circles disassociated from this snug little family abode, which was removed from the bustle of city life. From the porte cochère, Joséphine would step into her dashing little carriage drawn by black Hungarian horses, wearing a gray Italian silk taffeta that set off her radiant complexion and her luminous eyes, enhanced by the longest lashes that Constant (the man who would become Joséphine's valet) had ever seen. Off to the theater she would go, to applaud the theatrical idol Talma in his latest role. Like Vivant Denon, Talma had been saved from the Revolutionary Tribunal by the intervention of the painter Jacques-Louis David.

Suddenly, Joséphine's precious tranquility was shattered when, following the insurrection, the dreaded tocsin sounded again throughout Paris and drums beat the alarm. On October 14, 1795, the journal *Moniteur* had carried a notice by Director Barras stating that all unauthorized weapons must be surrendered to the authorities. When a commissioner knocked at Joséphine's door to enforce the edict, the fourteen-year-old Eugène protested in a manly way that he could not possibly give up the sword of his father, who had been General de Beauharnais of the Republican armies. He was told that his only recourse was to apply to the commander of regular troops in the capital, General Bonaparte, at his headquarters in rue des Capucines.

When Eugène was ushered into the general's office by the aide-de-camp, he was surprised to see how thin and pale the commander was. Bonaparte kindly told the boy to sit down, and as Eugène explained his mission, his eyes fell upon his father's precious saber (confiscated by the commissioner), and tears rolled down his cheeks. As Lavalette recorded, Bonaparte was moved by the

Jacques-Louis David (1748–1825), Bonaparte (Musée du Louvre). David met General Bonaparte at the end of 1797, just after the latter's return from the first Italian campaign. At the first sight of this youthful celebrity who was to become his new hero, David made his famous pronouncement: "Mais, il est beau, comme l'antique." Unwilling sitter though he was, Bonaparte remained quiet long enough for the painter to achieve this brilliant head. Bonaparte's classical features—conveniently satisfying the canons of "antique" beauty—provided a source of endless satisfaction for the imperial painters, as well as the greatest sculptor of the age, Antonio Canova.

boy's demeanor, the warmth and naïveté of his request, so he allowed Eugène to keep his cherished arm. It was a crucial meeting, because "from that moment on, the fate of Eugène was never again to be separated from that of Bonaparte."[7]

The morning after her son's visit, Joséphine's carriage stopped at General Bonaparte's headquarters so that she could thank him for his kindness to her son. This was a simple courtesy visit, but Joséphine well knew the value of becoming acquainted with people in authority, having recruited as many protectors as she could. After all, this General Bonaparte occupied a significant post in the government and some day might be useful to her. Besides, her curiosity was piqued by Eugène's account of their meeting.

There was no way Joséphine could have imagined, as she swept into his office that day, what kind of man she was about to meet, although his charismatic personality must have caught her attention. Nor could she have failed to notice that "his smile was of an uncommon sweetness, and one might even say irresistible."[8] Yet in spite of his position, Bonaparte may still have appeared provincial in the eyes of the sophisticated vicomtesse—by now the most visible ornament of Directoire society—and the contrast between them must have been striking. To him, this captivating woman with the slender figure, bewitching blue eyes, and seductive Créole voice was unlike anyone he had ever met. True, he had come close to marrying Desirée Clary earlier that year, but when he left for the capital, he quickly forgot her, although she never forgot him.[9] His first encounter with Joséphine he described years later writing his memoirs as a captive on Saint Helena: "Elle avait un je ne sais quoi qui plaisait; c'etait une vraie femme" (She had something indefinable about her that was so pleasing; she was a real woman).[10]

In short, Joséphine was the incarnation of all that being Parisiènne meant then and now—distinction, understated elegance, and, above all, attention to detail. Bonaparte had not, he admitted, been oblivious to feminine charm before, but he always claimed that Joséphine was the first woman to give him self-confidence. Not only was he overwhelmed by her appearance and manner, but by her flattery as well. For she said just the right thing, mentioning France's admiration for his early military success, and according to Mme. d'Avrillion, Joséphine won Bonaparte over so completely that he henceforth attached himself to her as if magnetized.

A few days later, General Bonaparte appeared at the house on rue Chantereine, for the widow Beauharnais had invited him to visit. The gardener Gonthier, hastily putting aside his trowel to assume the role of butler, ushered the visitor into the dining room. Obviously, Bonaparte must have thought, here lives a woman of taste, refinement, and wealth. But as Janssens pointed out, Bonaparte was unaware of the superficiality of his surroundings. For the handsome sideboard and silver cabinet were nearly empty, the mistress's closet held only a few costumes, and the servants rarely received their wages on a regular basis. Even had he known the truth, it would have made no difference, for by their second meeting, Bonaparte had fallen hopelessly in love.

For Joséphine, however, it was a mere flirtation, and she found him amusing: "Il est drôle, ce Bonaparte!" Besides, she was still the mistress of Director Barras and inhabited a social world apart from Bonaparte's, even though Barras was often accompanied by military men, bankers, and contractors. By the latter part of January 1796, the Luxembourg Palace had been lavishly refurbished, and here the epicurean Barras was installed. Surrounded by the usual bevy of beauties, including Thérèse Tallien, and by flowers in abundance, Barras staged lavish parties over which Joséphine (still known as "Rose") reigned supreme. Nothing vulgar, of course, but all governed by good taste, with the most delicate dishes, finest wines, and ices sent over from the fashionable house of Velloni.

Joséphine also did the honors for Barras at parties in the country, staged in the small villa she still rented near Croissy, where Barras would arrive on horseback. Her neighbor Etiènne Pasquier (later prefect of police) was amused, and annoyed, by the way Joséphine entertained. In the extravagant manner for which Créoles were known, she would order huge quantities of food from the Paris catering establishments, including fruits out of season, platters of game, and exotic dishes arranged as still lifes that were appealing to both eye and palette, but she never seemed to have on hand such mundane items as plates and glassware. Inevitably, she would turn to the Pasquier family at the very last minute, asking to borrow these necessities from their own meager ménage.

On the evening of January 21, 1796, against their wishes, Hortense and Eugène were required to accompany their mother to a banquet in the Luxembourg. Hortense, ever the aristocrat, said she could not imagine associating with the people she had heard would be there, but her mother replied that they had to show gratitude to those who had protected them during their misfortunes. And there were other compelling reasons: Barras was expecting her; she wanted to present her children to certain people of good family; and besides, she knew she looked particularly attractive in her robe *à l'antique* of Indian muslin, which fell in generous folds and was caught at the shoulders by two lions' heads enameled in black, leaving her shapely arms bare. Some of the guests were ladies of the ancien régime, and some were men moving into prominence in the new one. Hortense sat between her mother and a man she gradually realized was Eugène's new hero, the general who had allowed him to keep their father's sword. General Bonaparte became increasingly animated and kept leaning across Hortense to talk with her mother, who responded with her slumberous, caressing voice, which seemed to excite him even further. He was obviously smitten, and Hortense wondered uneasily how this would affect her love for herself and Eugène.

Bonaparte had now evolved from the timid, gauche provincial he had once been. Even in this select society, his extraordinary gifts as an orator were already surfacing. After dinner, the ladies retired to the salon, taking the general with them; his conversation pleased them so much that they sat in a circle around him. In fact, Hortense admitted that "he seemed to be the soul of that little society. . . . He had the art of telling [stories] in such a way as to make them interesting by the originality of his recitals."[11]

Soon Joséphine was seeing more of the general and even considering his proposal of marriage. Bonaparte wanted a wife, not a mistress, for he had been reared by a strong, devout, realistic mother, Laetizia ("Madame Mère"), and as Joséphine hesitated, her friends pointed out that Bonaparte was obviously a man of unusual talent. The one person on whom she could rely for an honest opinion was her tiny gnome of a notary, M. Raguideau, whom she and Bonaparte went to visit to review the terms of the marriage contract. While the general waited outside the room, she consulted M. Raguideau about the wisdom of this marriage, and the notary reminded her she had already lost one soldier husband, so he could certainly not understand why she would marry another, especially one who could bring nothing to their union except "his cloak and his sword."[12] Bonaparte overheard the conversation, but instead of being offended, he rushed into the room and clapped the little notary on the shoulder, declaring such pleasure in his logic that he guaranteed Raguideau would continue taking care of their business—and so he did. But, for the moment, Joséphine deferred making a commitment of marriage to Bonaparte.

In February 1796 something happened to force Joséphine's hand. It was precipitated by the directors' growing concern over the armies of Austria that were threatening the French frontier. So they turned to an audacious plan submitted by Bonaparte. Although success was unlikely against an army of 50,000 Austrians with only 35,000 men and scant artillery for the French, it was nevertheless agreed on March 2 that Bonaparte, at age twenty-six, should be named commander of the Army of Italy.

OPPOSITE: *Robert Lefèvre (1755–1830),*
Madame Mère (Château de Versailles). In 1808
the king of Spain commissioned from Lefèvre, one
of the Bonapartes' favorite painters, this portrait
of the dignified family matriarch Laetizia
Bonaparte. The canvas at Versailles is a copy
ordered by Napoléon in 1813. His mother wears
court apparel and stands before an imperial
armchair decorated with lions' heads supporting
the arms. Lefèvre refers to her Corsican
homeland by offering a glimpse of the gulf of
Ajaccio through the curtain.

RIGHT: *Jean-Baptiste Isabey (1767—1855),*
Joséphine, c. 1795 (Malmaison). Isabey was
exactly the kind of man Joséphine liked to have
near her—well-dressed, versatile, urbane, and
refined. She may have first encountered him at
Madame Campan's school as Hortense's drawing
master, and this sketch of Joséphine might have
been executed there. He remained in her service
for many years, designing costumes and schemes
for important occasions such as the coronation
and making informal sketches of family scenes.

While the Directoire was deliberating this decision, Bonaparte was bombarding the widow Beauharnais with haunting love letters: "Quel est donc ton étrange pouvoir, incomparable Joséphine?" (What is your strange power, incomparable Joséphine?).[13] This escalating pressure upon her to marry him stemmed not only from his passionate love for her, but also from his eagerness to rejoin the army. Joséphine's eroding resistance crumbled, and the marriage was set for March 9.

The pared-down,"republican" demeanor that Joséphine had prudently adopted three years earlier had now given way to an up-to-date turban wrapped round the chic disarray of her new coiffure, matching a thin white dress with its atypically high collar. Jean-Baptiste Isabey, Hortense's drawing master at Madame Campan's school, most likely caught this likeness of Joséphine when she visited her daughter there. Four years later Isabey would become Joséphine's resident artist and a virtual member of her family, first at Malmaison and then at court; he even went along on her travels, pen in hand.

The groom knew his bride to be older than himself, although he did not know her exact age, so Joséphine, who had (conveniently, as it turned out) lost her birth certificate, arranged to have a new one made by Etiènne Calmelet, who was persuaded to "improve" a bit on her age. Calmelet recorded her birth year not as June 23, 1763, but as 1767, which would have meant that she gave birth to Eugène at the tender age of fourteen! (Napoléon's birthday on the marriage certificate was given as August 15, 1769.) Calmelet and Jean Tallien stood as her witnesses at the civil marriage, and for Bonaparte there was Barras himself and a Captain Lemarrois. The time was set for 8 p.m., but Bonaparte did not arrive until 10 o'clock, without offering even a word of apology.

Their two-day honeymoon in the house on rue Chantereine was hardly satisfactory. First of all, it was marred by the inhospitable Fortuné's attack upon his mistress's new husband, for the little dog bit Bonaparte's leg on the evening of their wedding. Then most of the bridegroom's time was spent in the study, poring over his maps as he planned a campaign destined to become one of the most astonishing in military annals and shouting through the door to Joséphine that their real honeymoon would have to wait. On the evening of March 11, a carriage drew up to the door bearing Bonaparte's aide-de-camp, General Andoche Junot, and the commissary-general, Chauvet. As Joséphine stood in the courtyard of her house, Fortuné barking at her side, she waved to Bonaparte as he drove away to Italy and to glory.[14] Although she may have begun to suspect that she had married no ordinary man, Joséphine was as yet unaware that her husband was a genius such as the world had never seen, that he was about to carry her to unimaginable heights of grandeur, and that he would confer upon her a unique and enduring place in history.

Only a few weeks after Bonaparte's departure, reports from the victorious Army of Italy under its indefatigable commander began to reach Paris. The tidings of French soldiers led by their seemingly invincible general began to fill the newspapers, were shouted loudly in the streets, proclaimed in the official bulletins, ecstatically discussed in the cafés and salons, hailed and saluted by the proud citizens of Paris, and mulled over (with mixed feelings) by the directors in their offices at the Luxembourg. Even Joséphine herself must have begun to wonder.

4

Soaring with the Eagle

Eugène was disappointed by his mother's remarriage, but he did not yet know that the period about to open for him would be the happiest of his life, largely due to opportunities offered by his new stepfather. Hortense opposed Joséphine's marriage as well and was more vocal than her brother. At Madame Campan's school in Saint Germain, as the pupils were chatting excitedly about the remarkable victories won by Hortense's stepfather that spring of 1796, Madame Campan ecstatically read aloud the Bulletins that streamed in with the latest reports from the army. General Bonaparte had faced more than fifty thousand Austrians with their mighty cavalry, beat the Sardinians, then defeated the Austrians at Montenotte, Millesimo, and Mondovi. An armistice was signed April 28, and the French entered Milan on May 15.

Madame Campan forced Hortense to listen to the public readings of the Bulletins and asked her pupil: "Do you realize that your mother has just joined her destiny to an extraordinary man? What talents! What courage! At every moment, new conquests!" To which the obstinate Hortense replied: "Madame, I credit him with all those conquests, but I will never forgive him for the conquest of my mother."[1] Madame Campan thought this retort so witty that it was soon repeated in the salons of Paris. Now her school quickly acquired a long waiting list, and among those admitted (without waiting) was Bonaparte's sister, Caroline.

Surprisingly, France's new hero somehow found time to write to his stepchildren, his letters being accompanied by a splendid gold watch for Eugène and for Hortense a small round timepiece surrounded by pearls, as well as boxes of scent. These were brought by Bonaparte's aide-de-camp, in whom Bonaparte had confided how much he wanted his wife to join him. He poured out the immensity of his love for Joséphine in eloquent love letters, urging her to come to Italy as quickly as possible. He wanted to share with her his grief at the loss of a colleague, and he mused upon the mystery of life and death in a lyrical letter dated April 5: "It is an hour after midnight. . . . My soul is affected [by] the death of Chauvet. . . . My friend, I feel the need to be consoled . . . by writing to you alone. What is the future? What is the past? What are we. . . . We pass on, we live, we die in the midst of miracles."[2] Letter succeeded letter, begging her first to come with Junot, then (after no response) to leave with Murat. "Your rooms are ready."[3] Nothing, he added, could equal his love for her except his anxiety.

Implored by the victor of Italy to join him in his triumphal progression with an escort of the striking Andoche Junot (recently promoted to captain for his bravery)[4] or the glamorous cavalryman Joachim Murat (who had demonstrated his prowess at the battle of Mondovi), Napoléon's invitation was one no woman in her right mind could have refused. No woman, that is, except Joséphine, who remained as obtuse as her daughter when it came to appreciating Bonaparte. He once said there were three kinds of people: those who make things happen, those who watch things happen, and those who do not know anything has happened. Joséphine remained, for an infuriatingly long time, in the last category.

What was keeping her in Paris? Her children, of course, for Joséphine remained throughout her life a doting mother. Eugène and Hortense were in boarding school very near Paris, and she wanted to be close to them. Also Joséphine wanted time to enjoy her delightful home, in which she was conducting a salon modeled after Aunt Fanny de Beauharnais's literary soirées. Survivors of the old order were beginning to mingle with the new, and Joséphine was serving as catalyst.

A more compelling reason, however, for Joséphine's reluctance to leave Paris was a dishonorable one, a sudden infatuation with a young captain of less-than-mediocre military ability whom she met in April 1796. In his blue hussar's uniform with dolman slung over his shoulders and his shako adorned with a tricolored cockade, Captain Hippolyte Charles instantly caught her eye, perhaps for his party antics, such as gluing Andoche Junot's saber into its scabbard or appearing in the salon dressed as a Créole. It remains a mystery why Joséphine became so attached to such an inconsequential figure when she was married to a universal genius, now the toast of Paris. Her shameful behavior became general knowledge (to the chagrin of the Bonaparte family), and the worst of it was that, when she finally left to join her husband, her silly captain went along with her.

The directors were not anxious to have Joséphine join Bonaparte in Italy because they feared her presence might distract him from concentrating fully on the campaign. Nevertheless, by May 21, they granted Citizeness Bonaparte permission to join her husband, although she dallied for another month, as Bonaparte's letters became more desperate: "There is no greater torment than not to have a letter from *mio dolce amor* . . . They gave me a great fête here; five or six hundred elegant and beautiful figures sought to please me; none had that sweet and music-like countenance which I have engraved on my heart. I saw only you, I thought only of you!. . . And how goes your pregnancy?"[5] Joséphine had hinted to him that she might be pregnant, perhaps as a ploy to remain in France, but she was not.

Her recalcitrance is even more incomprehensible in view of the exalted new status she was now enjoying as wife of the popular commander-in-chief. During the month of May, Junot appeared in Paris, bringing twenty-one captured flags to the Directoire, which proudly staged a

Henri-Félix Philippoteaux (1815–1884), Andoche Junot (Château de Versailles). Junot came to Bonaparte's attention at the siege of Toulon in 1793. Known for his beautiful handwriting, Junot had just finished a letter for Bonaparte when an explosion covered the paper with debris. "Good," said the smiling Junot. "We won't need sand to dry the ink." Bonaparte was so impressed that he made Junot his aide-de-camp. As governor of Paris and duc d'Abrantès, Junot and his wife, Laure, were often in Joséphine's company, and Laure's memoirs are among the most interesting of the period.

public fête on May 10 to celebrate the occasion. The star of the occasion was of course Mme. Bonaparte, who brought along her friend the flamboyant Thérèse Tallien. Junot's wife, Laure d'Abrantès, recorded the great effect that Joséphine and Thérèse produced that day as "principal ornaments of this patriotic festival . . . both dressed after the fashion of antiquity. . . . Junot must surely have been proud to give his arm to two such charming women as they descended the stairs of the Luxembourg Palace."[6] The festival was punctuated with stirring martial music, patriotic orations, and shouts of "Long live the Republic!"

On the very day that Joséphine was being admired at the public festivities in Paris, Bonaparte acquired even more laurels when he crushed the Austrians at Lodi. As soon as the news reached the capital, people went wild, and the idolizing crowds were calling Joséphine's husband invincible, infallible. The triumphal entry of the French army into Milan on May 15 was followed by a brilliant ball in the evening, with the women of Milan wearing the French national colors. For the frustrated commander, however, the pleasures of conquest were anything but gratifying, for he longed to have his wife beside him, and he could not wait to finish the campaign to be with her again. "What a situation for a woman to find herself in," Claire de Rémusat wrote in her memoirs, "one of the motivating influences for the triumphal march of a whole army!"[7]

Despite the attractions of Paris, Joséphine was at last ready to set off under cavalry escort on June 26 or 27, as Joseph Bonaparte informed his anxious brother. The motley cavalcade boasted a fascinating cast of characters, each with a particular interest in the expedition. In the first carriage rode Joséphine, Hippolyte Charles (who kept her laughing along the way), Joseph Bonaparte (whose disapproval of Joséphine's conduct was unconcealed), and Andoche Junot. In the second carriage came Joséphine's maid, Louise Compoint (with whom Junot flirted at the stops), and two other servants; curled up beside Louise was the irritable little pug, Fortuné. Louise had her hands full caring for the impressive new wardrobe being transported for her mistress to wear in Italy (lots of gauze turbans and white dresses), and more delectable items would be added along the way. In the third carriage was the duke of Serbelloni, president of the Executive Directory of the Cisalpine Republic, to which several northern Italian states belonged; he had brought Joséphine more letters from Bonaparte, and she would occupy his beautiful palace in Milan.

Joséphine's journey was like the procession of a queen, for she was greeted with wild enthusiasm, impressive fêtes, lavish balls, and jewelry in profusion. As her carriage moved from city to city, escorted by Bonaparte's attentive cavalrymen, even she must have begun to realize that her life was assuming heroic proportions by the sheer plenitude of the offerings showered upon her— embodiments of obeisance rendered to the conqueror's wife. This was all very flattering, but her husband's spectacular success, which thrust Joséphine into a position of such public prominence, placed her in a tenuous position as well. Not only the French military but civilians as well knew there were fortunes to be made in the wake of this stunning campaign, and it was, above all, expedient to please Joséphine. Following her carriage was the merchant Antoine Hamelin (who acquired for her lovely veils from England), as well as an army supplier, Robbé de Lagrange, whose father ran the *Gazette de France*. Lagrange had been her friend since the days of Aunt Fanny's salon, and Joséphine especially favored men from that period in her life (such as Vivant Denon). She was now in a position to offer to Lagrange (and others) opportunities for contracts for government supplies, and he in turn felt obligated to return to her a part of the profits. It was, as Bernard Chevallier has pointed out, difficult for the minister of war to refuse to oblige Joséphine, and Chevallier even suggests that she "controlled the complete chain [of command] . . . from commissions from the offices in Paris down to Bonaparte's aides-de-camp."[8]

Receiving kickbacks on army supply contracts hardly redounds to Joséphine's credit, although public figures as prominent as Barras, Talleyrand, and the banker Ouvrard did make huge fortunes from currency speculation and loans as well. Nor can one overlook Joséphine's involvement in the financial dealings of the Bodin Company, which obtained lucrative army contracts and from which both she and Hippolyte Charles profited. This would all eventually come to light when Joseph Bonaparte informed Napoléon, and the two brothers would confront Joséphine in a painful interview upon their return to Paris.

On June 13, 1796, after a two-week journey, Joséphine's cortège drew up to Bonaparte's headquarters, the fine eighteenth-century Serbelloni Palace in Milan, the annexes of which housed the offices of the military administration. Bonaparte was so eager to please her that he had filled the marble halls of the palace with Italian paintings, the latest French furniture, and sculpture (his favorite medium) and had arranged operas to be performed by Italy's finest singers. The elaborate parties she would be expected to give for the French high command and prominent Milanese offered no problem for Joséphine, for the municipality had thoughtfully put at her disposal one hundred cooks and thirty servants. Although she was probably unaware of it, this stay in Milan marked the beginning of an official life that would tax her ingenuity, strength, and endurance almost to the breaking point. For the moment she was simply enjoying it, but soon we find her writing Hortense that she was homesick, longing for her children and her own little house.

Mme. Bonaparte was expected to be constantly on view, and so her seat at La Scala was in a prominent loge, where she saw Salieri's *La Secchia Rapita*, each act of which was followed by a ballet. The women in her suite repeated the latest gossip: Vivant Denon—in Italy to advise upon works of art to be sent to Paris as spoils of war—had lost no time in arranging rendezvous with the ballerinas for French officers. Bonaparte had eyes only for his "incomparable" Joséphine, and the Milanese were delighted to have the engaging wife of the commander-in-chief in their midst. The duke of Serbelloni was especially honored to have Mme. Bonaparte and the liberator of Italy under his roof, and in their salon in the evenings, the commander-in-chief would hold the assembled company enthralled with his fascinating conversation. One of the circle was a friend of Joséphine's, the poet Antoine Arnault, who noted that everyone was impressed by the general's ability to switch from military matters to an equally erudite discussion of philosophy and poetry. But the fleeting pleasures of those evenings in Milan—where Joséphine was beginning to see her husband in a new light—were overshadowed by her apprehension at the thought of Bonaparte's inevitable departure for the field. Arnault shared her concern and said, "He is born to command, as so many others [are] to obey. If he is not . . . carried off by a bullet . . . he will be in exile or on a throne."[9]

This pleasant interlude in Milan soon came to an abrupt end, for on July 15 Bonaparte left to survey the siege of Mantua, and in order to keep Joséphine nearby, he arranged for her to go on to Brescia, where Murat was ordered to prepare quarters for her. During her journey between Brescia and Verona, however, there occurred the first of several incidents that placed Joséphine in grave danger, for her convoy was suddenly fired upon by Austrian cannon. Junot, who arrived with a detachment of dragoons, quickly pulled Joséphine and her maid from their carriage and forced them into a ditch, drawing the fire upon himself and allowing them to escape. The merchant Antoine Hamelin was astonished at Joséphine's composure under fire and greatly admired her sang-froid: "This woman who is so frivolous, so occupied with her own pleasures . . . was (suddenly) metamorphosed into a chaste heroine."[10]

When Joséphine finally reached Florence, entering the city under escort of thirty dragoons, the French diplomat Count Miot de Melito placed his legation at her disposal. Miot

Antoine Gros (1771–1835). Bonaparte at the Bridge of Arcole (Château de Versailles). This celebrated portrait of Bonaparte was painted at Joséphine's insistence, for she discovered Gros on a short visit to Genoa in 1796 and brought him back to Milan. The forward thrust of the tense, youthful figure is accentuated by the sharp wedge shape made by the junction of the flag and the sword Bonaparte holds as he looks back to encourage his troops to follow. The meticulous attention given to the details of the uniform is typical of Gros's work.

described their meeting in August 1796: "I was now able to renew my acquaintance with her. I had . . . encountered her in the society of Paris, and I had [already] conceived an opinion of her that our closer rapports at Florence only confirmed. Never did a woman show more kindness and natural grace, or do more good with greater pleasure than she has. She honored me with her friendship."[11] Joséphine attracted everyone who met her, and she was well on her way to becoming Bonaparte's most effective ambassador.

She was also royally entertained by the Austrian prince, Ferdinand III, grand duke of Tuscany and nephew of Marie-Antoinette, although Bonaparte was in the process of reclaiming Italy from Ferdinand's compatriots. But courteous behavior remained an inviolable tradition in aristocratic Europe, even among enemies, and many of the men Joséphine would later receive in her salon had faced her husband on the battlefield.

As Joséphine waited anxiously for news of the army, Bonaparte was caught up in a terrible battle at the bridge of Arcole that lasted almost three days, from November 15 through 17, but in the end, the Austrians capitulated. Even from the field the commander kept up his faithful letters to his wife, and after the battle he added: "I am a little tired."[12] During this hard-fought battle Bonaparte seized a flag and led General Augereau's grenadiers across the bridge in the face of Austrian fire, an incident that apparently fired Joséphine's imagination, for it was she who was responsible for the painting that would commemorate it.

Antoine Gros (1771–1835), Eugène de Beauharnais (Malmaison). This is one of several versions of the first known portrait of Joséphine's son. It was no doubt painted in Milan in June 1797, when he was made Bonaparte's aide-de-camp, which uniform he wears here: a hat with red, white, and blue plumes and a white armband (brassard). *Joséphine undoubtedly commissioned this portrait from her protégé, Baron Gros.*

Toward the end of November, Joséphine made a brief visit to Genoa, where there was an interesting French community and where a young artist named Antoine Gros was presented to her at the house of the French consul. Joséphine had admired the portraits Gros had painted in Genoa, and she whisked him off in her carriage to the center of power in Milan. Her first thought was to have Bonaparte sit for the gifted young artist, and the result was *Bonaparte at the Bridge of Arcole*, which has now acquired the status of an icon. Antoine Gros was one of the most impressive of Joséphine's many artistic coups, for from this moment his career began to soar, and Eugène Delacroix called her Gros's "fairy godmother."

It is doubtful that Bonaparte spent the Christmas of 1796 with Joséphine in Milan, for by January 7 of the new year, the Austrians were already closing in on Joubert's defenses near Verona. Marching day and night, Bonaparte arrived at the battlefield of Rivoli and achieved the most resounding victory of the Italian campaign. This was followed by the surrender of Mantua, which meant that the Italian campaign was drawing to a close, although Joséphine and her retinue must have been surprised when Bonaparte negotiated the peace without even so much as a nod toward the Directoire. Next, he tackled the complex problem of reorganizing northern Italy, where he demonstrated his skill as an administrator. Joséphine could not have foreseen the significance of this series of events for herself personally, but this large territory would eventually be committed to the rule of her own son, when Napoléon named Eugène as his viceroy of Italy in 1805 and gave him a sumptuous palace in Milan.

The summer of 1797 was perhaps the happiest of Joséphine's life, for Bonaparte was beside her, and he sent for her beloved sixteen-year-old Eugène to join them in the Villa Cerutti at Mombello (some four miles outside Milan), where they were installed for the season. Eugène received special attention from his stepfather, who made him a second lieutenant and an aide-de-camp, and it was certainly his proud mother who had Gros paint this first known portrait of Eugène de Beauharnais, proudly wearing the armband of an aide-de-camp. At this time Eugène came to appreciate fully the man his mother had married, and the experience matured him, for Hortense later wrote that her brother had gone to Italy a boy and returned a man. Hortense in the meanwhile stayed in France at school, enjoying the special privileges that came with being the stepdaughter to the hero of France, and now Italy.

Life at the villa near Mombello now took on the aspects of a court, where strict etiquette prevailed. The celebrated couple dined in public, while the aides-de-camp and officers sat at separate tables, and a guard of three hundred Polish lancers in blue and purple uniforms controlled the crowds. Joséphine presided as hostess, wearing a cameo necklace given her by the pope. In matters of protocol, she had the able assistance of the Austrian envoy, the Marquis di Gallo, a persuasive diplomat employed by the court of Naples in various negotiations. Fortuné frisked about his mistress's household tormenting the cook's large dog, which finally dispatched the annoying little pug. A tragedy for Joséphine, but surely a secret satisfaction for Bonaparte, who had been the dog's adversary since his wedding night. Perhaps it was an appropriate fate for this most diminutive of Bonaparte's enemies.

That summer in the Italian countryside saw their first real honeymoon, and now Joséphine began to return her husband's affection. They took excursions into the hills, to Lake Maggiore and Lake Como. A French playwright who was in Italy at the time observed that "she frequently caresses her husband who seems devoted to her."[13] Joséphine reported some of the events of the summer to her elderly Aunt Renaudin in a letter taken to Paris by Serbelloni: "M. Serbelloni will inform you, my dear aunt, of the way I have been received in Italy—fêted wherever I have gone, given receptions by all the princes of Italy, even the grand duke of Tuscany, brother of the emperor. Ah, well, I would prefer to be an ordinary individual in France. . . . I have the best husband in the world. I never lack anything, for he always anticipates my wishes. All day long he adores me as if I were a goddess. . . . M. Serbelloni will tell you how I am loved. He often writes to my children for he loves them very much."[14] It had taken time for Bonaparte to win them over, but it would prove an enduring attachment and significant compensation for Joséphine's inability thus far to produce an heir. The duke of Serbelloni served as Joséphine's personal courier, delivering gifts she sent her friends in Paris. Typically, she never forgot those who had helped her through rough times: liqueurs to Barras, sausages to Tallien, and a Leghorn hat for his wife, Thérèse.

It was at this time that her husband decided to "Frenchify" his name, no doubt for political reasons. In 1796, after having taken command at Nice, the former "Napoleone Buonaparte" became General Napoléon Bonaparte, and when he was named first consul three years later, he would become simply "Napoléon."

The grounds of the Mombello villa were thronged with generals, administrators, the highest nobility, and Italy's most distinguished citizens, all hoping to catch a glimpse of the famous couple. The throng became so insistent that a huge cloth pavilion was erected in front of the palace to accommodate the crowds, undoubtedly Joséphine's idea. Besides Italian and French dignitaries, many from the Bonaparte clan came to Mombello that summer, and Joséphine saw them all together for the first time. Napoléon was the second oldest child, with four brothers and three sisters. Their mother, Madame Mère, came to visit with her half-brother, Joseph Fesch, a prolific patron of the arts who was in charge of requisitioning paintings from the churches of Florence. She also brought her daughters to share their brother's glory: Elisa was married to a Corsican, Felix Baciocchi; Pauline was a dazzling beauty of seventeen; and plump, pink Caroline was Hortense's fellow pupil at Madame Campan's school. Joseph Bonaparte, the oldest brother, had been married to Julie Clary since 1794 and was now a commissioner of the Army of Italy; Lucien, who preferred Italy to France, was in Corsica on business; Louis would be tapped as an unsuitable husband for Hortense; and Jérome, the baby of the family, would eventually fall in love with the daughter of a rich Baltimore merchant.

Joséphine was inundated with gifts during her stay in Italy, among them valuable horses sent by Emperor Francis from his renowned stables in Vienna, and when the court of Sardinia was in Turin to sign the peace treaty on May 15, Charles-Emmanuel IV (brother-in-law of Louis XVI) had expressed his desire to render her any services she might require. Even with homage from high-ranking officials and the attentions of European rulers, Joséphine was anxious to go home, but her duties bound her until November 1797.

In September Bonaparte sent Joséphine to Venice for four days to represent him, again with a specially chosen escort, General Marmont (who would command the artillery at Marengo). Because the Venetians wished to ingratiate themselves with Bonaparte, for fear of losing their independence, Joséphine was honored with receptions and a ball in the doge's palace, where she received a magnificent diamond ring. Her taste for art was further stimulated by this opportunity to study Venetian painting, and eventually she would form a truly extraordinary collection containing works by Titian, Veronese, Bellini, and Giorgione. The bronze horses she saw in the Piazza San Marco, which the Venetians had taken from the Byzantines in 1204, would soon, in turn, be carted off to Paris.

Bonaparte himself was keenly aware of the immense political prestige to be derived from possessing such treasures, to say nothing of their incalculable intrinsic value, so he established five art commissions throughout Italy. Many of these treasures would be sent to Paris in 1798 as part of

Pierre-Paul Prud'hon (1758–1823), Charles-Maurice de Talleyrand-Périgord, Prince de Bénévent, 1817 (The Metropolitan Museum of Art, New York). Prud'hon suggests the wisdom and erudition of Napoléon's former minister by portraying him with busts of the ancients. The pose is the same as in two portraits painted by Prud'hon in 1807, showing Talleyrand in official court dress. After Napoléon's fall in 1815, Talleyrand's niece commissioned this revised image showing the diplomat wearing the buckled shoes, silk hose, and culottes of the ancien régime and standing in a modish salon furnished with chairs in the Neoclassical style of Louis XVI.

the spoils and would enter the new Musée Central des Arts, formerly the Louvre and soon to be called the Musée Napoléon (and even later the Louvre again). Here Joséphine always attended the Salons, lending pieces from her own collection, and she bought many works on these occasions from living artists she wanted to encourage. Napoléon decorated painters and sculptors at these Salons, and John Russell reminds us that Napoléon made it unthinkable that anyone would not be interested in painting, a concept with which Joséphine obviously agreed.

During her sojourn in Italy, Joséphine began to think that her little rented house on rue Chantereine (now rue de la Victoire) was no longer impressive enough for the victor of Italy. In this way she rationalized her indulgence in the art of decor she practiced so skillfully and wrote detailed instructions to the architect Corneille Vautier, informing him that her agent, Etiènne Calmelet, would advance the funds for remodeling it "in the latest elegance."[15] Receiving carte blanche from Mme. Bonaparte, Vautier followed through, ordering such luxuries as mahogany furniture richly embellished with gilt bronze from the atelier of Joséphine's favorite *ébénistes*, the Jacob brothers; a painted frieze featuring a suite of antique personages; a circular mirrored dressing room draped in lilac taffeta, and a salon hung with green taffeta curtains. On December 6, 1797, Bonaparte returned to Paris, and when he opened the door, he was initially stupefied and then—as the enormous bills came rolling in—infuriated. But he had little time to think about this, being so constantly in demand for public celebrations in his honor.

This protracted attention to the Bonapartes began to worry the directors, who learned that Joséphine, after leaving Milan in late November, was honored all the way back to Paris. The silk capital of Lyons offered her balls, illuminations, and receptions, where she received a crown of roses and a laurel wreath for her husband. Given Joséphine's extensive patronage of Lyons' fabled silk manufacture, it is certain she was shown (and indeed given) some of these unparalleled materials that lent such splendor to her clothing, walls, and furniture, especially in the imperial châteaux.

Among those eager to ingratiate themselves to the Bonapartes was the clever minister of foreign affairs, Charles-Maurice Talleyrand, who was planning a lavish soirée in their honor. Joséphine, who was due back in Paris on December 29 or 30, would reign as queen of the ball, and Bonaparte was happy that his wife would be honored, knowing full well the political value of such an affair. This party was a true sign of the times: a gala given by a former bishop in an aristocratic town house that had been made national property and was now a ministry.[16] The event did, however, severely challenge Talleyrand's patience, for he had to keep postponing the date until Joséphine's arrival, and her stately progression from Italy could not, of course, be hurried. So the Minister had to wait . . . and wait, watching one wilting floral arrangement replace another for three successive days, and his harried chef (probably the renowned Antoine Carême), was left to improvise as best he could. Mme. Bonaparte finally reached Paris on January 2, 1798, by which date her host's bills at florists and food purveyors had reached nearly astronomic proportions.

The event, which at last took place on January 3, was magnificent, with a collation for three hundred people, music by singers from the Opéra, and toasts such as only the articulate Talleyrand could propose. The grand staircase was covered with flowering plants, and the musicians sat in a cupola adorned with arabesques; standing in a small Etruscan temple built to house it was a bust of Brutus from General Bonaparte himself. This bust would prove an exquisite irony, for Bonaparte would in due course play Caesar to Talleyrand's Brutus.

At 10:30 P.M. Joséphine, on her husband's arm, entered the extensive garden illuminated with Bengal lights, orchestras playing in the bosquets, and tents accommodating soldiers from the Paris garrison. The guest of honor was dressed in a dignified, understated way, having chosen the type of dress most becoming to her, further identifying the régime with classical antiquity: a Greek robe showing off her beautiful arms and neck, with a fillet of laurels in her hair (perhaps the one given her in Lyons for her husband). Joséphine well understood the art of image-making in politics, and a murmur of admiration greeted her arrival. Laure Permon (the future wife of Andoche Junot) and her mother took in every detail of Joséphine's costume. Laure herself was wearing a dress appropriate to the new Republic: chaste white crêpe trimmed with broad satin ribbons and a wreath of oak leaves.

One woman in particular, Germaine de Staël, who was fascinated by Bonaparte, insisted that the poet Arnault present her to him, but Joseph Bonaparte's friend Louis de Girardin said it was obvious to everyone that the general was very much in love with his wife and extremely jealous. He stayed close to Joséphine all during supper and paid attention to her alone, which would be an ongoing source of annoyance to the talented Mme. de Staël. If she was the most expansive of Talleyrand's guests, the most reticent was the discreet Vivant Denon, who said little despite his vast erudition, observing the maxim "Celui qui parle ne sait pas. Celui qui sait ne parle pas" (He who talks knows not. He who knows talks not)."[17] As he offered Bonaparte a glass of lemonade, the rapport between the two—already established during the Italian campaign—was renewed. Later that spring, Joséphine would point out to her husband that Denon would be indispensable to one of his most audacious enterprises, the voyage to Egypt.

As expensive as Talleyrand's assembly was, Bonaparte thought the money well spent because it bore the stamp of good taste. Besides, it was a gracious symbol of reconciliation, bringing together the military, members of the Convention, and former Jacobins and aristocrats. In fact, this was exactly what Bonaparte would seek to do himself, and with the woman he loved beside him, a lady of quality at ease in St. Germain society, it was soon to become a reality. Bonaparte had become accustomed to the outrageous cost of the new splendor in which they lived, although he scolded her and warned her against future extravagance, with little effect. As for Joséphine, she was relieved that the debilitating campaign was over and that she would be reunited with her children. Hortense was flourishing in Madame Campan's school, and Eugène would soon be coming home from Italy.

If the time Eugène spent on the Italian peninsula as his stepfather's aide-de-camp had changed him from a boy to a man, Joséphine's experiences had been transforming as well. She remembered the magnificent palaces and picturesque villas placed at her disposal; the courtly attentions of monarchs and princes, each trying to outdo the other; the illuminated cities, triumphal arches, and vestal virgins bearing laurels and roses; the precious gifts of jewelry, paintings, sculpture, and rare materials heaped upon her in the cities through which she passed. As Joséphine reflected upon the glories of the past year and a half in Italy, she believed that the expensive decoration of her house on the renamed rue de la Victoire was entirely justified. After all, wasn't it the responsibility of the conqueror's wife to create a setting worthy of France's new Man of the Hour?

5

To Egypt and Beyond

In February 1798, the Directoire was determined to put an end to the contest with England, so it sent Bonaparte to inspect the Channel ports with a view to invading the island. He returned with an unfavorable report, but he had an alternate plan in mind—an expedition to Egypt to cut off England's trade route to India, a major source of British wealth. Talleyrand supported the idea, but Bonaparte had to win the directors over to his side, and to this end he enlisted Joséphine's support. Utilizing her gifts of diplomacy, she set out to break down the defenses of the opposition, although the directors were tough, shrewd men, unlikely to be influenced by a woman in matters of policy.

She began by approaching the two directors most adamantly opposed—Paul Barras and the lawyer Jean-François Reubell, a successful diplomat and an expert in foreign policy. As she launched her offensive, Joséphine sent a warm invitation to "mon cher Barras" to dine at their house with, among others, the poet Raymond de Verninac, who had recently served as an envoy to Constantinople and reported on the advantages for France of seizing control of Egypt. At dinner, Joséphine tactfully brought up topics that would interest her guests, such as Reubell's having served at Mainz with Alexandre de Beauharnais during the campaign of 1793, although she would have been careful to avoid any reference to its outcome (bad for France and fatal for Alexandre). Subsequently, Joséphine lay siege to other key figures hostile to the Egyptian venture, dining with the ministers of war and of the navy. Of course, one cannot claim that her social efforts made any real impact upon the directors' decision, which may in fact have stemmed from their desire to have the popular and ambitious young Bonaparte out of the country, but on March 5, 1798, they finally gave their blessing to the Egyptian venture.

What were Joséphine's motives for promoting this venture? Obviously, if the expedition were successful, it would precipitate Bonaparte to even greater heights, making her own position even more enviable. Perhaps her husband's absence would permit her to continue her illicit affair with Hippolyte Charles. It is even possible that the mysterious civilization described by Constantin

Volney, who had visited Egypt in 1792 and on whose report Bonaparte relied, had so piqued her interest that she really did want to see Egypt.[1] Certainly Bonaparte intended for her to join him once he had established the French presence there, and the fact that Eugène was going would surely have been a compelling reason for her to go along with the expedition.

Joséphine was looking forward to Eugène's return from Lombardy. He had been making a sort of Grand Tour, as his father had done at Eugène's age. Starting in the south, Eugène stopped to admire the antiquities of Herculaneum, spent six days in Naples, and then went on to Rome, where he studied artifacts of the ancient capital. Joseph Bonaparte was now the French ambassador, and Eugène visited his office in the Palazzo Corsini overlooking the Tiber. When he returned to the house on rue de la Victoire, Eugène hardly recognized it, but he had to admit that his mother's decorative extravaganza was in every way suitable for the family of a victorious general and certainly in keeping with the efforts of the French Republic to identify itself with classical Greece and Rome. There were fasces (Roman symbols of authority), Pompeian frescoes, military trophies, curule chairs like those of Roman senators, and striped fabrics supposedly favored by the ancients. Another decorative motif with a classical origin (the myth of Leda and the Swan) was the heraldic swan motif that would forever be associated with Joséphine, undoubtedly inspired by Giambattista Piranesi's influential books. In the event he should fail to return, Bonaparte purchased their rented house on rue de la Victoire on March 26, and although the price was unreasonably high, it was said to have been less than the sums Joséphine had just spent for its redecoration.

Now that it was clear Eugène's career would be in the military, Joséphine turned her attention to Hortense's debut into society, for she was almost sixteen. Joséphine provided the requisite ensembles for her daughter and, according to Mme. de Chastenay's memoirs, the costumes of both mother and daughter attracted favorable comments at every party they attended. Hortense was already being pursued for her good looks, her many social gifts, and especially for "the grace and suavity of her manners, which united Créole languor to the vivacity of France. She was gay, gentle, and amiable; she had wit . . . with just enough malice to be amusing."[2]

By the spring of 1798, the elaborate, classified plans for the expedition to Egypt were essentially complete, and the fleet that would convey the Army of the East had been fitted out at Toulon in just six weeks. Joséphine was to accompany her husband and Eugène as far as Toulon to see them off, so on the night of May 3, 1798, shrouded in the utmost secrecy, a carriage carrying Bonaparte, Eugène, Joséphine, and the secretary, Bourrienne, rolled out of Paris.

After reaching the port, they were detained for more than a week, so Bonaparte thought it best for his wife to go to Plombières-les-Bains after the fleet had sailed, until he could summon her to join him in Egypt. Plombières was a spa in the Vosges with a reputation for curing sterility, and Joséphine was becoming increasingly concerned about her inability to conceive a child. As much as she feared for the safety of her husband and Eugène, she nevertheless believed that this Egyptian adventure would further strengthen the bond between the two and somehow help compensate for the fact that she had not yet produced Bonaparte's heir.

Meanwhile, all of Bonaparte's considerable energy was concentrated upon the fleet at Toulon, which was about to embark upon a unique voyage that was to be "a mythical event, as important as the discovery of the New World or the first step onto the moon."[3] This is essentially true, for one of the consequences of this audacious enterprise was the awakening of the Western world to a civilization that was virtually unknown. Although its military and political aim was to establish a French base in Egypt in order to cut off England's commerce with India, its cultural objective was to create a record of the society of this ancient land. The fleet comprised 65 ships, 280 transports, 38,000 men, 1,200 horses, 171 cannon, and 200 experts in various fields to evaluate and record the findings.[4] The chemist Claude Berthollet was to direct the scientific-archaeological aspects of the expedition, conducted by astronomers, engineers, mathematicians, geographers, historians, and doctors. Many of them were members of the French Institute, to which august body Bonaparte had been admitted as a mathematician. As the German scholar Friedrich Kircheisen recorded, Bonaparte liked to associate with writers, scientists, and artists in order to show them his interests were much broader than mere politics, a fact to which Joséphine and many others could attest.

We have seen that she had her own ideas about the director of the team of artists to accompany the expedition: her friend Vivant Denon, who was also a member of the Institute and had always wanted to see this fabled land. Denon's protector, the painter David, was also invited, but he begged to be excused because of his delicate health. Both Denon and Bonaparte had long been fascinated with Egypt, and no one had ever systematically studied and recorded the objects they would see. In 1802 Denon would publish the results of the expedition, and many of the images he recorded for these publications would be adapted into designs for Joséphine's table service and the Egyptian *cabaret* from which she and her ladies were served tea.

Joséphine was well aware of the dangers that lay ahead, such as the British ships Lord Nelson had sent to patrol the Mediterranean and the possibility that supplies might not be awaiting them at Malta. Once the fleet reached Egypt, the French might even be forced to fight the fierce Mamelukes and endless hordes of Turks. But as the wife of the expedition commander, Joséphine had to present a confident demeanor: on May 19, she boarded the world-renowned flagship L'Orient, and after her ceremonial inspection, she was escorted ashore, where she ascended the balcony reserved for wives of the leading members of the expedition. As the fleet set sail in brilliant sunshine, it was an awe-inspiring spectacle, with bands playing, flags fluttering in the breeze, and warships exchanging salutes with the forts on shore.

By the middle of June, Joséphine was at Plombières, intending to take a cure for a month. She had hardly arrived before she wrote to Barras, describing the sulphur waters and saying how much she missed her husband. Ever the coquette, she dared to add that she wished "the waters of Plombières could be prescribed for you so that you could decide to come here. It would be most obliging of you to have an ailment in order to be able to cause me pleasure. I am very devoted to you."[5] She enclosed a letter for him to forward to her husband, telling Barras that she "loves [Bonaparte] well, despite his little faults."[6] Joséphine stayed at the resort longer than planned because of a bizarre accident caused by a dog. She was sewing in an upstairs room when she was called to the balcony to see a pretty dog passing in the street. The balcony collapsed, and Joséphine fell so hard that she incurred painful internal injuries. As a consequence, she had to remain at the resort for two months, and it has been speculated that, ironically, these injuries rendered her incapable of producing another child.

During her convalescence, Joséphine began to assume a role that she enacted the rest of her life, that of benevolent ruler to whom her "subjects" brought their petitions, for she could never refuse anyone she thought was needy. One was a chief of battalion, Victor de Lahorie, who asked for a recommendation to Barras. Joséphine happily complied, since Lahorie had been devoted to Alexandre, whose memory Joséphine reverently kept alive for the sake of her children. For Augustin-Laurent de Rémusat (future prefect of the palace), Joséphine obtained a place in the War Department, and her future brother-in-law, Félix Bacciochi (Elisa Bonaparte's husband), received command of the fort at Marseilles. Then there was Joséphine's former father-in-law, the poor old marquis de Beauharnais, whose last years the Marine Ministry eased with a small stipend. And so it went.

While Joséphine was taking the waters, the French fleet was enduring a rough six-week voyage, narrowly escaping Nelson's fleet just before landing at Alexandria on July 1. Here Eugène first encountered the Mamelukes, a warrior caste who had been imported centuries before from the Caucasus to serve as soldiers for Egyptian sultans but who later overthrew their masters and set up a dynasty of their own. In 1517 the Ottoman sultan Selim I had conquered Cairo, making Egypt nominally a Turkish province, although in reality the government remained in the hands of the Mamelukes. Talleyrand was to have assured the sultan in Constantinople that the French were going to Egypt to subdue their Mameluke rivals, but he never did so, which turned the Turks against the French. In the meantime, the Mamelukes were also prepared to treat the French as enemies. Eugène de Beauharnais was fascinated with these warriors and wrote to Hortense that they could sever a scarf floating in the air with their razor-sharp scimitars.

On July 21, the French faced the Mamelukes in battle array for the first time, in the Battle of the Pyramids, and Eugène was present. When they appeared on the horizon under a bright blue sky in shimmering heat, Eugène described it as the most picturesque sight imaginable. Mounted on splendid Arabian horses, which snorted and pranced, the Mamelukes wore armor inlaid with gems or tunics in brilliant silk, and gilded helmets or turbans dashed with egret feathers. However, they were not well disciplined and were soon overwhelmed by the French.

The triumphant French entry into Cairo was tragically short-lived, for on August 1, 1798, Admiral Nelson discovered the French fleet anchored in the open waters of Aboukir Bay and opened

*Anne-Louis Girodet-Trioson (1767–1824), Study for the Head of a Mameluke (*Musées de l'Ile d'Aix*). The destruction of the despotic Mameluke regime in Egypt gave Napoléon one justification for his expedition. He brought back two Mamelukes—Raza Roustam and Ali—to Paris, where people were enthralled by their extraordinary appearance and lavish costumes. The debonair Roustam slept in front of Bonaparte's door, but the unruly Ali was sent to Fontainebleau. Girodet, Gros, and other artists were fascinated by them, and Roustam followed Napoléon even into battle.*

fire. The majestic French flagship *l'Orient* caught fire and exploded, and in a dreadful night engagement, the French fleet was destroyed in what Nelson termed the Battle of the Nile, which left the French army stranded in Egypt. It also paved the way for an anti-French coalition, the last thing in the world Bonaparte wanted, although he remained in complete control of his emotions and concentrated upon the second aim of his expedition: the scientific exploration of the land of the pharaohs.

By a decree of August 22, 1798, Bonaparte created the Egyptian Institute, based on the French Institute and consisting of the most eminent scholars, and for the first time Egyptian culture was the subject of serious study. The object was to investigate all aspects of Egyptian civilization: art, architecture, zoology, mineralogy, botany, and medicine. Joséphine would have been enthralled by the gardens, museum, artists' studios, aviary, and especially the zoological and botanical specimens, for she would soon be assembling one of Europe's finest collections herself.

Before the terrible losses at Aboukir Bay, concrete plans were being made for Joséphine to join her husband and Eugène, but the accident at Plombières delayed her trip, and after the naval disaster, it was out of the question. So she set off for Paris, and by September 15 was once again in her house on rue de la Victoire. When she heard of the disaster at Aboukir, she was almost beside herself, so she asked Barras to give her any news he might have, for almost no letters had come through. Judging from her correspondence, she was living for the moment when she would be reunited with Bonaparte and Eugène, for she wrote to the latter: "I have nothing more to desire if only I can have Bonaparte again as he was when he left, and as he must always be for me."[7]

It was a mercy that Joséphine was unaware of the almost-daily forays on horseback that Bonaparte's aides-de-camp made into the deserts against the Mamelukes. Although Eugène was the youngest of them, he was particularly daring and had to be reproached by Napoléon, who was responsible to Joséphine for Eugène's safety.[8] In October 1798, a riot broke out, and several French officers were wounded. The culprits disappeared, but suspicion fell upon the harem of Murad Bey, so Eugène was ordered to investigate. He was kindly received by the first wife, but when this handsome young Frenchman entered the harem, the women wildly threw themselves upon him without restraint, and it was only the arrival of the eunuchs brandishing their leather whips that saved him.[9] This experience must have made a lasting impression, for scenes from this adventure would adorn the Turkish Room in his Paris house.

In her husband's absence, it was politically prudent for Joséphine to mingle with both royalist and republican society in Paris, so she went to the Directoire's entertainments and befriended the wife of Director Gohier, a woman of unblemished character who had once been Gohier's cook. Joséphine was not always so discreet, however, for there were people whom she should have avoided in the interests of her reputation. One was Director Barras, whom she still saw from time to time, but even more serious was her protracted association with Hippolyte Charles. This brash officer of the hussars had joined Joséphine on the route from Plombières and imprudently traveled with her almost as far as Paris. Gossip about Joséphine's behavior eventually reached Egypt, and according to Eugène, his stepfather, already under great strain because of the troops' low morale, was plunged into the depths of despair. He confided in Eugène, who took it upon himself to warn his mother. They had heard that Joséphine was seeing Hippolyte in Paris and had been to the theater with him; it was also said he had even given her a dog. "Although I was very young," Eugene later wrote, "my stepfather made me a part of his torment. It was usually in the evening that he poured out his grief to me as he strode up and down the tent. I was the only one with whom he was able to speak his heart."[10]

The distraught Bonaparte wrote not to Joséphine, but to his brother Joseph that he was completely disillusioned about his domestic life, for the veil had been torn away from his eyes, and that for him—at twenty-nine—glory had lost its attraction. Neither Eugène's nor Bonaparte's letters ever reached France, having been intercepted by the British, but this first crisis in their marriage set the stage for violent repercussions. At this point, one can only sympathize with Bonaparte and be appalled by Joséphine's frailty. In spite of it all, his love for her remained strong, but from this moment on, his letters are no longer marked by the same tenderness, passion, and jealousy as those written before "the veil was torn away." Joséphine's friend and lady-in-waiting Claire de Rémusat made this trenchant observation, as we have noted: "Perhaps he [Bonaparte] would have been a better man if he had been more, and especially *better* loved."[11] The voyage to Egypt marked a watershed in their relationship, and Bonaparte would most likely never have been unfaithful to his wife had he not been so deeply wounded by her infidelity. He summed up the dilemma of their relationship in one of his many eloquent letters: "You are the pleasure and torment of my life."[12]

Bonaparte was so badly shaken by Joséphine's affair that he sought revenge, and the means was close at hand. Although he had forbidden women (other than Joséphine) to sail with the fleet, Pauline Fourès, the wife of a lieutenant, was so determined to accompany her husband that she dressed in a cavalry uniform and donned her feminine apparel only after she reached Cairo. A pretty woman who openly displayed her charms, Pauline soon became the center of an admiring circle, including Bonaparte, who lost no time in dispatching Pauline's husband on a special mission to France. Eugène was sent off to Suez to explore the region, fortify the town, and establish wells, for

Antoine Gros (1771–1835), Berthier at the Bridge of Lodi (Château de Grosbois). Bonaparte was so impressed by the versatile Berthier's distinguished performance at the bridge of Lodi on May 10, 1796, that he informed the Directoire that the intrepid Berthier assumed the roles of cannonier, cavalier, and grenadier. Bonaparte himself performed so courageously at Lodi that from this moment on he was affectionately known as "the Little Corporal." Marshal Berthier went on to become Napoléon's indispensable chief of staff until Napoléon was exiled in 1814, but he fell to his death from a window in Bamberg on June 1, 1815, a prisoner of the allies who feared he would rejoin the emperor.

which he received a letter expressing the commander-in-chief's satisfaction with his performance. He was still only seventeen and was so discomfited by his stepfather's liaison with "Bellilotte" (as Pauline was called) that Eugène asked Berthier to transfer him to an infantry regiment. The result was a painful scene with his stepfather, but after this, Bonaparte's rides in the open carriage with Bellilotte stopped. When Pauline returned to Europe, she would find that Bonaparte was no longer interested in her, for his reconciliation with Joséphine and the subsequent coup d'état would change everything.

During that late summer and fall of 1798, it was just as well that Joséphine received only intermittent news from Egypt, for there was little encouraging to report, nor did she know that Eugène was in fact suffering untold hardships in the desert and exposing himself to grave dangers. The destruction of the French fleet ended their dream of colonizing Egypt, and although Bonaparte had explained to the Turks that his inroads into Egypt should not be taken as unfriendly, Turkey declared war. At the end of November, he decided to march eastward and attack the Turks at the heart of their empire, but this expedition into Syria was one that Eugène would barely survive. In the meantime, Joséphine played endless games of tric-trac, while Hortense composed the marching song that was to become a favorite of generations of French soldiers: "Partant pour la Syrie" (Departing for Syria).

If Hortense provided music to inspire the troops, Joséphine furnished Baron Gros, the artist who would kindle public admiration for the leader in his paintings of battle scenes and dramatic incidents. By March 14, 1799, the French army had pushed as far as Acre—"the key to Palestine"—but some troops had fallen victim to a virulent plague. In hopes of raising morale, Bonaparte visited a hospital at Jaffa, helping to carry out the corpse of a victim and even placing his hand on a patient's infectious lesion, a singularly brave act. Joséphine commissioned Baron Gros to depict the incident in his most celebrated painting, *Bonaparte Visiting the Plague-Stricken at Jaffa*. Although it met with thunderous acclaim at the Salon, it displeased Eugène, who indignantly declared that no French officer would ever place his handkerchief over his nose (as in Gros's canvas), against the strict rules that governed military deportment. Typically, Eugène never spoke of the Battle of the Nile, for it was bad form for junior officers to make reference to disasters.

At the bloody assault on Acre, which lasted from March 19 to May 20, when Bonaparte withdrew, Eugène was severely wounded in the head by a blast from a shell and almost buried alive; it was reported to Bonaparte that his stepson had perished. But Eugène was rescued, treated, and back on duty in less than three weeks. Of the eight aides-de-camp who went to Egypt, however, four died and Michel Duroc and Eugène were wounded. Although Bonaparte had defeated one of the Turkish armies at Mount Tabor, he was forced to retreat into Egypt. Another Turkish army— sailing from Rhodes—appeared in the Bay of Aboukir at Alexandria on July 15, determined to drive the French out of Egypt. So Bonaparte prepared to meet them, and Eugène was with him. Devising a plan that has been called one of the masterpieces of modern strategy, Bonaparte mustered

Antoine Gros (1771–1835), Bonaparte Visiting the Plague-Stricken at Jaffa (Louvre). Gros's authoritative, mature Bonaparte goes far beyond the young officer at Arcole whom Gros had quickly sketched for Joséphine in 1796. Armed with drawings of the site provided by Vivant Denon, the artist constructs an exotic architectural setting for the compassionate commander's visit to his suffering soldiers on March 11, 1799. The critic Étienne Delécluze considered this unprecedented work to be Gros's masterpiece.

10,000 men against the enemy and attacked the Turks on July 25. Jean Lannes greatly distinguished himself,[14] and Joachim Murat's cavalry drove the Turks into the sea, where many of them were drowned. After this Battle of Aboukir, Eugène was appalled by what appeared to be literally thousands of turbans bobbing up and down on the waves.

Joséphine and Hortense heard of the victory just as news reached them of the unfortunate expedition into Syria. At home, changes were occurring almost daily in the government, for the former popularity of the Directoire was quickly waning. One director who was dropped from office was the lawyer Reubell, who had been at Joséphine's dinner party when the Egyptian expedition was being planned, and further shuffling followed. The country was in a state of general confusion and insecurity, and industry and commerce lay almost paralyzed for want of effective leadership.

Meanwhile, Bonaparte was established at Alexandria with most of his troops, Eugène as his only aide-de-camp. They had had no news from home for eight months, but Bonaparte was able to obtain a packet of French newspapers from the commander of an English vessel and was deeply disturbed by their contents. "I was with him," Eugène wrote, "when he learned . . . of the loss of Italy and imminent collapse of France. . . . We read all night . . . and he swore me to the most absolute secrecy, [but] I was convinced that he decided to return that night, although he did not confide to me his plans."[15] Bonaparte turned his army over to General Kléber and prepared to return to France. On August 22, 1799, two French frigates were waiting offshore for the party to board: Bonaparte, Eugène, Berthier, Marmont, Lannes, Murat (the last two severely wounded), Vivant Denon (laden with drawings), the savants Monge and Berthollet, and Admiral Ganteaume. Bonaparte now had a new attendant: the Mameluke Raza Roustam, who was about nineteen years old, armed, and luxuriously dressed, a gift from Sheik El-Bekri.[16]

The commander-in-chief announced happily to Eugène: "You are going to see your mother again!"[17] and they sailed at dawn the next day. Eugène had in his pocket a letter from Hortense that he had picked up in Cairo, and one hopes he shared it with his stepfather, for it contained a full report of Joséphine's circumspect behavior. Hortense wrote that her mother had bought the château of Malmaison, where she was living very quietly, seeing almost no one except Madame Campan and her two nieces, the Auguié sisters, who were Hortense's best friends. Aglae would become the wife of the eminent Marshal Ney, and Adèle—also an artist—became Hortense's constant companion. Hortense also mentioned to Eugène that their mother had invited the whole Bonaparte family to visit but that they always refused; only Madame Mère was amiable toward her. She concluded her note with a "hearty embrace for Bonaparte," which meant that now he had won the affection of both his stepchildren, for the trying sojourn in Egypt had drawn Eugène even closer to him, as Joséphine had hoped.

After a harrowing voyage, during which they sighted several British ships, on October 9, 1799, the small party entered the bay near Fréjus, where the inhabitants came out in barques to welcome the victor of Arcole, Rivoli, and the Pyramids. No one seemed to remember the siege of Acre, the plague, the reversals, or the army left behind in Egypt, for from the military standpoint the expedition to Egypt would have to be counted a disastrous failure. In spite of all this, Eugène recorded: "We were proud to belong to the one who would put an end to the misfortunes of our country."[18]

Fortunately, when Joséphine received the electrifying news by semaphore of her husband's landing in the south of France, she was not at the theater with Thérèse Tallien but dining discreetly with the reputable Mme. Gohier and her husband. The frustrating tragicomedy that followed has often been related: Hortense and Joséphine quickly set out by one route going south, and Bonaparte and Eugène advanced north by another, so the two carriages missed each other. The commander was dressed in civilian clothes, and all along his route flowers were strewn and bells were rung in each village as the populace called upon him to save France. In Paris, performances in the theaters were stopped for an announcement of the glad tidings from the stage.

When the hero of the Battle of Aboukir reached the rue de la Victoire on October 16, he discovered that his wife was not there and was swept into a towering rage. This time Joséphine was innocent, but when she returned after midnight on October 18, she found the door locked and her husband refusing to see her. Reconciliation seemed impossible, but Bonaparte finally relented after Eugène added his pleas to Hortense's tearful, impassioned entreaties. When Lucien Bonaparte was announced the next morning, he was sent upstairs, where he found the happy couple in bed. Bonaparte had agreed never to see "Bellilotte" again, and Joséphine never even considered risking her position with another senseless love affair.

The house on rue de la Victoire was bursting at the seams after Bonaparte and Eugène returned. Ensconced in the small lobby was the general's private secretary, Louis-Antoine Bourrienne, who kept tabs on the constant stream of politicians and soldiers who called on his master, hoping for a change of régime. Three Bonaparte brothers—Joseph, Lucien, and Louis—came regularly. Joséphine had found a servant for Eugène with the reassuring name of Constant Wairy,[19] a superior young man three years older than Eugène. She had met him at Plombières through an eccentric but inventive hairdresser, Carrat, whom she brought back to Paris as one of her coiffeurs. Eugène had clearly matured during the Egyptian ordeal, but he was still a gregarious young man, fond of dancing and the theater, and he often invited his fellow officers to breakfast parties with actors from the Théâtre Français. They were entertained by the gifted ventriloquist, Thiemet, who kept them amused with his imitations of the now-discredited directors.

Not since the founding of the Republic had France so longed for an ordered government as in that spring of 1799, and people on the street, in the salons, and in the coffee houses were yearning for peace. Bonaparte was cautiously studying his next move, and by November he and his able cohorts had decided upon a coup d'état. The plot was hatched during what appeared to be social gatherings in the house on rue de la Victoire. Joséphine was, of course, aware of each stage of the preparation, and General de Ségur avowed that she "was in on the secret. Nothing was concealed from her. In every conference at which she was present her discretion, gentleness, grace and the ready ingenuity of her delicate and cool intelligence were of great service. She justified Bonaparte's renewed confidence in her."[20]

Of the five directors, the only two who could be considered significant were Émanuelle-Joseph Sièyes and Pierre Roger-Ducos. Paul Barras had become so corrupt that he would go to almost any lengths to support his pleasures; Louis-Jérôme Gohier, president of the Directoire, was a timid lawyer, and Jean-François Moulin was a nonentity. If those three could be persuaded to resign, then an appeal could be made to the legislature—the Council of Ancients and the Council of Five Hundred—and a new régime appointed. The civilians brought into the plot were Jean-Jacques-Régis Cambacérès, a distinguished minister of justice, whom Joséphine would later see almost daily; Talleyrand, who would stand by her side at receptions; Joseph Fouché, minister of police, who would later turn against her; and two of the Bonaparte brothers—Joseph and Lucien, now president of the Council of Five Hundred, although he was its youngest member.

Late in the evening of November 8, 1799, Eugène was sent off by his mother to the house of the president of the Directoire with a perfumed invitation for M. and Mme. Gohier to join Joséphine for breakfast the following day, probably so she could persuade Gohier to resign as director. The wary Gohier suspected that something was afoot and sent his wife in his place. When she arrived, Mme. Gohier saw that Joséphine's salon and courtyard were filled with soldiers. Joséphine tried to calm the frightened woman, whom she finally had to send home in a downpour.

In the meantime, the president of the Council of Ancients announced a possible terrorist plot and advised that their meeting the following day be transferred to Saint-Cloud, outside Paris. The Ancients nominated Bonaparte military commander of Paris, and Sièyes and Ducos submitted their resignations (although, of course, they supported the coup). Gohier and Moulin were forced to resign, and Barras's resignation was obtained by Talleyrand. Barras became an implacable enemy of both Napoléon and Joséphine, and after he retired to his estate at Grosbois, he wrote his memoirs, which were full of vicious remarks that were later used by some of Joséphine's biographers to discredit her.

The next day at Saint-Cloud, November 10, was to prove decisive. Napoléon, as military commander of the city, rose to speak, warning first the Council of Ancients and later the Five Hundred of the alleged terrorist plot and requesting the creation of a new provisional government. His oratorical ability failed him, but Lucien Bonaparte stepped in to save the day for his brother by persuading the Council of Ancients to nominate three consuls (Sieyès, Roger-Duclos, and Bonaparte) and then collected enough of the Five Hundred to ratify the nominations.

Eugène was back in the rue de la Victoire house before midnight to reassure his mother and to give his version of the day's events. As for Hortense, the news was brought to Saint-Germain in a way that the proper Madame Campan found singularly inappropriate, but which Hortense thought romantic: "General Murat, a true knight-errant, sent us four grenadiers of the Guard, of which he was the commander, to tell us what had taken place at Saint-Cloud, and the appointment of General Bonaparte to the Consulate. Imagine the effect of four grenadiers knocking on the doors of a convent in the middle of the night! Everyone got a terrible shock and Madame Campan condemned this military method of sending news. But Caroline read it as a proof of love."[21] Caroline had met Murat when Bonaparte and Joséphine were holding court that summer of 1797 at Mombello, where the young general of brigade was part of her brother's entourage. Murat paid Caroline a great deal of attention, but Madame Mère thought her daughter should have a good education before she became serious about a man, so Caroline was promptly sent back to Madame Campan's school with Hortense.

That evening, rumors were flying about the capital and there was an unusually large

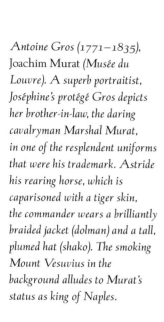

*Antoine Gros (1771–1835),
Joachim Murat (Musée du
Louvre). A superb portraitist,
Joséphine's protégé Gros depicts
her brother-in-law, the daring
cavalryman Marshal Murat,
in one of the resplendent uniforms
that were his trademark. Astride
his rearing horse, which is
caparisoned with a tiger skin,
the commander wears a brilliantly
braided jacket (dolman) and a tall,
plumed hat (shako). The smoking
Mount Vesuvius in the
background alludes to Murat's
status as king of Naples.*

number of troops in the street. But this was Paris, and it took more than a political crisis to prevent devotees of comic opera from flocking to the Feydeau Theater to hear a new piece, *L'Auteur dans son ménage*. At 9:30, in the middle of the performance, the actors stopped in their tracks, and the author (who was playing the leading role) moved close to the edge of the stage and cried loudly: "Citizens! General Bonaparte has just escaped being assassinated at Saint-Cloud by traitors of our country!" Panic ensued, and a loud cry issued from loge number 2, where Pauline Bonaparte was suddenly overcome with emotion. With her were Mme. Permon, her daughter, Laure Junot, and Madame Mère, who was just as disturbed as Pauline but remained in control of herself. They rushed to rue de la Victoire, where Joséphine assured them that all was well.

On December 12, 1799, Bonaparte would be named first consul, which elevated Joséphine to an even more exalted position, but there was a price to be paid: "Like France, she lost in liberty what she gained in grandeur . . . [and] for all her success, wealth, and greatness, Joséphine could not recall the days of the Republic without emotion. Then she was young; and nothing can take the place of youth. Then she was powerful; and is not hope always sweeter than reality? Then she was

Auguste Couder (1789–1873), Installation of the Council of State (Musée de Versailles). On December 12, 1799, Bonaparte was named first consul of France, with the learned jurist Jean-Jacques Cambacérès as second consul and the financier Charles-François Lebrun as the third. Here the ministers swear allegiance to the three consuls in the Luxembourg Palace. Although theoretically the three shared equal powers, the initiative for drafting laws and legislation almost always came from Napoléon himself.

beautiful; and for a woman is not beauty the only true power? . . . In her plain dress of white muslin and a white flower in her hair, she seemed to [her husband] more beautiful than in her coronation robes of silver brocade. . . . She had no equerries, chamberlains, or maids of honor; but her youth adorned her more than a diadem."[22]

Joséphine would now be called "Madame" like the ladies of the ancien régime as she moved onto an even more spacious stage and assumed ever more demanding responsibilities. She would now be compelled to leave her delightful house for far more elaborate establishments—first the Luxembourg Palace and then the Tuileries. The brilliant period of the Consulate had begun.

6

"More Than a Queen"

The momentous year that opened the century in 1800 changed Joséphine's life in many ways, the most challenging of which were her changes of residence. Five days after the coup d'état in November, she was obliged to leave her beloved house on rue de la Victoire, where she had lived for more than five years, and move to the new official residence of the consuls, the Luxembourg Palace. As early as February, Napoléon would declare their lodgings at the Luxembourg inadequate and select the Tuileries, abandoned since the fall of Louis XVI, as their new home. Joséphine missed the chic martial decor of her old house, since it represented both her taste and her history, a graphic expression of the métier of both her husbands and her son, as well as the increased militarism of the régimes under which she lived. Yet much as she regretted leaving the rue de la Victoire, she would shortly be achieving a similar effect—on an even grander scale—in the decoration of the château of Malmaison at Rueil outside Paris, which she had purchased in 1798, and in the refurbishing of the Tuileries, which would be her official residence for the next ten years. In any case, the Paris house, which she still owned, was now too small to accommodate the family's swelling entourage and the works of art that Joséphine had been accumulating since the Italian campaign.

The old Luxembourg Palace was familiar to Joséphine as the scene of Barras's parties and, more grimly, as having been a prison during the Terror, where Alexandre had been held when he was first arrested. She and Bonaparte moved into the wing known as the Petit Luxembourg, which overlooks the rue Vaugirard, and she must have shuddered as she glanced from the window toward the Carmelites, where she and Alexandre had been imprisoned. Only six years earlier, she had stood on that very street after her release, wondering how to begin life again, and now here she was ensconced in the Luxembourg Palace as consort to the first consul of France.

This was a period of adjustment for Paris as well as for Joséphine. Early signs of rehabilitation after the coup were the reappearance of more carriages in the streets, the patronage of luxury establishments such as Berthélemot (the pastry and sweets shop in the Palais Royal), and the restora-

Jean-François Bosio (1764–1827), Bal de l'Opéra (Art Gallery of Ontario, Toronto). Bosio's view of one of the masked balls that became popular social events after 1801 shows the fantastic costumes and masks worn by the revelers: at the left is Harlequin, a stock figure of the Commedia dell'Arte; at the right is a chasseur; and at the far right, a man in white wig with a sword, aping the dress of the ancien régime. The rulers' reserved box, hung with velvet trimmed in gilt passementerie, is just right of center, above the Neoclassical frieze.

tion of traditional holidays such as Carnival. The revival of Carnival in 1801 marked the return of masked balls, and the gaiety attending these popular amusements spilled over into the streets—not necessarily an agreeable situation, for one of the unresolved problems was that many of the still-unpaved, gutterless streets were impassable, especially during wet weather, when they became seas of mud. This and many other civic challenges would be efficiently addressed by the unusually able minister Jean-Antoine Chaptal, who was especially drawn to Joséphine; he admired the exemplary botanical collection she would form at Malmaison, and he urged the professors at the Natural History Museum in Paris to collaborate with the wife of the first consul. "May I congratulate you, Madame, for your taste in the natural sciences," he wrote. "You are contributing to their progress, and we thank you in the name of the naturalists."[1] One of them, Professor André Thouin, sent her figs and bananas to acclimatize in her hothouses, which Joséphine told him reminded her of her native land. These would figure among the specimens that Joséphine later commissioned Redouté to commemorate in his watercolors on vellum.

Jacques-François Swebach-Desfontaines (1769–1823), Review of the First Consul at the Tuileries (Musée Carnavalet). Joséphine enjoyed watching these colorful reviews that took place in the courtyard of her official residence. The regiments in formation, the soldiers home from the field, the bands playing, and the presence of both Bonaparte and Eugène invariably attracted large crowds. Bonaparte was well aware that external splendor decisively affected public opinion.

On February 19, Joséphine and her family moved into the Tuileries Palace, which had been built by Philibert Delorme for Catherine de Médicis in 1563. It was in shambles, having been stormed in August 1792, so Napoléon had engaged his architect, Félix Lecomte, to clean it up and begin redecorating, putting Joséphine in charge of their personal apartments. Because she was not allowed to spend large sums for new furniture, she compensated by choosing imaginative materials for the upholstery of old pieces and for wall hangings. She used a violet silk taffeta in her first salon, in which she hung about seventeen paintings from her collection. Her second salon was decorated in yellow and brown satin and furnished with console tables that held porphyry and marble vases. The furniture in the bedroom was covered in blue-and-white striped material trimmed with gold passementerie.

Moving day was bright and sunny, and a showy military procession marked the occasion. Joséphine and Hortense watched from a vantage point in the Pavillon de Flore, and beside them sat two of Joséphine's nieces, Émilie and Stéphanie de Beauharnais, who proudly observed their cousin Eugène astride his prancing horse below. Everybody was in a wonderful mood, for Bonaparte's new constitution had been overwhelmingly approved the previous day. His coach was pulled by six magnificent white horses given him by the Austrian emperor, and when it reached the courtyard, Bonaparte descended to deafening applause and mounted a horse for the military inspection. Eugène later noted that the women wore antique-inspired muslin gowns and light shawls, and he wondered how they dared invoke the master's disapproval, for Bonaparte knew such materials came by way of England rather than from French manufacturers. When her stepfather asked the origin of their mousseline, Hortense replied that it was "linon de Saint-Quentin"—a fib she probably picked up from her mother. These impressive military reviews in the courtyard of the Tuileries were to become a tradition that "la grande troupe de Paris" (Balzac's phrase) anticipated with the wildest enthusiasm, greatly fortifying support for the new régime. Besides the feeling of security the huge military establishment provided, the populace was thrilled to have their ruler and his consort in their midst. Parisians and foreigners alike scrutinized every detail of Joséphine's costumes, for her sartorial authority was widely recognized.

As the first consul plunged into his work,[2] applying his astounding energy to the organization of a Council of State and a legislative body, Joséphine herself was serving in a major political as well as social capacity. One of her husband's major objectives was to absorb the old nobility into his new "aristocracy of merit," and he freely admitted that he never could have achieved this without Joséphine. So successfully did she attract to the Tuileries those who bore the most ancient names in France that Victorine de Chastenay, who later became one of her attendants, exclaimed: "Bonaparte had become a prince, and already Mme. de La Rochefoucauld, in the role of friend or relative, was performing for Mme. Bonaparte the functions of a lady-in-waiting."[3]

In short, a consular court was being put into place, so Joséphine had to turn her attention to the ceremonial routines and patterns of decorum that would govern it. Protocol was modeled on that of the Bourbon court, expressly addressed to the ancient quarter of Faubourg Saint-Germain, whose residents, like Mme. de Chastenay, represented either real or potential royalist opposition and whom Joséphine intended to put at ease. Then there were the "new" people of less illustrious lineage who had to be made to feel part of the *beau monde* exemplified by the wife of the first consul. This institution and codification of consular etiquette was one of her major contributions to the advancement of her husband's ambitious plans. Happily, Joséphine had knowledgeable friends to help her, among them Mme. de La Rochefoucauld, Mme. de Montesson, Talleyrand, and Madame Campan, an authority on the finer points of the etiquette that had governed the Bourbon court at Versailles.

First of all, there was the matter of Joséphine's entourage. Some of her previous female associates were now prudently replaced by ladies with gentler upbringing, such as the haughty Lucie Dillon (Mme. de la Tour du Pin), a distant relative who considered Joséphine fortunate to have her at court. In her memoirs, Lucie remarked upon Joséphine's assignment: "I saw clearly that the first consul had entrusted to her the department of the ladies of the court and the task of conquering . . . them.

The duty was not very difficult, for all were rushing toward the ascending power."[4] There was also some truth in Princess Dolgoruki's pronouncement: "It was not exactly a court but it was no longer a camp."[5] Joséphine was happy to bring women of the old nobility into her company, and she was kept very busy writing letters on behalf of the émigrés who were now returning to France in large numbers. At the time of the Revolution about 100,000 people had emigrated, forfeiting their property and civil rights, and their names were kept by the state on a list of "enemies of the Republic." Although the émigrés on the list would be granted amnesty in April 1802, until that time official action was still needed for names to be removed. Joséphine worked tirelessly for those who wished to be repatriated, and when their names were stricken from the list, she would let them know. Many became Joséphine's ladies-in-waiting, and her sympathetic personality made it easier for those associated with the ancien régime to overcome their resentment. As Constant remarked: "You felt yourself drawn to her by an irresistible power. . . . Her lovely countenance, expressing sweetness and good nature, and the angelic grace diffused around her person, made her the most attractive of women."[6] Bonaparte put it more succinctly: "I win battles; Joséphine wins hearts."

Besides decorum, another issue to be addressed by Joséphine was the all-important matter of dress, which in this period was particularly symbolic. The revealing white dresses that Joséphine, Thérèse Tallien, and Juliette Récamier favored so highly during the 1790s were a deliberate evocation of the ancient world with which the new régime wished to identify, but they were about to become a thing of the past. Like many other women, Joséphine was loathe to give them up, and she appeared in this type of gown at one of their first official receptions. Constant recorded that most of the women appeared in splendid formal gowns, plumes, and diamonds, but when Joséphine entered on Talleyrand's arm, she was wearing a simple white Indian muslin in the Directoire mode. However, she apparently never did so again, since for both political and economic reasons, it was expedient for the first consul to forbid the importation of Indian muslins (especially through England) and to promote French-made materials. Elegance was gradually returning to the capital and Joséphine was ushering it in: women began to wear sumptuous gowns and family jewelry; important foreign visitors appeared in their decorations; and the first lady of France ordered silk and velvet from Lyons.

Another duty the first consul thrust upon Joséphine was one she performed with particular finesse—thanking people who had rendered some special service. One such was the grenadier Thomas Thomé, who had saved Bonaparte from daggers on the day of the critical coup d'état. Joséphine invited Thomé to breakfast, gave him a bonus of 600 francs, and presented him with a diamond ring. Another exceedingly delicate responsibility was the painful task of informing the family of an officer who had fallen in battle and offering solace to the family. Many of the widows were known to her personally, which must have made this arduous task even more agonizing.

A number of family matters also preoccupied Joséphine early in 1800, such as the marriage of Caroline Bonaparte to the cavalier Joachim Murat, who had made a name for himself in the Italian and Egyptian campaigns and had played an important role in the coup. The marriage contract was signed on January 18, 1800, followed by the civil marriage in Joséphine's old house on rue de la Victoire, and a church wedding on February 20. Caroline was maturing quickly and would become a suitable partner for the ambitious Murat, who was named commander-in-chief and inspector general of the new Consular Guard and would in due course become king of Naples. The Consular Guard was an elite corps to which Eugène de Beauharnais was admitted, although he was not yet twenty-five, and in which he received what he thought was the finest position in all the army—command of the mounted regiment known as Chasseurs à Cheval de la Garde.

By the late spring of 1800, an alarming military situation had developed in Italy, for the French had been driven almost entirely out of the peninsula during Bonaparte's absence in Egypt. So he conceived a bold strategy that would demand his personal leadership, and for the third time in their four years of marriage, Joséphine saw her husband off to the battlefield. On May 6, he said good-bye to her and Hortense at Malmaison and with an eager stepson at his side, set off to participate in a campaign that would be among the most inventive and surprising of his career.

After the army achieved the audacious crossing of the St. Bernard Pass to surprise the Austrians, Eugène recorded that the monks of the hospice gave bread and wine to the passing soldiers and that their enormous dogs brought in several near-frozen French soldiers. What followed was another victorious campaign on the plains of Lombardy, culminating in the battle of Marengo on June 14. Eugène escaped with only two saber cuts on his saddle cloth and was promoted to *chef d'escadron*, as Joséphine soon learned. Bonaparte told her of his satisfaction with Eugène's performance, how he had covered himself with glory in every action, and that he expected Eugène to figure among the first commanders in Europe. But the tone of Bonaparte's letters to Joséphine had changed. The impassioned ardor of his first love letters from Italy had given way to a courtly homage: "My first laurel must be for my country, my second will be for you."[7]

During her husband's absence, Joséphine continued to supervise the redecoration of the Tuileries Palace, but her greatest interest was the embellishment of Malmaison, the country house she had bought in December 1798. During the Terror, when she was living at Croissy on the right bank of the Seine, Joséphine had noticed across the river a property that appealed to her—an old manor house set in the woods. Early in 1798 she took Bonaparte to see it and later that year, while he was in Egypt, she made a low offer, which was accepted. She borrowed the money to make a down payment, and the balance of the purchase price was paid by Bonaparte on his return. The house was in a dilapidated state, so she turned to the architect Pierre Fontaine, who with his partner, Charles Percier, began in November 1799 to demolish the old walls and to embark on a complete renovation. The work was sufficiently advanced by March 1800 for Bonaparte to inspect it, and he pronounced it a real success. This would soon become the place where Bonaparte most liked to relax, and where the family could live informally, away from the protocol of the Tuileries. Hortense thought Malmaison a "delicious spot" because she (like her mother) loved the country.

If the private apartments at the Tuileries represented what could be called the "consular style," Malmaison was its epitome. The dining room, for example, was decorated in neutral tones, with wall panels painted by Louis Lafitte with motifs inspired by Herculaneum dancers; the idea was to provide a quiet backdrop for the superb porcelain services from Sèvres and the Paris porcelain manufactories she patronized. The music room was sparsely furnished with a suite made by the Jacobs, covered in deep red with black passementerie. Here she hung many of her paintings by contemporary artists, most of which she had bought at the official Salon. The music room opened into her gallery (now destroyed), where her old master paintings and sculpture were displayed. She had acquired works by many well-known artists, especially Northern European painters, such as Hans Memling, Gerard Dou, and Paulus Potter (she owned at least sixteen Potters), and Italians, including Giovanni Bellini, Ghirlandaio, Andrea del Sarto, Giorgione, Perugino, Leonardo (four of them!), Veronese, Raphael (three), and Titian (four). In addition, she owned paintings by Rubens, Rembrandt, Claude le Lorrain, Nicolas Poussin, and about 125 works by living artists. Her sculpture collection included the work of contemporaries, such as Bosio, Chinard, and Cartellier, as well as an unparalleled group of Canovas. Antiquities of the highest quality were given her by the king of Naples, including Greek vases and objects excavated at Herculaneum and Pompeii, which were shown on console tables in the gallery.

Joséphine's interest in collecting art was equaled by her love for rare specimens of flowers, shrubs, and trees. Botanists had brought back exotic plants from the Egyptian campaign, and ship captains transported plants and carried seeds with them from foreign lands. Egyptian poppies eventually brightened the fields, their seeds reputedly brought back from the Nile in Bonaparte's boots. Always in Joséphine's mind was the dream of bringing to France the tropical flora she had known as a child, and eventually, in 1805, she would build a large conservatory for her extraordinary collection, which attracted some of the most renowned scientists in Europe. Even from the beginning, she intended to give the château a garden setting, and she soon transformed the gardens into a landscaped park of lush green lawns punctuated by statuary, pools, pavilions, and follies, such as the Temple of Love, in which classical urns held flowering plants. This was Joséphine's significant contribution to the art of gardening, and the eminent garden historian Alexandre de Laborde so admired her achievement that he called it "the true Jardin des Plantes of France."[8] Laborde was a frequent guest at Malmaison and a close friend of Hortense, for whose marching song "Partant pour la Syrie" he had written the lyrics.

Laborde no doubt attended the amateur theatricals at the Malmaison theater, which was inaugurated May 12, 1802. Professional troupes came out to perform, including singers from the

*Joseph Chinard (1756–1813),
Bust of Joséphine (Malmaison).
The Lyonnaise sculptor Joseph Chinard
brought a Canovian sensibility to his
own work. Joséphine's portrait presents
the empress in her official capacity,
wearing a diadem, a gown adorned with
classical palmettes, and the imperial eagle
spread across the bodice. Chinard also
sculpted a large bust of Eugène in the
uniform of the Chasseurs à Cheval;
it was commissioned by the state,
shown at the Salon of 1806, and is
now at Versailles.*

Opéra and performers from the Théâtre Français, including Louise Contat, Mlle. George, and the great comedian Talma, who preferred tragedy. He was Joséphine's age, a perennial member of their suite, and Bonaparte never seemed to tire of the actor's conversation.[9] One of the stars was Hortense herself, who was a talented singer and actress, as well as a composer and painter.

Vivant Denon often visited Malmaison, where he advised Joséphine on her growing art collection, and he was often joined by other intellectuals. On the rolling lawns, young officers played games with Hortense, Eugène, and the artist Jean-Baptiste Isabey, who remained always in Joséphine's service. Isabey was endowed with a multiplicity of gifts—enlivening theater and dinner functions; painting informal watercolors of the family and guests; and designing and organizing Joséphine's private parties, not only at Malmaison but in the other residences as well. The first consul, who declared that he could not think except in the open air, loved to stroll about Joséphine's gardens, and he prescribed that the ladies were to wear only white dresses in the garden because they were perfect foil for the greenery. Before he and Eugène had left for Italy in May, Bonaparte and Joséphine planted a cedar of Lebanon just behind the château, its dark silhouette visible from her

Eugène Delacroix (1798–1863), Talma as Nero (Musée de la Comédie Française). Talma was another artist who barely escaped the Tribunal, thanks to the painter Jacques-Louis David. In 1792 Talma met Bonaparte, who appreciated the prodigious talent of this actor, who is among the immortals of theater history. He and Joséphine brought Talma into their family circle, and he performed regularly for them at Malmaison often during their travels.

bedroom. After the battle of Marengo, she regarded the lofty tree as the horticultural symbol of this victory, and the "cedar of Marengo" flourishes there to this day.

The annual celebration of Bastille Day on July 14, 1800, should have been a wonderful day for Joséphine. Bonaparte had returned from Italy on July 2, and Eugène appeared on the 14th, having been assigned the honor of bringing the captured enemy flags to the capital. There was a festival and a review on the Champ de Mars, and although the Paris garrisons were impressive as they filed past, the most enthusiastic ovation was reserved for veterans of Marengo, who marched onto the field in their dusty uniforms still smeared with the stains of battle. The deposition of the flags was followed by a duet sung by the tenor Bianchi and the soprano Grassini, the toast of Milan, who had been Joséphine's guest at Mombello three years earlier. Joséphine discovered, to her horror, that the reason Bonaparte had brought Grassini to Paris was a romantic one. As it turned out, Joséphine had no cause for worry, since Bonaparte was so busy he hardly glanced in Grassini's direction, and the disappointed diva had to turn to a violinist for consolation.

Joséphine's star, like her husband's was in the ascendant. The transformation of the Tuileries into a proper seat of government and official residence for the first consul impressed even the critical Mme. de la Tour du Pin. Lucie thought Joséphine had risen admirably to the task and conducted herself with distinction: "All the young people from this moment turned their eyes toward the rising sun, Mme. Bonaparte, who was installed at the Tuileries, where the apartments had been entirely refurbished as if by magic. She already put on the airs of a queen, but of a queen most gracious, most amiable, the most kind-hearted."[10]

Everyone was in high spirits after the battle of Marengo, and Joséphine told Pierre Fontaine she was going to celebrate with a supper under the trees at Malmaison—a legitimate excuse to order her beloved tents to shelter the tables. One of the baths in Malmaison was already hung with white cotton; the door from her husband's study into the gardens Joséphine endowed with a white awning; and in ten days Percier and Fontaine put together the famous Council Chamber, a room much like Joséphine's tent-shaped boudoir on rue de la Victoire (see pages xx–xxi). This blue-and-white striped military tent held by fasces, its doors painted with antique emblems and its walls fitted with martial wall lights, was such an instant success that it would be copied far and wide (as at Charlottenhof), and a version of this celebrated feature of the Malmaison interiors is commemorated in Eugène Delacroix's painting of 1833, *The Chamber of Count Mornay* (Louvre).

The château and gardens at Malmaison would eventually become so crowded with official visitors that the nearby château of Saint-Cloud, which Louis XVI had bought for Marie Antoinette, would be designated the official summer residence for the Bonapartes. The château, surrounded by a vast park descending to the Seine and punctuated by glorious cascades, pleased Joséphine because her private apartment opened onto the terraces and gardens that contributed so much to its ambiance. By September 1802—after an enormously expensive restoration—the Bonapartes would be able to move in. One of the most admired features in the park was the so-called Lantern of Diogenes, which Joséphine had purchased at the Salon. Like an antique monument, the lantern was placed on an obelisk at the top of a hill and lighted when the family was in residence. Sadly, the magnificent château at Saint-Cloud was destroyed in 1870 during the Franco-Prussian War.

In the fall of 1800 came an incident that shattered the composure of the entire household. On October 10, Hortense was preparing to attend the première of a ballet called *Dansomanie* when Eugène suddenly appeared, greatly agitated because he had just learned that the first consul was to be assassinated that evening. The conspirators were planning to kill Bonaparte as he left the Opéra and had installed themselves in the loge just under his box, but the plot was discovered in time and thwarted. Such attacks were invariably the work of royalist extremists in the pay of English agents.

Another unsettling thing happened that month, at least for Hortense. Now that she was seventeen, her mother was beginning to think about a suitable marriage for her. Despite her infatuation with one of Napoléon's aides-de-camp, Michel Duroc, Josephine and Napoléon intended for her to marry Napoleon's younger brother, Louis. As Louis Bonaparte was leaving for a tour of Germany in October, he called at Malmaison to say good-bye and surprised Hortense with a passionate kiss. She hoped this did not mean he was serious, but he soon followed up with a long letter detailing the history of his emotional life, making it abundantly clear that he was interested in her, although Hortense hoped in vain that his desire would quickly pass.

The year ended with a terrifying episode, for another attempt was made against Napoléon's life on Christmas Eve, and it came perilously close to succeeding. Everyone was traveling in two carriages to a performance of Haydn's *Creation* at the Opéra: the first consul and three of his generals in the first carriage, followed by Hortense, Caroline Murat, and Joséphine in the second. Joséphine was wearing for the first time a superb shawl from Constantinople, and Bonaparte—who had wanted to stay home that evening—stopped a moment to criticize a detail of her ensemble before they left. Hortense believed that this delay saved their lives, for just as they reached the rue Nicaise, a barrel packed with gunpowder exploded, throwing about twenty people into the air, wounding sixty, and blowing up two or three houses. Broken glass fell on Joséphine's carriage and cut Hortense's hand. Although badly shaken, they proceeded to the Opéra; Joséphine's face was ashen, but Bonaparte displayed his usual sang-froid. Eugène noted in his memoirs that they were received with a tumultuous ovation from the audience.

With all these assassination attempts, Joséphine became increasingly troubled by the fact that she had not yet produced Napoléon's heir, although other women in the family were delivering offspring on a regular basis. One evening, she told a party of ladies that she was certain she could become pregnant, for she had given birth to Eugène and Hortense, but her sister-in-law, Elisa, tactlessly responded with, "You were younger then, sister." So Joséphine planned another trip to Plombières in the summer of 1801 for a cure, inspired by the fact that Julie Bonaparte had taken the waters and, after six years of sterile marriage, had given birth to two daughters.

ABOVE: *Anonymous artist,*
Assassination Attempt in the Rue
Nicaise *(Musée Carnavalet). As
Joséphine and Napoléon were on their way
to the Opéra on December 24, 1800, one
of several attempts on the first consul's life
almost succeeded and cost the lives of
twenty-two people. These repeated attacks
were perpetrated by royalists still hoping
for a restoration of the monarchy and paid
for by English supporters of their cause.*

LEFT: *Charles-François Jalabert
(1819–1901),* Louis Bonaparte
*(Napoleon Museum, Arenenberg).
This painting of Napoléon's brother
in the costume of the Fifth Regiment of
Dragoons must be a copy of a miniature
of Louis by Isabey. The unstable Louis
was unable to cope with the overwhelming
personality of Napoléon or the compelling
social presence of his attractive wife,
Hortense, but Louis sincerely endeavored
to be a good king of Holland.*

By late 1801, despite Hortense's objections, plans for her marriage to Louis Bonaparte had been made, and the wedding took place on January 3, 1802. Joséphine was delighted, for this union of a Bonaparte and a de Beauharnais might produce a son whom Bonaparte would accept as his successor. Hortense's marriage was (in Bernard Chevallier's phrase) "a victory and a sacrifice." The victor was Joséphine, who chose to ignore the fact that her daughter and Louis Bonaparte, who suffered from a neurasthenia that often caused irrational behavior, were a singularly ill-matched couple. The first consul gave his stepdaughter a magnificent set of diamonds, and on July 27 he bought for Louis and Hortense one of the most celebrated town houses in Paris: 16, rue de la Victoire, a small perfect building constructed in 1777 by the architect Alexandre Brongniart for the dancer Mlle. Dervieux. But nothing could compensate for the ensuing years of misery.

Six days later, on the bitterly cold morning of January 9, Joséphine set off with her husband on an official journey to Lyons, the city of silk, where Eugène joined them, along with delegates summoned from Italy. While Bonaparte met with the Italian delegation, Joséphine was treated with the usual princely honors at Lyons—concerts, receptions, and balls—and she received an expensive gift as well, a parure of sapphires and diamonds; Napoléon was displeased and told her to return it, but she managed to keep it anyway. A triumphal pyramid was put up in the new square in honor of their visit, and Talma arrived to play four classical tragedies that were among the first consul's favorites. The silk manufactory was particularly honored by the visit, and Eugène reported that mountains of silks and rolls of precious carpets were spread out for their delectation. Both he and Hortense shared their mother's taste for beautiful things, and since Eugène would be acquiring his own Paris town house the following year, he joined Joséphine in taking a special interest in the latest designs.

When they returned to Paris, Joséphine was kept busy with official events, such as a diplomatic reception during which Bonaparte announced with great satisfaction the signature of the Peace of Amiens on March 25, 1802, which marked, temporarily, the end of hostilities with England. This meant that, for the first time since April 20, 1792, France was no longer at war. The stream of English visitors that had begun to pour into Paris late in 1801 had now become a torrent. They stood in line to see the Venetian horses from St. Mark's, the Venus de Milo, and the Apollo Belvedere; squeezed into countless private and public ballrooms where the waltz was the dance of the moment; waited for tickets to performances at the nearly two dozen theaters; and took ices at cafés that had once been private houses. French cuisine was, as always, a focal point of every gathering, and the chef who set the standards was the legendary Antoine Carême. It was doubtless Joséphine—ever watchful for culinary talent—who enlisted this extraordinarily inventive chef for the court, and during this happy time of celebrating the peace, Carême was in constant demand.

On the evening of the Tuileries reception, Paris became a fairyland. Fireworks burst over the Seine; public buildings blazed with colorful, symbolic illuminations; and between the tall, twin towers of Notre Dame hung an immense shining star mirrored in the river. Everyone was eager to catch a glimpse of the first consul and his wife, who was particularly radiant on this occasion, wearing one of her magnificent gowns of Lyons silk with a suite of glittering jewels, while her husband wore a silk habit, silk stockings, and buckled shoes—yet another intentional link with the glories of the French monarchy.

An English visitor watched Bonaparte review his troops on the parade ground of the Carrousel, and noted that as he passed the hussars, he nodded familiarly to his stepson, Eugène de Beauharnais, whose military bearing and trim uniform excited the spectators. Women were completely captivated by Eugène; the duchess of Gordon, who had brought her daughter, Lady Georgiana, placed Eugène at the top of her most-eligible list. He was an accomplished dancer like his late father, and at the ball following the military review, Lady Georgiana was swept off her feet, both literally and figuratively, when Eugène swirled her round the dance floor. Besides, Eugène de Beauharnais was to own one of the finest town houses in Paris the following spring—the splendid Hôtel de Beauharnais on the rue de Lille—the expensive decoration of which was no doubt supervised by Joséphine and Hortense.

Some visitors, such as the portly statesman Charles James Fox, were asked to dinner at the Tuileries or out to Malmaison.[11] Fox was as anxious as Bonaparte for a lasting peace and approved a rapprochement with France in opposition to his eternal rival, William Pitt. Fox was entertained in the renowned town house of Joséphine's friend, Mme. Récamier, where he met two young officers of the hussars, Philippe de Ségur and Eugène de Beauharnais. Eugène extended Fox an invitation from his mother to visit Malmaison, and the English politician no doubt arrived with a horticultural offering for her greenhouse.

On April 11, Bonaparte held an unusual conference at Malmaison for the purpose of preparing an act of amnesty for almost every class of émigré still on the list, a move that Joséphine would certainly have encouraged. Amnesty went into effect on April 26, and many of these émigrés would play a considerable role in Bonaparte's increasingly "monarchical consulate,"[12] as Mme. de Chastenay called it. She noted Joséphine's undisguised pleasure in welcoming such distinguished repatriates as the baron de Breteuil with his daughter and granddaughter, and Mesdames de Matignon and de Montmorency. Even such people as these "made a point of mentioning that they had been received by Mme. Bonaparte—not necessarily an easy thing to achieve—and that this made it even more desirable."[13]

One of Joséphine's favorite haunts in Paris was the nearby museum, where Vivant Denon was playing host to an international community of visiting artists, including prominent Americans such as the painter John Vanderlyn (the first American to exhibit at the Salon), the poet Joel Barlow, and his partner, Robert Fulton, who would demonstrate on the Seine a version of his steamboat for the first consul the following summer. Denon was already the unofficial director of fine arts, and on

November 19, 1802, he would be named director of the Musée Centrale, certainly at the urging of Joséphine. She and Bonaparte had presided over the inauguration in 1800 of the splendid sculpture salons refurbished to receive the fabled treasures from Italy. In August 1803, the museum would be renamed the Musée Napoléon and a colossal bust of Bonaparte placed high above the central doorway. Denon played a key role in forming its incomparable collections and at the same time helped to enrich Joséphine's personal art collection at Malmaison. She never failed to attend the Salons that Denon arranged to be held every other year after the Empire was proclaimed.

August 4, 1802, was a day Joséphine never forgot, for it marked another step in her husband's ascension to power. He was proclaimed consul for life, so he now signed with his Christian name, Napoléon, although she always called him Bonaparte. Joséphine, not surprisingly, was at the center of the ceremonies, including a reception at the Tuileries at which she received legislators and ambassadors. A concert followed the reception featuring music by Cherubini, whose work she supported, performed by at least three hundred musicians. Fireworks and amateur theatricals, including an appearance by Hortense (seven months pregnant at the time), preceded a dinner for two hundred.

On September 24, Joséphine and Napoléon moved to Saint-Cloud, where they spent a month receiving foreign dignitaries and performing official duties. Life at the official summer palace was very formal, and Joséphine would preside over ambassadorial receptions for as many as two hundred people, who were presented to the ruler by Talleyrand, now properly married to his mistress, Josephine's friend Madame Grand. Special uniforms were designed for the prefects of the court, and attendants wore fine green livery. Joséphine's pleasure in holding court at Saint-Cloud was, unfortunately, spoiled by the fact that Mlle. George of the Académie Française visited Napoléon by night, as Joséphine was well aware.

On October 10, 1802, Hortense gave birth to Napoléon-Charles Bonaparte, a grandson for Joséphine and a possible heir for Napoléon, who saw in this child a way to resolve the dynastic problem of his succession. He was in an unusually jovial mood as he and Joséphine set out for Normandy on October 29; he even permitted her to order whatever she desired from her *modiste* in order to be well dressed for their triumphant procession through the towns of France. They visited the manufactories at Beauvais and Rouen in November, and Isabey painted their visit to the textile atelier of the Sévène brothers. Wearing an exquisite lace scarf on her head, Joséphine was shown various samples of Sévène manufacture, as Napoléon and his officials were greeted by the proprietor. When they reached Amiens, the people were so enthusiastic that they pulled the carriage themselves, while Eugène trotted alongside as they pushed on to Antwerp. Brussels was ablaze with lights to welcome them, and Talma extended himself to present his usual evening performances.

By the time Joséphine returned to Saint-Cloud on November 14, a new era had begun, for her husband was moving ever closer to an hereditary empire, and the hierarchical structure of the palace already reflected it. Along with a governor and prefect of the palace, Joséphine was now attended by four ladies-in-waiting chosen for their fortunes and good reputations. Their husbands advanced in their careers as well: Mme. de Luçay's would become a count of the Empire and prefect of the palace, Mme. de Lauriston's a marquis and a marshal of France, and Claire de Rémusat's the first chamberlain.

A succession of events during the spring of 1803 was to alter Joséphine's life significantly. On May 16, England broke the Peace of Amiens by declaring war, which plunged France into a bloody struggle for the next eleven years and forced Napoléon to place an embargo on English goods. Now that war again loomed on the horizon, Napoléon went with Joséphine in June to inspect the troops and ships assembled on the channel at Boulogne for a possible invasion of England. On his subsequent tours, however, she had to remain at the Tuileries for the official receptions, attended by her ladies-in-waiting. In addition, there were family weddings, such as the marriage of Pauline Bonaparte, Napoléon's favorite sister, to the Italian Prince Camillo Borghese on November 5 at Joseph Bonaparte's château, Mortefontaine, where Joséphine was obliged to represent Napoléon. She found time, however, to answer his affectionate letters from the Iron Coast at Boulogne with equally warm replies: "How grateful I am . . . for giving so much time to your Joséphine! . . . A letter is a portrait of the soul, and I press this one to my heart. . . . I wish to keep it always! It will be my consolation during your absence. . . . My wish is also to please you, to love you—rather, to adore you!"[14]

Bonaparte returned on January 6, 1804, but in February another dark shadow clouded Joséphine's happiness, as the secret police uncovered a new plot hatched by French royalists to assassinate her husband, and she became intimately involved in the painful repercussions. Some conspirators were given warnings or exiled; eight of the twenty were pardoned at Joséphine's behest, but others were condemned, including the duc d'Enghien, son of the last prince de Condé and a cousin of the royal family. Joséphine did her best to save him, as she had done in innumerable other cases, believing not only that Enghien's death would be a miscarriage of justice—because of the lack of evidence against him—but also that his execution would alienate so many of the former nobility whom she had tried so hard to incorporate into the new régime. Her efforts were fruitless, but she was successful, as were Napoléon's sisters Caroline and Elisa, in persuading Bonaparte to spare the lives of other suspected conspirators.[15]

Joséphine was so stricken by Enghien's death that she tried to think of something practical to do, and as usual she succeeded. Her informants discovered that the woman Enghien had loved was Charlotte de Rohan, so a few days after his death, Joséphine managed to gather together a few souvenirs of the prince to send to Charlotte: Enghien's last letter and the little dog who refused to leave his grave. It was this kind of endearing personal touch that won Joséphine so many friends, not just from members of the former nobility but from all classes. Eugène, too, was deeply grieved by the

Enghien affair, and recorded in his memoirs: "I suffered greatly because of the esteem and love that I felt for the first consul; it seemed to me that his glory would be tarnished."[16]

Among the many who were alienated from Napoléon by the Enghien affair was Victorine de Chastenay, who was placed in an awkward position because, although she liked Joséphine, she did not want to serve the wife of the man who had executed the duc d'Enghien. Mme. de Chastenay was prepared to decline her appointment as lady-in-waiting, but she greatly underestimated Joséphine's powers of persuasion and her irresistible magnetism:

> I had to go myself to see [Joséphine] in her palace of Saint-Cloud. When I arrived, she had with her Mme. de Lavalette [her niece, Emilie de Beauharnais] and one or two ladies in her intimate circle, several men and M. d'Harville, who had been named a few days before as her first postilion. She came to me and said that she had learned from the minister of police that I had consented to accept a place as *dame du palais*. . . . I was on the point of composing my words of thanks [and to refuse] . . . but I found that I could not get them out, and if I had seen an open door, I think that I would have taken flight. The thought of myself, following Mme. Bonaparte, whose husband's actions and character I had come to detest! . . . To act the role of mannequin in the demi-circle of her salon! The past, the present, all of it was revolting to me. However, as was usual with her, the empress was so charming, spoke to me in such an appealing way, and had such flattering things to say about our future relationship that I felt myself drawn toward her little by little, even against my will.[17]

Just as the consular house was assuming its definitive shape, decisive measures were already being taken to elevate Joséphine's husband to the highest rank possible. In the spring of 1804, the valet Constant noted in his memoirs that the army and many French citizens who idolized the hero of Italy had openly expressed their desire to see him bear a title worthy of his fame. Now that he controlled such vast areas of Europe (the Netherlands, the Rhineland, much of Italy), the title of king would not do; nothing less than the imperial title would be sufficient. It all happened very quickly as plans were set into motion through the efficient operating machinery of the consular régime. The principal of heredity was adopted in April by the tribunate, the title of emperor for Napoléon Bonaparte was approved, and in early May the Senate gave its assent.

On May 18, the second consul, Jean-Jacques Cambacérès, arrived at Saint-Cloud, accompanied by troops and members of the senate, to announce the proclamation of the Empire (see pages xvi–xvii). The scene was painted by Georges Rouget, but the artist took artistic liberties, for Joséphine was not actually standing by Napoléon's side when the delegation arrived. Protocol

demanded the announcement be made first to him, then the Senate proceeded to Joséphine's apartments to formally announce it to her. Claire de Rémusat watched both of them closely, noting that Bonaparte took the novelty of being addressed as "Your Majesty" quite coolly, and that Joséphine responded to her new title with customary grace, although she must have had mixed emotions. She had opposed the concept of empire because imperial dignity was hereditary—a dreadful idea, since she had not been able to produce an heir and would now be haunted by the specter of divorce. Her one hope for retaining the throne of France was that Bonaparte would be able to adopt as his heir Napoléon-Charles, the first son of Hortense and Louis, although Hortense had refused their adoption request in April. Nevertheless, Napoléon's brothers had no suitable heirs themselves (Joseph had only daughters and Lucien and Jérôme had both disqualified themselves by marrying unsuitable women), and Napoléon had expressed his intention to pass a law that would make him master of his family, by which he could control his succession. Joséphine remained hopeful, therefore, that her grandson would one day be in line for the throne of France.

This was not the only family problem. Bonaparte's three sisters, who had reason to dislike a sister-in-law who had carried on with another man in their brother's absence, were becoming increasingly jealous of Joséphine's prospective title as empress. Her peccadillos were now in the past, and she was doing all she could to make amends, but when news of the forthcoming coronation reached the ears of her three married sisters-in-law—Elisa Bacciochi, Caroline Murat, and Pauline Borghese[18]—the Corsican clan vehemently demanded that they receive titles befitting their new importance as sisters of an emperor. When it was finally officially announced in *Le Moniteur* that each would be called "princess," the furor subsided somewhat, although echoes reverberated throughout the entire coronation period.

But titles were not the only issue that concerned Joséphine. How would Hortense be affected as the emperor's sister-in-law, the mother of a child who might become the imperial heir? And what of Eugène, who would certainly be going off with his stepfather to the field and for whom an appropriate princess would have to be found? Joséphine also realized that the demands on herself would become ever more relentless, with each day governed by exacting formality, prescribed ceremony, and few moments for herself. We know that she found this kind of restricted life unappealing; even while she was receiving the adulation of the princes of Italy in 1797, she had written to Hortense that she preferred to be a private person, at home with her family. She had repeated the same sentiments to her daughter in the autumn of 1802 during her official tour with

Pauline exemplified the élégantes *of the Empire in her exquisite white gown (probably embroidered by Picot), her crimson cashmere shawl thrown over a Directoire chair, resting her hand upon a pianoforte most likely from the Erard factory. The marble group on the pedestal are Cupid and Psyche, and the tripod table with bronze winged figures is based upon models excavated in Italy, an enterprise generously supported by the Borghese family.*

Bonaparte. Seated beside him in the theater, wearing some of the most spectacular crown jewels and accepting the enthusiastic homage that greeted them in every city through which they passed, she felt that "I was not made for so much grandeur. I would be happier in some retreat, surrounded by the objects of my affections."[19]

It has been claimed that Joséphine herself bore a share of the responsibility for the dramatic changes in her life, by having gained the love of the people. "The 'citizen wife of the First Consul' was everywhere at his side, participated in the honors bestowed upon him, and took part in his official voyages," wrote historians Nicole and Gérard Hubert. "Everyone was seduced by her amiability, her generosity, and the courtesy of her manners which contributed so much to the growing popularity of the First Consul, and opened for him the way to the throne."[20] Was Joséphine really so fortunate, after all, to have become "something more than a queen"?

7

Coronation and the Court

As Joséphine had anticipated, the proclamation of the Empire in May 1804 was a mixed blessing, for it meant that imperial succession was to be vested in Napoléon's family unless she were able to come up with an heir. The evening of Cambacérès's announcement Joséphine was faced with a Bonaparte family dinner that she found particularly trying. The weather was an atmospheric metaphor for the mood of those gathered around the table—hot, threatening, stormy, and punctuated by flashes of lightning. The quarreling that ensued centered mainly on the titles each Bonaparte sister was to receive. Hortense already stood in a favorable position as Napoléon's stepdaughter, Louis's wife, and the mother of Napoléon-Charles, the emperor's favorite. Eugène would achieve distinction as colonel-general of the Chasseurs à Cheval, a general of brigade, a prince of the Empire, and an arch-chancellor of state. Joséphine's new status would mean an inescapable commitment to an increasing number of public functions, balls, operas, concerts, rounds of diplomatic receptions, elaborate dinners, ceremonies for visiting heads of state in the Tuileries, royal processions, and the responsibility of representing the court in foreign capitals. It also meant that the intimate Consular style would give way to formal apartments, with glorious imperial silks on the walls and suites of stately gilt furniture around the perimeter, upholstered to match the walls as an appropriate setting for state functions. Joséphine's costumes, too, befitted an empress. Richly embroidered Lyons silks were set off by parures of diamonds, emeralds, and sapphires.

The spread eagle of the Roman legions was now adopted as the emblem of the Empire, marking the official seal, topping the flagstaffs, and crowning the gilded baldaquin of Joséphine's bed at Malmaison. This formal bedroom was Joséphine's last tent room, and perhaps her most impressive (see pages xviii–xix). From the windows she could look out upon her gardens, and against the drapery hung eight of Redouté's beautiful watercolors depicting the flowers she grew there and in her greenhouse. Everyone who visited Malmaison wanted to see Joséphine's bedroom, and a British officer, General Alexander Mercer (who saw the room in 1815, after Joséphine's death), avowed that he "never saw any room so remarkable for its decoration and so interesting from every point of view.... The walls, instead of being hung with paper, were covered in [fine material], with lace used as a border around the panels. There, I truly appreciated Joséphine's taste."[1]

As empress, Joséphine would have even more opportunities to help people in need, for when Cambacérès led the delegation to Saint-Cloud in May to proclaim the Empire, he seized the occasion to deliver a flowery speech, in which he praised Joséphine for her continued accessibility to the needy and conveyed the gratitude of the French people for her compassionate heart. Although probably intended as official flattery, it was nevertheless well deserved, for among her many acts of charity, we remember her efforts to save the lives of condemned prisoners and her tireless work on behalf of the émigrés. Joséphine saw Cambacérès often, and it was said that he and Joséphine were the only two people capable of assuaging the emperor's anger.

During the summer of 1804, the eyes of all Europe would turn to France, where the coronation of the imperial couple, scheduled to take place at Notre Dame on December 2, would catapult the most illustrious military figure on the Continent to even loftier heights and Joséphine would become the first empress France had ever known.

On June 27–28, 1804, Napoléon and Joséphine journeyed out to Fontainebleau, which would be used as another imperial residence (along with Saint-Cloud) outside Paris. The château had been built by François I before his death in 1547, and it had been a royal tradition for the court to move to Fontainebleau each autumn for the hunts. Because of its importance in French history, it was deemed a temporary country residence for the pope, who was coming to France for the coronation, although renovations would have to be made before his arrival.

As the usual Bastille Day celebration rolled around, Joséphine—a devotée of the theater—made her first public appearance as empress on July 10, when she and Napoléon attended a performance of *Ossian*, an opera in five acts by Jean-François Le Sueur based on the life of the legendary Celtic poet.[2] The subject was familiar to Joséphine, for one of her husband's favorites was the book of poems published by James McPherson as Ossian's work, an interest shared by Goethe, Talleyrand, Madame de Staël, and other intellectuals. Ossian was also the subject of two controversial paintings (by Gérard and Girodet) that hung in Joséphine's salon at Malmaison, depicting dead French warriors received by Ossian in a vague, moonlit Valhalla complete with a Napoleonic eagle. Joséphine must have noted that the costumes worn by the characters in these canvases were almost identical to those draped around the singers in Le Sueur's popular opera, the theme of which was principally political. The opera was such a resounding success that Le Sueur presented it one hundred times, and thanks to the support of Joséphine and Napoléon, the composer's reputation was secured. After *Ossian*, Le Sueur essentially became the official musician of the reign and even composed religious works for the chapel in the Tuileries, being the first composer in France to show interest in the Latin oratorio. On July 15, 1804, Napoléon honored those who had made sacrifices for

Anonymous artist, Celebration of the Emperor's Birthday at the Camp of Boulogne *(Museo Napoleonico, Rome). This celebration, in which the emperor was awarding the Légion d'Honneur to 2,000 soldiers, took place on August 15, 1804, in a large meadow near his military encampment on the French coast as preparations were being made for an invasion of England that was ultimately abandoned. When Austria attacked Bavaria in the fall of 1805, Napoléon redirected the Grande Armeé—a living, invincible machine of war—toward Ulm.*

their country by distributing for the first time crosses of the Légion d'Honneur. The ceremony began with a volley of cannons in the morning, and Joséphine watched Napoléon leave the Tuileries, riding between hedges of troops that lined the route all the way to the Invalides,[3] led by marshals (the first rank of officers of the Empire) and Hortense's husband, Louis Bonaparte, as grand constable. The comte de Ségur, grand master of ceremonies, awaited them at the Invalides as Joséphine arrived with her own suite, which was greeted with warm acclamation. She took her place in a special tribune facing the emperor as he distributed the crosses, and Claire de Rémusat thought "her costume was admirably selected and in perfect taste . . . a robe of rose-colored gauze, spangled with silver stars, and cut very low, in the prevailing fashion. Her headdress was a tiara of diamond wheat-ears, and this brilliant attire, the grace of her carriage, the charm of her smile, the sweetness of her countenance, produced such an effect that I heard many persons present say 'the empress of the French outshines all the ladies of her court.'"[4] The evening concluded with a performance at the Théâtre Français, the illumination of public edifices in their honor, sparkling fireworks displays on the Tuileries terrace below, and a myriad of brightly colored missiles launched out over the river from the Pont Neuf.

Napoléon and Eugène left for Boulogne on July 18, and on August 1 Joséphine went to Aix-la-Chapelle to take the waters before rejoining her husband for a trip to Belgium and the Rhineland in September. Aix was a much-needed respite before she plunged into the frenzied activity and emotional tension that accompanied preparations for the coronation. A journey by carriage from Paris to Aix in 1804, however, was not a carefree jaunt, because the roads were in disrepair. Joséphine never forgot the deep ruts on the route between Sedan and Rethel that bounced her off the carriage walls. As they approached Feulen, the ruts became even worse, and the only way to get her vehicle up a steep embankment was for men to tow it with heavy ropes as it rocked precariously back and forth.

Almost the worst part of Joséphine's trip to Aix that summer of 1804 was the jubilant reception awaiting her, which she dreaded in her weakened state, but as usual, she pulled herself together. Despite her longing to sink into bed and remain there, she dutifully appeared, perfectly composed, beautifully dressed, smiling cordially, and personally addressing everyone presented to her. Hortense heard from the couriers that her mother made herself as much loved at Aix as elsewhere, and even those not expected to join the chorus of praise attested to Joséphine's appeal. Surprisingly, one was an actress from the Comédie Française, the statuesque blonde Mademoiselle George, who had caused Joséphine grave concern when she visited the First Consul one night in the Tuileries. Yet, Mademoiselle George said that "[the empress] puts you at ease with her distinction, with the elegant simplicity that belongs to her alone. There is in all her person a suavity which is magnetic."[5]

While Joséphine was winning friends at Aix-la-Chapelle during August, her husband was making a tour of inspection in Boulogne, where plans for an invasion of England were now gaining momentum since the breaking of the treaty. As usual, he wrote to "his" Joséphine frequent, loving, newsy letters, complaining that his bachelor life was wretched and that, since she could not join him, he was sending for Hortense to spend two days with him beside the sea, bringing with her the child he and Joséphine so loved, Napoléon-Charles. Hortense was expecting her second baby early in October, and it is amusing to envision the doting stepfather, his pregnant stepdaughter, and a two-year-old in the setting of a vast army camp bristling with the largest mortars yet made, a flotilla of 1,700 vessels in the sea below, confronting an English squadron as the English coast shimmered on the not-too-distant horizon.

Hortense described Napoléon's headquarters at the military encampment on Boulogne's Iron Coast as a pavilion with a Council Chamber, its ceiling painted with an eagle flying into a sky of cerulean blue and its simple furnishings a chair of green Moroccan leather and a folding campaign desk. She and her son must have had to perch on folding stools. The bedroom, its walls papered in a trellis pattern with a classical border, was also of Spartan simplicity: the folding iron camp bed, a writing desk, a splendid dressing-case, and a telescope, which would have intrigued the toddler.

There was even a garden with ornamental water upon which floated two black swans, probable offspring of the Australian black swans that fascinated Napoléon-Charles in his grandmother's garden at Malmaison, a touch of Joséphine on the Iron Coast.

Napoléon rejoined Joséphine in Aix on September 2 to embark upon a trip she would number among the most satisfying of her life. The couple were shown the glories of Aix-la-Chapelle—the relics of the Emperor Charlemagne—and Joséphine asked for a reliquary holding a bone from Charlemagne's arm, along with a small statue of the Virgin reputedly carved by Saint Luke. This reliquary has an unusual history, for it passed from Joséphine to Hortense, whose daughter-in-law, Empress Eugénie, inherited it.[6] As Napoléon and Joséphine were considering which artifacts would be appropriate for the high offices they were about to assume, Napoléon borrowed an emblem from another emperor, Childeric, king of the Franks, namely the objects in the shape of bees found when his tomb had been opened in 1653. Thus the bee became a symbol for the Empire, signifying industriousness and identifying the new régime with the Merovingian-Carolingian past.

After leaving Aix on September 11, Napoléon and Joséphine proceeded up the romantic Rhine to Cologne, where sixty-seven different clocks sounded the hours from a host of ancient churches. Joséphine received special attention all along the way, and at Bonn she occupied a house Constant thought just right for her, for there was a garden filled with fairy-lights running down to the banks of the broad and lovely river on which had been stationed a boatload of musicians to serenade her. At Coblenz, the prince of Nassau offered the new empress and her suite two yachts in which to ascend the river to Mainz, while the emperor took the new riverside highway. Despite the pleasurable voyage, Joséphine was anxious to reach Mainz, because she knew there would be maneuvers by four cavalry regiments on September 30, with her Eugène commanding them.

Joséphine and Napoléon entered the city on September 21. Besides the usual complement of marshals, generals, and councilors were foreign minister Talleyrand, secretary of state Maret, grand marshal of the court Michel Duroc, and grand master of the horse Caulaincourt. This marked the first time Joséphine would preside over the French court in a foreign city, and henceforward she would occasionally do so without her husband beside her. In 1805 she would officiate alone at Strasbourg while Napoléon was fighting the Austerlitz campaign, and in 1806 she would reestablish the court in Mainz while he fought the Prussians at Jena. Among the German Electors who came to pay their respects this September were the margrave of Baden, the Bavarian ambassador in Karlsruhe, and the prince-archbishop of Mainz, Karl Theodor von Dalberg, who now became one of Joséphine's admirers and would frequent her court in Mainz in 1806.

Hortense remarked that everyone thought there were plans to unite her brother with one of the German royal families, so sundry female offspring were trotted out at Mainz in hopes of attracting Eugène's attention. One was the awkward daughter of Prince Leopold of Bavaria, a young woman Con-

stant thought not even faintly attractive, and worse still, badly dressed. Although the girl was seated between the emperor and Eugène de Beauharnais, she naively chattered away during the entire meal. Napoléon lost patience and soon turned away, but Eugène, with his impeccable manners, listened politely. He was considered the most eligible bachelor on the continent and rising in his profession, having been made a member of the Legion d'Honneur the previous December; he had been promoted to commandant in June, and on October 17 he would become colonel-general of the Chasseurs à Cheval. Besides his other attributes, Eugène was endowed with a full, resounding baritone voice, which Constant thought was the reason his stepfather chose him to command the military reviews.

After Mainz Napoléon continued his tour of inspection, but Joséphine returned home on October 7 because Hortense's second child was due imminently. Joséphine's route back to Paris took her through Nancy, where the glorious Place Stanislas shone with illuminated houses, transparencies in the windows, lighted triumphal arches, and welcome placards in her honor. She reached Paris on October 12, the day after Hortense gave birth to her second son, and was pleasantly surprised to find Louis in an almost expansive mood. When Louis thought Hortense needed him, he was capable of tender affection, and Joséphine was relieved to see that his attitude toward his wife seemed more considerate than usual. When he became grand constable, Hortense had thought the house on the rue de la Victoire too small for the official receptions she would be expected to give, so Louis had purchased the splendid Hôtel Saint-Julien on rue Cerutti, complete with extensive gardens. When Joséphine saw it, she was impressed although shocked to see the barriers Louis had erected around his wife: a sentinel was stationed under her windows, and her ladies-in-waiting were not allowed to advance any further than her salon. It was here that the new baby was born, a boy named Napoléon-Louis, and in a fit of generosity, Louis founded a hospital at Saint-Leu, where they owned a summer house, in honor of his latest heir. In spite of his habitual irritability, Louis was always attentive during Hortense's confinements and he ordered a parure of diamonds for her at the birth of each son. Much of the time, however, he was morose, given to petty accusations, and generally made life miserable for his wife.

It was not so much her volatile son-in-law who concerned Joséphine that fall but Hortense herself, who had been having an affair with an officer two years her junior by the name of Auguste-Charles de Flahaut.[7] Among the émigrés in Joséphine's circle was the novelist Mme. de Flahaut, who had returned from exile in 1797 with twelve-year-old Auguste-Charles (widely believed to be the illegitimate son of Talleyrand) and immediately attached herself to Hortense and Joséphine, whom she had known during the Directoire. Ironically, Charles later served in the regiment of Louis Bonaparte, who perceived his unusual military ability and took him to Marengo; in 1802 Joachim Murat had made the young man his aide-de-camp.

As unsettling as this affair was in light of the forthcoming coronation and the possibility of

François Gérard (1770–1837), Auguste-Charles-Joseph Flahaut de la Billardie (1785—1870) (Bowood). Charles de Flahaut not only moved in the highest ranks of society in France, and later in England, but he was also an unusually precocious soldier, highly valued by Napoléon. Flahaut became a hussar in the consular guard at the age of fifteen and Joachim Murat's aide de camp two years later. He fought at Ulm, Jena, Auerstadt, Eylau, Friedland, Wagram, as well as in Spain, Leipzig, and the Russian campaign of 1812. He attended Hortense's funeral in 1838 and lived long enough to attend that of their son, the duc de Morny, in 1865.

scandal, Joséphine now had to turn her attention to other matters. The Bonapartes, whose animosity toward the de Beauharnais family was exacerbated by the birth of Hortense's second son, continued to express their displeasure at the prospect of Joséphine's being crowned empress, presumably because of her earlier infidelity. Napoléon, however, stood firm, making his position clear to comte de Roederer, the secretary of state : "They are jealous of my wife, of Eugène, of Hortense. . . . I love these children. . . . My wife is a good woman [who is] willing to play the empress . . . [and] if I had been thrown into prison instead of mounting a throne, she would have shared my misfortune. It is right for her to share my success."[8] So it was announced that Joséphine would be crowned as well as anointed, and the pope himself was coming to do it. She would become the only Frenchwoman ever to bear the title of empress,[9] a decision Napoléon never regretted, judging by his reflections on Saint Helena. One historian even extolled Joséphine as "the principal ornament of the imperial court."[10]

Ever since May, Paris had been preparing for the great event, but a formidable challenge was the condition of the city itself: cramped, narrow streets with no sidewalks; no supply of good drinking water except from wells; in efficient street lighting. When Joséphine left the theater in the evening, she was lighted as members of Louis XIV's court had been—by an attendant carrying a torch. Certain areas in Paris were so dark that the carriage of the unfortunate marquis de Caulaincourt suddenly plunged into a huge hole as it crossed the Place Vendôme. The dismal condition of the streets was an onerous fact of life, even for those now occupying the most prestigious residences in Paris, such as the Murats in the Hôtel Thélusson, Elisa Bonaparte Bacciocci in her eighteenth-century Folie de Saint-James, and Hortense, now ensconced in the splendid Hôtel Saint Julien (later the Hôtel de Lannoy). When these privileged few departed from their elegant portes cochères, they took the same chances in the streets as everyone else.

Napoléon now began a campaign of amelioration, ordering Pierre Fontaine to demolish the old houses encumbering the premises of Notre Dame, where the great event was to take place on December 2. New streets were opened up to accommodate crowds attending the festivities, and street names were chosen by the emperor himself to commemorate battles: the paved rue de Rivoli that ran along the Tuileries gardens, with arcades to protect pedestrians; the nearby rue des Pyramides; rue de Castiglione, running from the Luxembourg gardens to Place Vendôme; rue de Mondovi, and rue du Mont-Thabor. He would continue to transform Paris with public monuments such as the Bourse (stock exchange); the monumental façade of the Corps Legislatif; the new fountain of the Châtelet; and four new bridges across the Seine. The quai Bonaparte was finished to facilitate the passage of the coronation procession, and visitors to Paris during the summer of 1804 were amazed at the number of improvements made since 1800.

Since July the newspapers had been announcing that merchants were anticipating brisk business, people were refreshing their apartments for rental to visitors at good prices, and jewelers were besieged by clients desiring parures as much like Joséphine's as possible. The price of diamonds of good quality was the highest it had been in many years, but one person who did not need any (other than Joséphine) was Pauline Bonaparte Borghese. Laure Junot was stunned to see Pauline adorned on one occasion with all the diamonds of the house of Borghese, a blazing mass of jewels. Fashion industries that had fallen with the monarchy were now revived to accommodate the demand for gauzes, plumes, embroidery, buckles, buttons, pearls, paillettes, and passementerie. Artisans who had struggled to survive suddenly found themselves gainfully employed, and Joséphine herself more than did her part, ordering dozens of pairs of shoes, gloves, and silk stockings.

Laure Junot saw the streets thronged from morning to night. Some stood in line for tickets to the coronation ceremony, while others clambered to find places in windows. One man even paid 300 francs for a second-floor window near the cathedral gate. There was much to delight the eye even before the great day. One could visit the famous embroiderer, Dallemagne, who was preparing the emperor's mantle; at the shop of the jeweler, Foncier, the crowns of Napoléon and Joséphine were on view, along with the emperor's sword made by Boutet and decorated with the fabulous Regent Diamond worth six million francs. There was such a throng and press on the walkway in front of Foncier's, however, that it was all but impossible to get near it. Etiènne Nitot was the jeweler who enjoyed most of Joséphine's patronage and was granted the envied title "Jeweler to Her Majesty the Empress and Queen." So everyone rushed to see the window of Nitot's establishment on the Place du Carrousel near the Tuileries, hoping for a glimpse of one of the empress's spectacular parures of emeralds or carnelians. Jewelry was a passion, and she was quickly assembling the most beautiful collection in Europe.

On September 12, on the occasion of the first Salon held under the Empire, the Musée Napoléon had offered a day of free admission to a special exhibition of paintings, sculptures, and engravings by living artists. Among the paintings was the canvas that had been commissioned from Joséphine's protégé Antoine Gros—*Bonaparte Visiting the Plague-Stricken at Jaffa*—a skillful bit of propaganda to remind the populace that the hero of Aboukir was now emperor of the French. Because Gros had not been on the campaign, Denon gave him sketches and directives regarding his treatment of the subject, and the picture was so enthusiastically received by the public that it was crowned with laurels and palms.

After Joséphine's return to Paris in October, she was kept busy approving designs for the forthcoming event that were presented to her by Percier and Fontaine and Vivant Denon. Fontaine had produced a drawing of the imperial throne, and Denon submitted sketches of coats-of-arms and various decorations appropriate to the Empire. The splendid carriages for the coronation were almost complete, and the architects added a provisional vestibule behind Notre Dame to shelter the imperial couple as they arrived. Since the cathedral had been damaged during the Revolution, Percier and Fontaine provided a neo-Gothic façade, and even more space was opened up around it to accommodate the lengthy procession and the huge crowds anticipated. Inside the church the decorations included imperial eagles placed in the arches, white silk hangings embroidered with gold bees, and special carpeting.

One of the key figures involved in carrying out the elaborate plans for the coronation was Joséphine's friend Jean-Baptiste Isabey, who had been asked to make a series of drawings setting forth each stage of the ceremony. Realizing there was no time for drawings, he began to ransack shops for every toy figure he could find. Dressing the dolls in their costumes, Isabey moved them about so the principals would know where they would be sitting, standing, or kneeling at any given moment. Pressed for time, this artist assumed a crushing burden, working closely with the comte de Ségur, master of ceremonies; the painter David, who was to record the event; and the architects Percier and Fontaine, who were transforming the premises. Not only was Isabey largely responsible for the pageantry, but he also had to design the costumes, including Joséphine's, which had to be appropriately rich, varied, and loaded with symbolism. The costumes would be executed by Louis-Hippolyte Leroy, the oracle of Paris fashion and Joséphine's *modiste*, whose shop at 89, rue de la Loi was thereafter inundated with women clamoring to be dressed by the empress's own dressmaker.

Jean-Baptiste Isabey (1767–1855), Claire de Rémusat (Ann S. K. Brown Military Collection, Providence, R. I.). Joséphine's lady of honor is shown wearing a court costume in this plate from Isabey's superb volume Le Livre du Sacre de S. N. l'Empereur Napoléon. *Mme. de Rémusat's memoirs favored her close friend Talleyrand at Napoléon's expense, so when he returned from Elba, she burned them and rewrote them in 1818. Chateaubriand called them "memoirs of memoirs."*

The emperor was to wear a crimson velvet robe weighing, it was said, over eighty pounds, and Joséphine's costume was a reflection of her husband's: a deep crimson velvet mantle with a long train decorated with gold bees and gold embroidery with interlaces of oak, laurel, and olive leaves, lined and bordered with ermine. Her dress was of silver brocade embroidered with golden bees. The bodice and the puff at the top of the sleeves were sprinkled with diamonds, and the high collar, the *chérusque*, was of gold lace inspired by Médici collars of the sixteenth century.[11] It was a style particularly becoming to Joséphine, Laure Junot thought, for "one of [her] chief beauties . . . was not merely her fine figure, but the elegant turn of her neck, and the way in which she carried her head; indeed, her deportment was altogether conspicuous for dignity and grace. I have had the honor of being presented to many *real princesses,* to use the phrase of Faubourg Saint-Germain, but I never saw one who, to my eyes, presented so perfect a personification of elegance and majesty."[12] Joséphine's chestnut hair had been arranged in tiny curls upon which her diadem (four rows of pearls interlaced with diamond leaves) rested perfectly, and Claire de Rémusat remarked that it made the empress look twenty-five years old. In addition to the diadem, she would have a crown of diamonds and emeralds and a girdle made of thirty-nine rose-colored stones. Even the pope received a tiara of pearls and colored stones set in vine leaves, probably designed by Joséphine's jeweler. Napoléon's brothers were to wear knee breeches, lace cravats, and plumed berets in the manner of Henri IV, as was Eugène, whose taste was simple and who spent much of his life in uniform on horseback. He must have been

Pierre-François-Léonard Fontaine (1762–1853) and Charles Percier (1764–1838), View of the Principal Façade of the Church of Notre Dame de Paris and of the Portico Decorated for the Coronation Ceremony (Ann S. K. Brown Military Collection, Providence, R.I.). The façade of Notre Dame had suffered during the Revolution, so Fontaine and Percier designed a temporary neo-Gothic structure at the entrance, with wings extending from the sides. Fontaine reports in his journal that they worked almost up to the moment the imperial carriage arrived.

relieved that David (in his painting of the coronation) depicted him bareheaded, his hand resting on his sword.

An important position yet unfilled was director of the Garde-Meuble, an indispensable branch of the imperial household that provided furnishings for the residences, so Joséphine was quick to recommend her old friend, Etiènne Calmelet, who was duly appointed on November 4. (This was the same Calmelet who had been her business adviser since the dark days of the Revolution and falsified her birth certificate at the time of her marriage to Bonaparte.) By November 15 Calmelet was already at the Sèvres manufactory choosing a large number of vases to embellish the imperial apartments at Fontainebleau. The pope would stay only briefly at Fontainebleau, and in Paris his residence would be in apartments in the Pavillon de Flore of the Tuileries, under Joséphine's solicitous eye. A complete renovation of this part of the old palace was therefore in progress, and the work of uniting the Grande Galerie of the museum to the Pavillon de Flore would have to be finished before the pontiff's arrival.

In the midst of these feverish preparations, Joséphine found time to visit Hortense, who was slowly recovering from childbirth. The emperor too was pleased to find his stepdaughter well and was obviously gratified by Napoléon-Louis's birth. During her convalescence, Hortense caught up on her journal, in which she reflected on the political implications of the coming coronation. She thought that all parties should rally around the emperor because the honors he bestowed were based on merit and not class, and she believed that the return to royal protocol and attire would be more in harmony with the European monarchical system. Now that all was set in motion for the coronation, Hortense hoped her stepfather would no longer have any enemies, except for "England because of rivalry, some royalists because of old memories, and some republicans [due to] their character."[13]

While Hortense was musing upon the state of the nation, she received a visit from her old friend Caroline Murat, who came to complain that her own children might well be ranked below those of Hortense. Joséphine was annoyed that Caroline would bother Hortense with such matters, but for the moment she had no time to smooth ruffled feathers, for Napoléon needed her to assist him with the list of invited guests, which was due on October 26. On the 28th Joséphine came in from Saint-Cloud with him to attend a military review, and they stopped by the museum, which was overflowing with visitors more excited about seeing the glamorous couple than the works of art.

As the significant day approached, it was inevitable that Joséphine would have to endure the spasms of another Bonaparte reunion. It came on November 17 at Saint-Cloud, and the controversy centered, as usual, upon imperial prerogative. When the emperor's sisters were told unequivocally they would have to carry the empress's train, they wept with rage, and Napoléon exploded. Joseph and Louis jumped into the fray, humiliated after being told they were to appear as "grand dignitaries" and not as princes, in which event their wives, Julie and Hortense, should not be asked to help carry the train (although Hortense would have been delighted to do so). After a week-long stalemate, Napoléon finally conceded his brothers the privilege of participating as princes and their wives as princesses. This meant that they would only be required to hold up the robe and not to carry the train, apparently a meaningful distinction. Madame Mère averted any potential problems that might have arisen in her case by simply remaining in Rome with her independent son, Lucien. He had been living there since April after an unpleasant interview with Napoléon, who wanted him to marry the queen of Etruria, but Lucien refused to leave his second wife, Alexandrine de Bleschamp. Although the Bonaparte women were mollified for the moment, Joséphine had to endure their wrangling throughout the events preceding the coronation.

On the morning of November 22, Joséphine took the road to Fontainebleau with her husband to look over the final renovation of the palace. There was delicious irony in that she had once been an ordinary resident in her Aunt Renaudin's small house nearby and now she was would occupy the imperial apartments of the château itself. Furthermore, the man beside her in the carriage was the leading monarch of Europe, and her mission was unprecedented—to check arrangements for the arrival of the pope, who would officiate at her own coronation. Everything appeared to be in order, and Fontaine reported that he and his staff had prepared forty apartments, two hundred lodgings for attendants, and stables for four hundred horses, and that the apartments had been superbly furnished. The bare stone walls were hung with magnificent tapestries from Aubusson, Savonnerie, and Tournai, the time-honored French manner of preparing a residence to receive a ruler or prince of the church. This was all accomplished in only nineteen days, thanks to the efficacious attentions of Marshal Duroc and Calmelet. The populace of Fontainebleau was delighted, declaring that the old palace was even more magnificent than it had been under the monarchy.

The complex negotiations with the pope had been carried out principally by Napoléon's uncle, Cardinal Fesch, now French ambassador to the Holy See, who had helped open the way in 1803 for the Holy Father's participation, accompanied by the writer René Chateaubriand.[14] By inviting the pope to France, Napoléon wanted to imbue the ceremony with religious significance, thereby stamping it with the seal of legitimacy.

For the sixty-two-year-old Pope Pius VII, crossing the Alps in winter was not an easy journey, either physically or emotionally. He had exchanged letters with Joséphine and sent her a papal ring in appreciation for a surplice she had had made for him. After a tearful farewell from his flock, who feared they would never see him again, the pope set out for Paris with an imposing cortège of thirty wagons and coaches bearing six cardinals, ten bishops, and more than one hundred officials. It was such a difficult voyage that the oldest cardinal died on the way, but the others were about to witness, for the first time in French history, the effulgent spectacle of an imperial coronation.

The pope's arrival presented slippery problems of protocol, for the emperor could hardly take second place to the Holy Father. So it was decided in advance that they would meet "by chance" in the royal forest near the château, where Joséphine would be waiting on the steps to receive him. On the designated date of November 25, Napoléon, wearing his favorite green uniform, "just happened" to be riding on horseback through the forest of Fontainebleau when he came upon the papal carriage. The leader of France gallantly dismounted to greet his aged guest, who descended with difficulty, in his white robes and delicate silk shoes, into a sea of black mud. After the greetings, an imperial carriage appeared as if by magic. Host and guest stepped in simultaneously, with Napoléon entering on the right, thereby attaining the traditional seat of honor. This first encounter established the protocol for the rest of the visit, and it set the precedent for all the events surrounding the pope's stay in France. Joséphine awaited them on the palace steps, composed as always in the face of a potentially awkward situation, and she performed the honors with her usual tact, putting the Holy Father at ease, and making certain that his apartments were arranged to his satisfaction.

Ever since the founding of the Empire, Joséphine had been deeply concerned about a matter as yet unresolved, her fear that the re-establishment of the church might cast a shadow over her civil marriage in 1796. This emboldened her to seek a private conference with the Pope during his three days at Fontainebleau, where she solicited him to persuade her husband to sanctify their marriage with a religious ceremony. Napoléon agreed, somewhat reluctantly, and their marriage was solemnized the afternoon before the coronation in a small chapel of the Tuileries. Cardinal Fesch officiated, and Talleyrand and Marshal Berthier stood as the two witnesses. It was a double triumph for Joséphine, for her marriage was now blessed by the Church, which would presumably make divorce much more difficult.

After his brief rest at Fontainebleau, the pope and his party were escorted into Paris, where the papal rooms in the Pavillon de Flore of the Tuileries had been converted into an exact replica of his Vatican apartments. His huge retinue of attendants required fifty-six rooms on the floors above, and imperial records reveal that staggering sums were expended to provide the abundance of food they consumed. They must have eaten competitively, as the ascetic Pope in his apartment below dined circumspectly. Each day the populace crowded beneath the Tuileries windows and called for the pope's appearance, for his kind, dignified manner and his benevolent demeanor had won their hearts. As she watched this phenomenon, Joséphine must have recalled the horrible scenes that had taken place a decade earlier, when mobs had hunted down priests without mercy and massacred them by the hundreds, many in the prison where she had been incarcerated. Now, in 1804, her husband had established peace with the church through the Concordat, and the Pope was in Paris on a mission she could never have imagined.

Joséphine was delighted by the honors granted her own family during this historic visit, for Louis was present at the first interview between his brother and the pope, and Hortense and her son were received at the Pavillon de Flore, after which she recorded her reaction: "This venerable figure, head of a religion that recognizes so much suffering and forgiveness, inspired within me a deep emotion."[15] She added that a large crowd came daily to be blessed by him in the galleries of the Louvre, except for one arrogant egotist who refused to receive a blessing. The pope paused and gently said to him: "The blessing of an old man never does any harm," so the young man, ashamed, knelt down for the benediction.

At six o'clock on the frigid morning of December 2, the long-awaited ceremony was announced by cannon, repeated each hour until the evening, and the ringing of bells, although hundreds of people had been up all night and hardly needed awakening. The officials set out from the Palais de Justice, then the legislative body and diplomatic corps, followed by the Pope with his retinue, although the shivering pontiff had to wait for the imperial couple for almost two hours in the bone-chilling cold of the cathedral. Finally, to the explosion of cannon, escorted by twenty squadrons of cavalry, Napoléon and Joséphine arrived, accompanied by Louis and Joseph, in a carriage with large glass windows. The interior of the cathedral blazed with lights from countless candelabra and crystal chandeliers, and the dazzling costumes with flashing jewels created a spectacle of astonishing brilliance.

After the pope's charge to the ruler, the imperial couple were led to the altar to kneel for the sacred act of anointing. Then Napoléon (by pre-arrangement) laid aside his golden wreath, took his own crown and placed it upon his head. What followed was the most memorable moment of the entire ceremony, according to Laure Junot, at least, the "magical scene" in which Napoléon crowned Joséphine, the focus of David's painting (see frontispiece).

If anyone ever doubted Napoléon's love for his wife, it was now confirmed before 20,000 spectators, including the Bonaparte family. Laure Junot was in a position to see every detail, and she was struck by the affection and tenderness written on Napoléon's face as his wife advanced toward him. "When she knelt down . . . both . . . appeared to enjoy one of those fleeting moments of pure felicity which are unique in a lifetime, and serve to fill up a lustrum of years. . . . When the time arrived for placing the crown on the head of the woman whom popular superstition regarded as his good genie, his manner was almost playful. He took great pains to arrange this little crown, which was placed over Joséphine's tiara of diamonds; he put it on, then took it off, and finally put it on again, as if to promise her she should wear it gracefully and lightly."[16]

The ceremony finally ended at 3 p.m., and as the imperial procession was returning to the Tuileries in the gathering darkness, thousands of torches were set aflame, and a gigantic lighted "N" appeared at the Porte Saint-Denis. Along the streets the crowd responded with a deafening ovation, so the day ended as an apotheosis. The tallest buildings glowed with Bengal lights, the Champs-Elysées and Tuileries gardens shone more brightly than ever, and at 6:30 Joséphine and Napoléon appeared on the balcony as the city saluted them with joyous shouts. While a concert was played under their windows, they watched as the skies and the river exploded with fireworks launched from the Place de la Concorde. Napoléon could hardly wait to fling off the bejeweled robes so foreign to his personal taste; Joséphine was even more uncomfortable in her tight dress and heavy diadem and visibly staggered under the weight of her ponderous mantle.

On December 16, the city acclaimed its sovereigns with a fête staged on the Place de Grève, where the imperial couple were presented a spectacular silver-gilt table service made by the famous silversmith Henri Auguste. Yet another fête, accompanied by a Haydn symphony, ended with fireworks launched from the Rive Gauche, during which an effigy of the emperor and a ship representing the city of Paris appeared in lights. Joséphine herself was honored at a reception that took place in a "huge salon decorated with silver gauze, gardens of fresh flowers, a great profusion of candles that lighted up the women's splendid parures . . . that sparkled with fiery diamonds. [The women wore] robes embroidered so heavily with jewels that one had to half close one's eyes not to be blinded. . . . The air was filled with the fragrance of flowers in the midst of a rigorous winter."[17]

Anonymous artist, The Fireworks Display *(Ann S. K. Brown Military Collection, Providence, R. I.). These fireworks celebrating the coronation, launched from the river bank opposite the Place de Grève, perpetuated a royal tradition. The ephemeral structure represents Bonaparte's crossing the Alps and the French army's descent into Italy for the second Italian campaign. The illuminated vessel obviously refers to the ship that appears in the arms of the city of Paris, which offered this tribute.*

This continual round of celebrations made the December of 1804 truly unforgettable, but the memory Joséphine must have cherished most was the crystal-clear evening of the coronation itself. A wonderfully decorated balloon bearing a constellation of lights was launched into the heavens, traversed half the continent, crossed over the Alps, and splashed down fifteen days later into Lake Bracciano to the amazement of fishermen.

In Paris the weary couple were at long last divested of their cumbersome robes, but as they sat down to dine informally, Napoléon asked Joséphine not to remove her diadem, for it suited her perfectly. Far into the night, they heard crowds milling about the terrace, with hurrahs and cries of "Vive l'Empereur," and from the tall windows of the palace, they looked out upon the extravagantly illuminated gardens. All along the *grande allée* stood shimmering columns of light, with colored lamps swinging from the branches of the trees, and further along—high above the square where the loathsome guillotine had once darkened the horizon—hung a bright, symbolic star.

8

"Aux Armes!"

$\mathcal{P}$aris was in a state of jubilation for weeks after the coronation, and 1804 ended with a dramatic ceremony on the Champ de Mars, during which the emperor distributed eagles to the army, after an oath of loyalty from his marshals. The ceremony had been planned for the day after the coronation, but Joséphine was so weary that it had to be postponed until December 5, when it took place under an elaborate pavilion designed by Pierre Fontaine especially for the purpose, echoing the ancien régime. The day was miserably cold, with snow melting on the ground and turning into puddles, to the dismay of officers in gold-trimmed uniforms and women in silk dresses. The frigid dampness forced people in the stands to leave, and Joséphine herself had to take to her carriage, leaving Caroline Murat to represent her. Although bare-armed and shivering, Caroline was proud of the prominent place her husband was playing in the ceremony, for he was now a marshal of the Empire, the governor of Paris, and for some unaccountable reason, prince and grand admiral, despite his total ignorance of naval affairs.

Joséphine never felt completely at ease in the Murats' presence, but she had to admire the fine works of art they were amassing—an impressive manifestation of their status and, Joséphine admitted, a well-chosen collection. In fact, the Murats already owned at least two works by the leading sculptor in Europe, the Italian master Antonio Canova, whose atelier Murat had protected while he was with the army in Italy in 1798. In the summer of 1802, while Joséphine and Napoléon were visiting the Murats at their château in Villiers-la-Garenne, she had seen two masterpieces by Canova that Murat had acquired in 1800: the standing *Cupid and Psyche* and the recumbent *Cupid and Psyche.* From that moment on, she was so enthusiastic about Canova's work that she began to build the finest private collection of the Italian master, which she displayed in her gallery at Malmaison.[1]

The year 1805 opened with the emperor's promise of a great year ahead. He did not imagine for a moment that the imperial title conferred some sort of magical security, for he once remarked that "a throne is nothing but planks covered with velvet." Yet he did share Hortense's hope that the

Antonio Canova (1757–1822), Cupid and Psyche (State Hermitage Museum, St. Petersburg). Joséphine's perspicacity in patronizing the leading sculptor in Europe, Antonio Canova, was praised by connoisseurs during her lifetime. The somewhat naive Cupid and unusually chaste Psyche look like a brother and sister concentrating upon a butterfly, emblem of the soul. The sculpture is based on the tale by Apuleius.

restoration of monarchical forms would reconcile France with the rest of Europe, and Joséphine was optimistic as well. But the year was still young when rumblings of future conflicts were heard, such as the cold reply from George III of England to Napoléon's letter expressing his desire for peace. King George warned that a new storm was brewing in the north, by which he meant Russia, where Catherine the Great's grandson, Czar Alexander, now ruled. Most Russian trade rested in the hands of some 4,000 English merchants in St. Petersburg, and England was prepared to use its considerable influence with Russia to defeat Napoléon's blockade, which hurt English commerce. In April a secret treaty would be signed in St. Petersburg that paved the way for a new coalition led by England; this would become stronger each day, so by the end of the summer France would once again become an armed camp.

After the coronation, Joséphine was kept unusually busy at the Tuileries and Saint-Cloud entertaining the many consequential foreigners who had come for the festivities and remained for the season. The pope continued to occupy his quarters in the Pavillon de Flore, along with his attendants, whom the French thought noisy and excitable. The papal contingent was awaiting the return of warm spring weather before again tackling the Alps. Joséphine decided to take advantage of the pope's presence by having him baptize her latest grandchild, Prince Napoléon-Louis, who was five months old in March. The ceremony took place on March 24 at Saint-Cloud, where the château's gallery was transformed into a chapel; afterwards the entire château was illuminated, with a fireworks display launched from the Lantern of Diogenes.

Hortense hosted numerous parties as the wife of the grand constable, and Caroline, as wife of the governor of Paris, kept the Elysée Palace aglow with her evening receptions that invariably required Joséphine's presence. Although most of the empress's attendants had been chosen for their family connections, one who entered Joséphine's service at this time was so attractive that she created an unusual stir among the men, including the emperor. While chatting one evening with the ladies-in-waiting, he was seen to pause before Mme. Duchatel, a young woman with huge blue eyes, dark hair, and perfect teeth. Joséphine was acutely embarrassed, especially since she had accepted Mme. Duchatel for the position on Eugène's recommendation, as he was himself interested in her. Joséphine's lady-in-waiting, the ever-alert Claire de Rémusat, believed that the newcomer had been planted by the Murats in hopes of detaching the emperor from his wife. After she was installed at court, Mme. Duchatel surprised Eugène by showing him no gratitude whatsoever, and she all but ignored him when they met, a novelty for someone as sought after as Eugène. Her mysterious behavior was explained by Marshal Duroc, who confided to both Eugène and Hortense that the emperor had taken an interest in Mme. Duchatel himself, and the reason Murat danced with her the entire evening at one of the court balls was to divert attention from Napoléon.

Eugène now forgot his own disappointment in light of his concern for his mother, because the harmony between Joséphine and her husband that had reigned since the coronation was threatened. For once, Eugène seemed at a loss, but his clever sister rose to the challenge. Hortense found a moment to be alone with her stepfather and was able to resolve the matter by appealing to his pride. She summed up their interview in her memoirs: "Too much master of himself to give way to a sentiment, and too severe in his moral code for a liaison, [the emperor] renounced his interest in Mme. Duchatel."[2] Besides, it was his duty to set a good example for his government by setting standards that were above reproach.

Marital concerns were not Joséphine's only troubles, for just over six weeks after the coronation, Eugène left suddenly for Italy with his regiment. He had to prepare so quickly that there was time for only a parade on January 13 and a ball in his town house on rue de Lille, which the emperor had bought for him but which Eugène hardly had time to enjoy. This fine Paris dwelling underlined the fact that Eugène was now housed in a manner appropriate to his rank, as was Hortense in the sedate old Hôtel Saint-Julien. Whether consciously or not, the emperor was perpetuating a deeply entrenched eighteenth-century custom whereby one's residence (a town house in Paris and a château in the country) spoke volumes for one's social status, in much the same way that appearance and cuisine did (and still do).

Eugène's departure at the end of January 1805 was made more distressing for Joséphine by the cool manner in which her husband bade her son farewell, for the emperor had always shown him the warmest affection. But this enigma was resolved ten days out on the road to Milan, when Eugène was overtaken by a courier bearing a letter from the emperor: "My cousin, I have named you prince and arch-chancellor of state. . . . This change offers no obstacle to your military career. . . . Your title is: Prince Eugène de Beauharnais and you will receive the attribute of serene highness. You are no longer colonel-general of the Chasseurs à Cheval; you will be general of brigade with the command of Chasseurs à Cheval of my Imperial Guard."[3] Joséphine heard the news when Napoléon addressed the Senate; she had always imagined that her husband had some special post in mind for Eugène, and she was thrilled to have this dream come true.[4] Neither she nor her son could have asked for more, and he would go on to merit his stepfather's complete confidence. Napoléon had been impressed by Eugène's willingness to play a relatively minor role in the coronation, knowing that self-effacement was a salient feature of the young man's character.

One of Joséphine's most challenging duties as Napoléon's wife was to deal with difficult officials. In early February, she attended a ceremony in which the emperor appointed various grand dignitaries. One was Jean-Jacques Cambacérès, once a consul, now an arch-chancellor. Although highly valued for his solid legal knowledge, eloquence, common sense, and devotion to Napoléon, Cambacérès was given to eccentric behavior that occasionally compromised the dignity of the court. He had recently developed the disagreeable habit of parading in the evening around the Palais-Royal in an outlandish uniform with a costumed entourage that attracted a great deal of attention. Since Napoléon had to make a quick trip to Boulogne in early February, it fell to Joséphine to speak with Cambacérès. Besides, the emperor knew she could handle the situation diplomatically and told her that only a woman could tell a man when he was being ridiculous. But not even Joséphine could cope with this particular problem, even with the help of Joseph Fouché, minister of police. In the end, Cambacérès's buffoonery had to be tolerated, but then, unusual behavior and novelties of all sorts were traditionally part of life under the arcades of the Palais Royal. The Tuileries Palace was another matter, however, for there Cambacérès's deportment was expected to conform to the circumspection befitting a court official, especially one close to the ruler.

Early in the year, a delegation of leading citizens from Lombardy was received in the throne room of the Tuileries to ask Napoléon to become king of Italy. The group was led by comte d'Eril Melzi, whom Napoléon considered one of the most valuable members of what would become

Jean-Louis-André-Théodore Géricault (1791–1824), An Officer of the Chasseurs Commanding a Charge (Musée du Louvre). Géricault's portrait was shown at the 1812 Salon where he made his debut, and in 1814—with the invasion of France—Denon commissioned Géricault to paint the incident of Eugène rescuing a Polish officer. Eugène himself, an officer of the chasseurs, wore a uniform identical to Géricault's chasseur, even down to the leopard skin caparison. Both Géricault and Eugène died in 1824.

Eugène's domain. For Joséphine, it meant that she would become a queen as well as an empress. The ateliers of Joséphine's *modistes* rose to the occasion. Their task was made easier by her knowing exactly what was required, for she was fully aware of her influential position in the realm of fashion. For the ceremony in Milan, she wanted sibilant silks heavily embroidered with silver and gold, enhanced by a sparkling diamond parure appropriate to her role as empress.[5] The jewels had to meet with the master's approval, for he always carefully scrutinized her costumes, and we know that he never failed to notice what other women wore. Even on his coronation day (when he might have been expected to have his mind on other matters), his eagle eye picked out Laure Junot in a black velvet dress. Afterwards, he chided her for its being "somber, almost sinister," alert as he was to any hint of political opposition. But Laure defended herself by insisting it was not somber at all, having been embroidered all over with gold and enhanced by her diamonds.

No woman outshone Joséphine in the jewelry department, though, for it was her favorite accessory and her authority in this domain was paramount. "It was Joséphine herself whose personal taste and patronage was so influential in establishing the character of jewelry design during the First Empire."[6] She had been especially enthusiastic about cameos since her first trip to Italy, when she sent Hortense a cameo of engraved amethysts. One intaglio, depicting the Three Graces, was mounted to hang from a pearl, coral, and gold necklace; in 1812 she would commission Antonio Canova to execute a sculpture of the same subject for her gallery. Eugène was always on the lookout for cameos and intaglios for both Hortense and his mother, and it was Eugène's daughter (who would become Queen Joséphine of Sweden) who inherited Joséphine's superb cameo-and-pearl diadem. The Empress Joséphine owned gems of every kind, and the inventory of 129 items of jewelry made after her death reveals it to have been the extraordinary treasure of a woman of extreme elegance and extravagance.

Although she may have been extravagant, Joséphine knew how to spend her money wisely, as demonstrated by the art and botanical collections at Malmaison.[7] By January 1805, her gallery already contained forty-four canvases, and six of her botanical paintings by Pierre-Joseph Redouté (called "the Raphael of roses") had been shown at the Salon of 1804. Her patronage of this great flower painter alone would have been enough to assure Joséphine's position as an important collector.

Joséphine was delighted when Napoléon decided to stay at Malmaison for a while during the spring, even though he had to make frequent trips into Paris. An English visitor, James Forbes, had visited the small château in 1803, made a somewhat naive watercolor of it, and praised its mistress for what he called her exquisite taste in combining comfort with beauty. Joséphine especially wanted to be at Malmaison at this time to supervise the garden work, for a small war had broken out between Pierre Fontaine and her garden architect, Jean-Marie Morel (whose design ideas prevailed). The gardens were being expanded and embellished with lakes, pavilions, and pieces of sculpture.

Malmaison was also acquiring a model farm to provide products for the table, similar to Marie-Antoinette's dairy at Rambouillet, and Joséphine's extraordinary conservatory was in the design stage. This enormous transparent structure, housing an almost unparalleled collection of rare plants and exotic flowers, would be a drawing card for specialists (who were always impressed by the empress's knowledge of the Latin names for the plants), and for visitors who wanted to experience, during the cold, damp winters of Paris, a warm and inviting tropical environment miraculously re-created under glass. Napoléon could not enjoy the delights of Malmaison for long, however, as official business called him back to Paris, where he worked around the clock. One of his secretaries, Agathon Fain, said that when all other lights were extinguished in the huge palace on the banks of the Seine, the emperor's lamp could still be seen burning in his study.

The aesthetic aspect of Napoléon's nature developed dramatically under Joséphine's influence. In Lincoln Kirstein's opinion, "the 'good' taste, that really excellent taste which we may come to praise in the emperor, was a reflection of the empress's education, experience, and knowledge."[8] Certainly she encouraged his participation in improving the appearance of Paris: expanding the national art collections (although she sometimes confiscated works for her own gallery); refurbishing the Musée Napoléon, encouraging public interest in the Salons, and patronizing the theaters. As we have already seen, it was Joséphine who brought to Napoléon's attention the key figures who gave pictorial expression to the achievements of the Consulate and Empire, from Baron Gros to Vivant Denon, whose vital direction of art in Napoléon's France made it "the envy of the Western cultural elite."[9]

Joséphine and Napoléon set out for the coronation in Milan on April 2, but he was determined to be back in France by early June, as the projected cross-channel invasion of the British Isles was still on his mind. Although Joséphine rarely anticipated long carriage rides, she did look forward to this trip because she wanted to see Eugène again, and Napoléon was eager to show her some places along the way that held special meaning for him. They stopped first at his old military school at Brienne, to which he had been admitted in May 1779, when he was not yet ten. He undoubtedly recounted for his wife how terribly homesick he had been, leaving warm, fragrant Corsica for the isolated confinement of a strict French military school on the windswept plains of Champagne. She must have understood his unhappiness, for she had given up Martinique's gentle climate to marry Alexandre de Beauharnais in the cold church at Noisy-le Grand in December 1779, the same year Bonaparte had been admitted to Brienne.

On April 10 they found themselves again in Lyons, where they were presented the keys to the city and attended a large exposition of silks held in their honor. The silk industry occupied a prime place in the French economy, its products considered essential for both clothing and hangings, not only in France but in the rest of Europe as well. Joséphine was fascinated by the manufactories, and they examined the new weaving mechanism invented by Joseph-Marie Jacquard, to whom the emperor would present an award in 1807. The usual ceremonies and public affairs staged by the Lyonnais detained the imperial couple a full week, but now they faced the difficult crossing of the Mont-Cenis Pass. There was no actual road, so the baggage had to be carried by mule, Joséphine's heavy jewel coffer was strapped to the shoulders of a strong Savoyard, while the ladies mounted improvised sedan chairs and the men rode mules. This was another nostalgic moment for Napoléon, as he described to Joséphine the challenge of crossing the St. Bernard Pass with his army four years earlier, when Eugène had been with him. On April 24, to Joséphine's immense relief, they found refuge at the former hunting lodge of Stupinigi, six miles outside Turin, which the kings of Sardinia had enlarged into an enormous dwelling. It housed not only the large imperial cortege from Paris, but also Pope Pius VII and his jovial party, which had left Paris on March 30 to return at last to Rome. Eugène was waiting at Stupinigi to meet them, and that evening, four places were laid at the table for a quiet family dinner with the Holy Father. Eugène told them about the month of torrential rains in Milan and feared that the spell of bad weather would spoil the fine ceremony the emperor had planned for May 5, but his stepfather cheerfully assured Eugène that weather had always favored him. Surely they remembered that the sun had come out by noon on coronation day in Paris, in spite of an unpromising morning. The pope needed no reminder of the weather that morning, for he had spent hours in the cold church awaiting the arrival of the imperial procession.

The emperor's prediction was fulfilled, for May 5 was a perfect spring day, and they set off for the plains where the battle of Marengo had been fought and where Napoléon was staging a review of 30,000 troops for Joséphine and veterans of the battle. As they rode in the carriage toward the site of the great victory of June 14, 1800, Napoléon must have recounted to Joséphine the story of Eugène's great performance, as well as their deep sorrow at the death of Louis-Charles Desaix, an outstanding scholar and general to whom Eugène had become attached during the Egyptian campaign. When they reached the historic spot, they were driven onto the parade ground in a fine chariot drawn by eight horses, hailed by thousands of voices, the blare of countless trumpets, and rousing music. A high throne had been erected for the imperial couple to watch the parade of uniformed troops on their richly caparisoned horses, accompanied by the thunders of artillery that sent billowing clouds of smoke rolling over the plain.

The immaculate uniforms contrasted markedly to Napoléon's appearance, for as usual, he appeared in his war-worn coat, with a battered felt bicorne on his head and the saber he had worn the day of Marengo at his side. Both Joséphine and General Rapp noticed that the emperor was the most shabbily dressed man in the army, and the bright sunlight revealed to all eyes the holes in his moth-eaten uniform. She knew there were some things about her husband she could never change, such as this ostentatious modesty and his devotion to the misshapen hat he always wore or carried with him, even during receptions. The hat suffered not only in battle but when anything greatly upset the emperor. Then he would hurl the poor old hat to the floor and trample on it. The bicorne and the famous gray riding coat were ideas he had borrowed from Frederick the Great of Prussia, but the sword was another matter. Someone once asked Napoléon why he had not taken Frederick the Great's sword when he had the opportunity, to which he is supposed to have coolly replied: "I had my own."

After the exhilarating parade at Marengo, the imperial party pushed on to Milan, where the emperor and empress made their triumphal entry on May 10 to the pealing of church bells and discharge of cannon. Everything was being arranged by Cardinal Caprara, archbishop of Milan, who had been in Paris and knew how things ought to be done. Eugène, commanding detachments of the Imperial Guard cavalry, was quartered with his staff in the uncomfortable barracks at the Castello, just outside the city. He had prepared the Palazzo Reale in the cathedral square for his parents and had a temporary gallery constructed to connect it to the cathedral. The interior of the palace contained many splendid apartments, but the noise of the traffic and cathedral bells made sleep all but impossible. Joséphine could not manage without a bathroom adjoining her room, so she had to accept a smaller bedroom. Eugène offered the larger bedroom to his mother's *dame d'honneur*, Mme. de La Rochefoucauld, who was notoriously outspoken, even with Napoléon.

The coronation in Milan cathedral on May 26, 1805, was much like the ceremony in Paris, except that Joséphine was not a participant in the ceremony. She entered the cathedral first, beautifully dressed and glittering with diamonds. Then Napoléon appeared in purple and gold velvet with a diadem upon his head and the scepter of Charlemagne in his hand. Joséphine took her seat in a box prepared especially for her, but with some reservation, for she was attended by the emperor's oldest sister, Elisa Bacciochi. Like her sisters Pauline and Caroline, Elisa had never liked Joséphine and had remained aloof at the coronation in Paris, so the empress hardly expected a cordial greeting in Milan. On March 28 Napoléon had given Elisa the principality of Piombino, which commanded the straits between Tuscany and Elba; she was an ambitious young woman and proved to be a worthy governess of her territory. In 1806 she would receive the principality of Lucca, and in 1809 Napoléon accorded her the title of grand duchess of Tuscany, and she moved into the Pitti Palace in Florence. Elisa immersed herself in her duties, gathering about her the most competent people, creating schools and hospitals, developing mines, promoting silk and velvet manufacturers, opening quarries, and becoming a major patron of the arts. In fact, the Grand Duchess Elisa Bonaparte Bacciochi is still remembered as a conscientious sovereign, whose primary concern was for the welfare of her people. Joséphine might have thought more highly of Elisa had she known that her sister-in-law's competence as a ruler would ease Napoléon's mind about the governance of at least one part of his kingdom. For the moment, however, there they sat, side by side in their box in Milan cathedral, watching the emperor receive the Iron Crown of Lombardy from Cardinal Caprara. It was not really iron, but a circlet of gold and gems covering an iron ring allegedly formed from one of the spikes that had pierced Christ's hands at the Crucifixion.

Joséphine saw little of her husband during their stay in Milan, for he was reorganizing the government, renovating buildings, supervising beautification projects, and—good news for

Joséphine—improving the route between Milan and Paris. He did take time to join her and Eugène for an evening at La Scala. The famous singers Banti and Marchesi gave concerts at the palace during their stay in Milan, and when his parents attended a *Te Deum* at Sant' Ambrogio, Eugène commanded the cavalry escort. Joséphine was with her son almost daily, and the fêtes organized by the Milanese for their new king and queen were held in the arena at the Castello. The festivities evoked the days of imperial Rome: games, chariot races, and a balloon ascent by the wife of the famous aeronaut Gainerin, who ventured aloft to scatter flowers upon the new sovereigns. In the large crowds an old man was knocked over, and Joséphine stopped instantly to assist him and to soothe him with comforting words.

In early June Germaine de Staël stormed Milan to continue her fourteen-year duel with the emperor, hoping to catch him in a clement mood after the second coronation. Any thoughts she might have harbored about cornering him, however, were ill-begotten, so Joséphine interceded, received Germaine kindly, and salvaged their friendship. After all, nothing was to be gained by further provoking a woman whose salon was a hotbed of opposition, although it was not in Joséphine's nature to offend Germaine in any case.

Before they were to leave Milan on June 10, Joséphine received a marvelous surprise. The emperor called a session of the Legislative Assembly and announced that he was appointing his stepson viceroy of Italy, the highest honor he could confer upon Eugène. But if Napoléon thought this would be cause for family rejoicing, he was mistaken, for it precipitated instead a torrent of feminine tears. As they were preparing to depart for France, he found Joséphine weeping, and, according to Mlle. d'Avrillion, he guessed the cause and was so displeased that he gave way, somewhat petulantly, to his feelings: "You are crying, Joséphine . . . because you must part with your son. If the absence of your children causes you so much pain, you can only guess what I must always feel. The affection you display for them makes me feel bitterly the unhappiness of having none myself."[10]

Joséphine was stoic, however, compared to Hortense, whose dependence upon her brother was legendary. Every time a crisis arose in either household, the call went out: "Send for Prince Eugène!" When Hortense received Eugène's letter about his appointment, her first thought was not of the honor conferred upon him but of herself, wailing that he was her only bulwark against Louis's capricious temperament, since she knew that if Eugène had to stay in Italy, she would be left utterly at Louis's mercy. Hortense was not forgotten, however, by either her mother or her brother. Joséphine had generously patronized the Milanese jewelers, and upon leaving, she selected an amethyst necklace engraved with classical figures for Hortense, and Eugène found one in malachite for his disconsolate sister. Before leaving the young viceroy, Napoléon dictated instructions and fatherly advice, and Joséphine hinted that there might soon be a young woman to mitigate his loneliness, for Napoléon had taken the matter of Eugène's marital status in hand as well. Soon Eugène received a letter telling him to prepare for his first royal guest in early August—Prince Ludwig, the son of Maximilian I Joseph, Elector of Bavaria, and a brother of the ravishing Princess Auguste-Amélie.

Late in June, Joséphine and Napoléon were in Genoa, the ancient republic that would now become part of France. A marvelous jubilee was staged for them on the waterfront, where they embarked on a barge in the form of a floating temple and were rowed out into the bay. That great Italian specialty, the fireworks display, showered colored fire over the water, and the entire town was set aglow. Especially to honor Joséphine, florists had painstakingly created a floating garden of orange trees, for all Europe knew of her fondness for flowers and her consuming interest in botany. The leisurely journey through Italy that Joséphine was enjoying with her husband was winding down, and when they reached Turin, it stopped abruptly. Here they received news that England had successfully formed another coalition, this time with the courts of Austria, Naples, Sweden, and Russia. Napoléon had to leave at once, and Joséphine begged to go with him. After a short stop in Turin, they traveled incognito at top speed, traversed the Mont-Cenis Pass, and reached Fontainebleau on July 11 in the remarkably short time of eighty-five hours. The emperor plunged, as usual, into his work, but Joséphine was exhausted, her feet too swollen to wear shoes. In spite of her fatigue, she had to rouse herself for the celebrations in Paris marking the Italian coronation: illuminations of the Hôtel de Ville and public edifices; a religious ceremony celebrated with the usual pomp at Notre Dame; theaters offering free performances; and the Murats entertaining with their usual flair.[11]

On July 17 Joséphine and the emperor made an appearance at the Opéra, and the "brilliant and numerous" audience was so preoccupied with the couple in the imperial box that hardly anyone glanced at the stage.[12] So elated were they to have the emperor and empress in their midst after several months of absence that they kept breaking into spontaneous applause. Neither would be in the capital for long, however, for Napoléon was off to the Iron Coast, where a huge operation was being planned at the camp of Boulogne that was intended to bring England to her knees and restore peace. He advised Joséphine to make her annual pilgrimage to Plombières during his absence, and she proceeded to do so on August 1, but she was overcome with depression along the way, writing to Hortense that her life was sad, "always distant from the person I love."

At the end of August Joséphine returned to Saint-Cloud and warned Eugène that the situation at Boulogne was shrouded in mystery and that it was impolitic to refer to it. She was as indulgent a grandmother as she was a mother, and she had Hortense's second baby, Napoléon-Louis, come to stay with her at the château. She wrote Eugène that he was a sweet child, adding rather grimly that Louis was the same as ever. She was aware that her husband was prepared for the invasion of England, with the army under the command of four of his ablest marshals, Lannes, Davout, Soult, and Ney. Now he had only to await the arrival of his fleet, and the officers anxiously watched the coast for the arrival of Admiral Villeneuve. Villeneuve, however, had put in at Cadiz, having heard that Admiral Nelson had an immense fleet in the vicinity, which was not true. The emperor's carefully laid plans were thus destroyed, for by the end of August, it was too late in the season to invade England. Napoléon was furious and undoubtedly indulged in justified raving, punctuated by another flattening of the little black hat.

He recovered quickly, however, and with characteristic agility redirected his energies toward preparing to meet the Austrians, who were assembling in the north. By mid-September he issued his final marching orders, setting the Grande Armée on its long, wearing march to take the field against Russia and Austria, while Czar Alexander, who had provoked the war, hastened through Poland with 116,000 men to join forces with the Austrians, assuming that Napoléon was still a thousand miles away at Boulogne and unaware of their movements.

Once his army was on its way toward the Danube, Napoléon returned to Joséphine, reaching Malmaison on September 3. On September 23, he went before the Senate to denounce the coalition and to announce his departure for the army. He appointed his brother Joseph to preside over the Senate and councils of government in his absence, and he named Louis chief of the reserve army. Joséphine was to go with her husband as far as Strasbourg, where she would set up court with her ladies and Talleyrand, for the emperor depended upon her to represent him in this city that would become a crossroads of Europe during the campaign. They traveled at breakneck speed, leaving Saint-Cloud on September 24 at 5 A.M. and pulling into Strasbourg only two days later.

As she said an emotional good-bye to her husband, Joséphine was concerned for his health, knowing that many lonely, anxious months lay ahead. She knew that his life on campaign was difficult, with sleepless nights and ceaseless work during the long marches, and that he had little regard for his own safety. In the forthcoming campaign, he would recklessly expose himself to the greatest hazards at the front. Although his officers were most likely discreet in the presence of the empress, their wives were sometimes less so, and Joséphine was well aware that her husband rode up and down the lines on his white horse in full view of his men (and the enemy) to encourage his troops before battle and to perpetuate his carefully designed self-image.

In Italy Eugène received instructions from his stepfather regarding the hostilities about to commence against Archduke Charles, brother of the Austrian emperor, who was advancing from Padua to the aid of Vienna. Napoléon was sending Marshal Masséna to lead the troops, and Eugène was greatly frustrated to be so far removed from the main field of action. He was disappointed not to have a command of his own, and his anguish intensified when Napoléon outlined for him the division of the Grande Armée, with Jean-Baptiste Bessières at the head of the Imperial Guard.

Having her husband away was hard enough for Joséphine, but the absence of her children was doubly trying. Hortense had to remain in Paris, and it was rumored that Italy was going to be the principal theater of the new war, which meant Eugène would be in grave danger, but this proved to be a false alarm. In Strasbourg Joséphine occupied a strategic spot, for at this advance post on the

Rhine she could receive the first dispatches from the battlefield, and when letters arrived from the emperor, she could relay them to Hortense. Strasbourg must have reminded her of Paris, for half the houses dated from the eighteenth century. The magnificent Rohan Palace served as the imperial residence during Joséphine's two-month stay, and in her honor the architect Boudhors constructed a small masterpiece as a tribute to her love of botany—a pavilion sheltering orange trees taken from the estate of the Landgrave of Hesse-Darmstadt. Joséphine, as the emperor's representative, spent not only this autumn of 1805 in Strasbourg but would spend three months there again in 1809.

As soon as Joséphine was settled, she summoned the composer Gasparo Spontini from Paris. He had attracted the attention of the sovereigns on November 11, 1804, at the Théâtre Italien, when Joséphine gave him the official title of composer of music to the empress, and on November 27 he scored a notable success with his *Milton*.[13] At her court in Strasbourg, Spontini also staged one of his newest religious works, *O Salutaris*, although her finest musical legacy was her support of Spontini's *la Vestale.*

In spite of her various duties in Strasbourg, Joséphine still had Malmaison on her mind, for she bought animals for her menagerie, plants and flowers for her gardens and greenhouse, and valuable objects for her art collection. There was a constant ebb and flow of visitors, with delegates from Paris always passing through and princely rulers of Germany eager to attach themselves to the emperor's ever-rising star. The most effective method of doing so was to offer unusual gifts to his wife, so Joséphine's collections were further expanded during her stay in Strasbourg.

An important feature of the city's geographical position was its proximity to the Confederation of the Rhine, which would be formed on June 12, 1806, when sixteen German princes attached themselves to Napoléon. Strasbourg would become a key city in an empire of seventy million people increasingly forced to become more centralized. For its governance, the emperor depended heavily on his own family, and Joséphine's presence at Strasbourg in the fall of 1805 was part of his plan. During these critical months, her social expertise proved more valuable than ever to her husband, for his own emotional, physical, and intellectual energies were being poured into a vital military campaign.

Even as they trudged along rain-soaked roads, dragging artillery through deep ruts, Napoléon did not forget his wife, often writing letters using the head of a drum or the pommel of his saddle; he sent at least thirteen letters during the six weeks after he left her in Strasbourg. "It rains so much that I have to change my coat twice a day,"[14] he told her, and in fact, he did not take off his clothes for eight days and nights.

The coalition underrated the speed of his advance into southern Germany, so Napoléon took General Mack by surprise at Ulm. His carefully constructed strategy for its encirclement proceeded just as planned, and by October 20, General Mack was ready to surrender. Again, just as Joséphine feared, her husband had placed himself in the foremost ranks, exposing himself to the gravest perils.[14] Still in Strasbourg, Joséphine received bulletins about the victory at Ulm, which she celebrated by attending a *Te Deum* at the great cathedral and offering a fête for the ladies of the city. Then came other bulletins describing the army's entry into Vienna, attended by a corps of musicians playing marches undoubtedly composed by the oboist Michel Gebauer, leader of the band of the First Grenadiers, who often performed at Joséphine's functions at the Tuileries. As thrilling as his marches were, however, they hardly held a candle to "La Marseillaise," which was composed by another friend of Joséphine's, Claude Joseph Rouget de Lisle. That march was, Napoléon said, the "best general of the Revolution." Joséphine was also pleased to hear that her husband had ordered a guard to protect the house of the staunchly patriotic Viennese composer Franz Josef Haydn.

For the moment at least, Eugène could breathe easier too, for on November 1, Archduke Charles began his retreat, and Eugène ordered the bells of all the cathedrals to be rung in joy, as he wistfully reflected on his own regiment marching without him to fight in the campaign. When the news of Ulm reached Paris, there were three cannonades of joy through the day; a *Te Deum* was celebrated at Notre Dame; and verses from Racine were recited at the Théâtre Francais comparing the emperor to Achilles, as the audience broke into thunderous applause.

Not all the news was uplifting, however. At the Palais Rohan in Strasbourg, Joséphine and Talleyrand had learned in late October that the French-Spanish flotilla commanded by Admiral Villeneuve had been completely destroyed by Admiral Nelson in the battle of Trafalgar, which so decimated Napoléon's maritime strength that the French navy never recovered. England remained mistress of the seas, pursuing the course of world domination upon which she had embarked even before the war of 1793 and reinforcing France's enemies with money, supplies, and men.

Joséphine's presence at the Palais Rohan in Strasbourg continued to lure distinguished visitors, such as the elector of Baden and his family and Ludwig, prince electoral of Bavaria, who spoke of his friendship with Eugène that had resulted from their meeting in Italy the previous August. From Frankfurt came the future prince primate of the Confederation of the Rhine, Karl-Theodor von Dalberg, who had come to Mainz in 1804 and whom Joséphine found particularly pleasing; she accepted an invitation for herself, Hortense, and little Napoléon-Charles to visit him in Frankfurt. Each time another of Napoléon's victories was announced, a *Te Deum* was celebrated in the cathedral, and Joséphine never failed to attend in ceremonial attire and to offer yet another ball.

On November 28, Joséphine was ordered to leave Strasbourg for Munich, where the emperor would join her, although his arrival date was as yet unknown. She thoroughly enjoyed her last days in Strasbourg. Napoléon had asked her to buy gifts for the ladies of the Bavarian royal family, because negotiations with Bavaria for Eugène's marriage into the ancient dynasty of Wittelsbach were still ongoing. Joséphine was in her element and happy to oblige, for the emperor had practically given her carte blanche to spend money. She had already seen a portrait of the intended bride, Princess Auguste, and she wrote Eugène enthusiastically that she was lovely as an angel, with a figure as beautiful as her face. When Joséphine learned that the elector, Maximilien-Joseph, was preparing a grand fête in her honor, she apparently became so caught up in this exciting affair that she remained as bad a correspondent as ever, not even sending Napoléon a word before leaving Strasbourg for Munich at the end of November. This provoked a little sardonic humor on his part: "Great Empress, not a letter from you since your departure from Strasbourg. . . . This is not very kind, nor is it very tender. . . . Deign, from the height of your grandeur, to concern yourself a little with your slaves."[15]

There were certainly enough reminders of him along the way. After leaving Strasbourg, Joséphine's caravan rolled through Stuttgart, Ulm, and Augsburg. One can only imagine what she saw in Ulm, where Napoléon had gained his remarkable victory only the month before. Now she was deeply concerned about the next phase of his campaign, for he was in critical danger, as the big battle against the Russians and their allies was shaping up. A cold winter was quickly setting in, and his line of communication was lengthening daily. Soon he would be 1,500 miles from Paris. His relentless advance appeared to be sheer, irresponsible recklessness, since the French were outnumbered by 85,400 troops and outgunned by two cannons to one, with the Russian army, a division of Austrians facing him at Austerlitz, and Italian and Prussian troops on the way. But Napoléon had calculated his strategy with the utmost caution and vigilance. His plan was to leave his right flank weak to tempt the Russians into striking him from the Pratzen Heights and to achieve a quick, decisive victory to avoid being overwhelmed.

The morning of December 2 dawned in heavy fog, but the mists began to lift about 8 o'clock, and the celebrated "sun of Austerlitz" broke through.[16] Knowing that the Russians and the Austrians had occupied the Pratzen Heights, the emperor asked one of his generals how long it would take to reach the site. The reply was it would be less than twenty minutes, whereupon the commander in chief supposedly delivered his famous remark: "Good. We wait twenty minutes. When the enemy is about to make a false move, we must be certain not to interrupt him." The moment the Russians attacked the French right flank, Napoléon ordered the ascent of the heights and stunned the Allies, splitting their army in two. He then turned his force on the Allies' left and decimated it; when he turned to their right, it was no more.

By piercing the allies' center, followed by the devastating thrust to take the heights, Napoléon's army—the most highly disciplined, best-trained instrument he would ever command—won this legendary victory. Even in the midst of the furor at Austerlitz, however, Joséphine pervaded her husband's thoughts, and the very next day he wrote to her, saying that he had beaten the two emperors (Russian and Austrian) and that he was somewhat tired. He wrote her twice again before she reached Munich (she was as yet unaware of the happy outcome), and his second letter reproached her for not having written him for so long: "Do the elegant fêtes at Baden, Stuttgart, and Munich make you forget the poor soldiers who lie covered with mud, rain, and blood?"[17]

Eugène heard about the victory at Austerlitz on December 9. There had been no word from his stepfather in several weeks, which was unusual, for he was normally bombarded with let-

François Gérard (1770–1837),The Battle of Austerlitz (Château de Versailles). Napoléon ordered Gérard's canvas of this classic battle on December 2, 1805, for the Council Chamber ceiling of the Tuileries. Jean Rapp, the emperor's aide-de-camp who had made an irresistible cavalry charge at the head of the Mamelukes, is bringing Nicolas Repnine, the Russian prince and colonel of the Russian imperial guard, as a prisoner to Napoléon. Roustam is the turbaned figure at far right; the officer behind Napoléon appears to be Berthier. Rapp was made General of Division on December 25.

ters filled with instructions. So he was greatly relieved when Marshal Mortier's aide-de-camp arrived in Milan with the report. The cavalry charges at Austerlitz, Mortier said, would be celebrated in history, but he added the sad news that Colonel Morland—who had commanded the Chasseurs of the Imperial Guard and had thrown back the cuirassiers of the Russian Guard—had been fatally wounded, and his body was en route to Paris.

When Hortense received the good news of Austerlitz in Paris, all her friends celebrated. Talma read the electrifying announcement from the stage of the Théâtre Français, and it quickly spread throughout the capital. Joseph Bonaparte proclaimed the glad tidings, Fouché had it announced with three salvos of artillery, and cries of "Vive l'Empereur!" livened every quarter. Hortense and Louis received a letter from the emperor shortly after the battle asking them to permit Napoléon-Charles to join him so he could show off his nephew to his victorious armies, but, predictably, Louis refused.

As always, war—even for the victors—delivers a tragic aftermath, and Joséphine's lady-in-waiting Claire de Rémusat recoiled from the damage she encountered along the route from Strasbourg to Vienna. On every hand, there were "devastated villages, roads encumbered by corpses . . . [and] the distress of the vanquished added an element of danger to the discomfort of this journey so late in the season."[18]

The momentous year of 1805, which Napoléon had previewed so auspiciously, ended with the (temporary) destruction of the Austro-Russian armies. The emperor had shattered the third coalition in the matter of a few weeks. The humiliated czar, who broke down and wept after the battle, went home, and by the Treaty of Pressburg on December 26, the Austrians resentfully surrendered the last of their Italian lands, gave up the Tyrol to Bavaria, and recognized the rulers of Württemberg and Bavaria. In Paris the year ended with public rejoicing and the requisite *Te Deums.*

On January 1, 1806, the French Senate would celebrate the new year and the victorious Austrian campaign with a grand ceremony, during which were presented the flags taken from the vanquished. The position so long held by the Habsburgs would shortly be filled by Joséphine's husband, for with the Treaty of Pressburg the Holy Roman Empire would officially be dissolved and Francis II would become simply Francis I of Austria. Napoléon Bonaparte, emperor of the French and king of Italy, had reached the summit of his military career at the age of thirty-six, without losing a single battle. On December 28, 1805, Napoléon left Vienna in triumph, and on the last day of the year "the new Charlemagne" joined his wife in Munich to prepare for the marriage of their beloved Eugène, a union that was destined to bring them great and abiding joy.

9

Empress of Europe

The principal reason Joséphine and Napoléon went to Munich in December 1805 was to make the final preparations for Eugène's marriage in January, a liaison of major dynastic importance. The bride-to-be was Auguste-Amélie, daughter of Maximilian I Joseph, the elector of Bavaria, whom Napoléon elevated to the rank of king after the victory at Austerlitz. This was the first marriage Napoléon had arranged with a princely house, and although it was politically motivated, he wanted it to be a happy one for both Eugène and his bride. As we have seen, the emperor seems to have found much more satisfaction in Joséphine's children than he did in members of the Bonaparte family: Eugène was faithfully fulfilling his duties in Italy, and Napoléon's affection for Hortense was the enduring love of a father for his daughter, so much so that when he finally came to realize the extent of Hortense's unhappiness with Louis, he allowed her a legal separation. After Eugène's wedding, the emperor would shower Auguste with attention as well, writing her warm letters filled with "paternal blessings" and assuring her of his concern for the smallest details of their domestic life. His unfailing attention to Joséphine's children (and Auguste would soon count as one) went a long way toward reassuring his wife about her own uncertain future.

The union of Eugène and Auguste required shrewd political negotiation. Talleyrand had been exploring the possibility of the Bavarian princess for Eugène since well before the summer, although he did not give Joséphine the news about Auguste until just before they left Strasbourg in November, when the arrangements had been secured. Joséphine agreed that the bride selected for her son would please him in every way, as did Hortense, who wrote to her brother on November 12: "Mme. de Cetto [a representative of Bavaria in Paris] came to see me last Monday. She spoke a great deal of Princess Auguste, and how happy she would make her husband, that she was certain this would also be true of you; and that, if the emperor still had this idea [of Auguste's marriage to you], it would soon be done."[1] Eugène was not consulted, but Napoléon knew that Auguste was beautiful, intelligent, and a Wittelsbach princess for whom several princes were vying, so he was certain that Eugène would be pleased (as in fact he was).

Even as late as November, however, the desired alliance was by no means certain, for it depended upon a number of factors, among them the agility of French diplomacy in winning over the ancient Wittelsbach family (who were interlocked by dynastic marriages with other European courts), the outcome of Napoléon's Austrian campaign, and the consent of Auguste herself, who was betrothed to Prince Charles of Baden. Auguste's father had been among the first German princes to congratulate Napoléon on his elevation to the rank of emperor, but this did not mean that the Bavarian court was ready to do everything the French asked. Especially opposed to the marriage was Maximilien-Joseph's second wife and Auguste's stepmother, Princess Caroline of Baden, who from her lofty height regarded the French emperor as a parvenu. She was a woman with formidable connections: her sisters were married to Czar Alexander of Russia and King Gustav IV Adolph of Sweden; her younger brother was Prince Charles of Baden, to whom Auguste was engaged.

Although intensely preoccupied with the war against Austria in September 1805, Napoléon was determined to have Auguste for Eugène, so he turned to Talleyrand, his principal agent in "amalgamation and conciliation," as his secretary Méneval put it, to manage this delicate affair. (As a reward for his work during the negotiations at Pressburg, Talleyrand was given the title of prince of Benevento, which was still part of the kingdom of Italy.) The imperial chamberlain, Count de Thiard, had already been dispatched to persuade the house of Baden to renounce Charles's engagement to Auguste. Although prospects looked bleak, Thiard found one ally in the Bavarian camp, the Margrave Louis (Charles's uncle), who was kindly disposed toward the French. Leverage was certainly provided by the emperor's resounding defeat of Austria at Ulm on October 20, followed by his triumphant entry into Munich, the Bavarian capital, on October 25. With the victor at his very doorstep, Auguste's father decided on November 8 to give in to Napoléon's request and to ask the house of Baden to renounce the hand of his daughter. Auguste wept at the news but told her father that she would be an obedient daughter, so she renounced Charles and cleared the way for her marriage to Eugène.

The elector had moved his family to Würzberg in late August, when the Austrians were marching south, but as soon as the marriage plans were set, Princess Caroline was ordered to return post haste to Munich to prepare for the arrival on December 15 of Empress Joséphine, who would be staying in special apartments in the elector's Munich Residenz, where the marriage would take place. It was important not to incur the displeasure of the man who now occupied the central position in Europe—or that of his wife. Even as Napoléon was marching upon Austerlitz in late November, the Bavarian representative, baron von Gravenreuth, was attached to his retinue, and the French victory at Austerlitz could only have confirmed the wisdom of Maximilian I's decision. From the field of Austerlitz, Napoléon wrote to the elector: "I hope to be able to [soon] manifest the

Luigi Rados (1773–1840), after Jean-Baptiste-François Bosio (1764–1827), La Princesse Auguste-Amélie de Bavaria, Vicereine of Italy (Bibliothèque Marmottan). This engraving was made from Andrea Appiani's official full-length portrait of Eugène's wife, which was commissioned by Vivant Denon in 1806, for Napoléon's gallery of family portraits at Saint-Cloud. The vice-reine stands before the Villa Bonaparte in Milan, wearing a diadem and a court robe similar to her robe in the collection of the Museo Napoleonico in Rome.

Etching by Morinet, after Henry Scheffer (1798—1862). Eugène de Beauharnais, duc de Leuchtenberg, Vice-Roi d'Italie (Château de Malmaison). The original painting, ordered in 1835 from the younger brother of Ary Scheffer, is today in the Musée de l'Armée. Historian Alain Pillepich has pointed out several anachronisms: for example, Eugene here wears his uniform as colonel-general des Chasseurs à Cheval de la Garde, which he had to give up when he became Archchancellor of State in February 1805.

Anne-Louis Girodet (1767–1824), General Duroc (Museé Bonnat, Bayonne). Girodet's sketch of Duroc was intended for his painting Surrender of the Keys of Vienna *in 1805, the year Duroc was made grand master of the palace. Typical of Girodet's style is the crisply curling hair, and he obviously delighted in the general's noble, assertive profile. This intimate friend of Eugène fought in Austria, Prussia, Poland, at Austerlitz, and in Silesia, where he was mortally wounded on May 22, 1813. Duroc lived long enough for Napoléon to be with him in his last moments.*

interest I have in you and your house."[2] At the signing of the Treaty of Pressburg on December 26, 1805, Napoléon would dictate the conditions: Eugène's marriage to Auguste was now considered a fait accompli; additional territories were ceded to Bavaria; the rulers of Bavaria and Württemberg were made kings; and from 1806 to 1810 Bavaria would be a favored ally of France.

Before that treaty was signed, however, there was still a lingering anxiety in Munich because of Auguste's broken engagement and because the contract had still not been signed. Fortunately, French was spoken at the Bavarian court, and a distinguished Frenchwoman who had preceded Joséphine to Munich had let it be known that the Empress Joséphine's son possessed all the qualities a woman could desire, a description seconded by Joséphine's *dame d'honneur,* the grumpy but influential Mme. de La Rochefoucauld, who was renowned for being difficult to please. She reminded the Bavarians that the de Beauharnais family was a noble one and that Eugène's father had been a virtual fixture in her own household since his youth. When Eugène's portrait was passed around, it was agreed that he was, in any case, exceedingly handsome. As to the contract, the officials involved continued to negotiate certain issues, and Joséphine was grateful to have the deft Talleyrand on hand to keep the marriage plans on track.

The Residenz was alerted on the evening of December 30 that the French emperor was due to arrive at any moment, so both the army and the court remained vigilant from 8 P.M. until midnight, when Napoléon's carriage and entourage finally reached the outskirts of the city. The emperor received a tumultuous welcome and proceeded to the palace, accompanied by a torchlight procession. Late as it was, he immediately inquired about the marriage contract and was furious to find it still yet unsigned, a situation that was remedied almost immediately so the official announcement could be made. After his first glimpse of Auguste, Napoléon was more determined than ever to have her for Eugène; accustomed as the emperor was to having comely ladies paraded before him, he was still dumbfounded by the young princess's majestic carriage and astonishing beauty as he bent to kiss her hand. She had a splendid figure (as Joséphine had already told Eugène), fine features, curly chestnut hair, blue eyes, and lovely skin. Later, Napoléon jested one day with Maximilian: "If you had not willingly agreed to accord us the Princess Auguste, she would have been kidnaped by a regiment of cuirassiers."

On January 1, 1806, in the presence of both Napoléon and Joséphine, Maximilian was proclaimed king of Bavaria, and Eugène's good friend Michel Duroc, grand marshal of the French court, made the official request for Auguste's hand in marriage. Three days later, Napoléon formally adopted Eugène as his son on January 4, 1806, and the marriage contract was signed.[3] Both Joséphine and Napoléon were delighted with the bride, and on January 9 the emperor wrote Hortense a flattering letter, promising her a sister who would in every way be worthy of her—a pledge that would be abundantly fulfilled, for Auguste was a young woman of exceptional qualities. Eugène's marriage contract stipulated that he would now be called "Imperial Highness" and "Son of France," signifying that Joséphine's son now took precedence over Joseph and Louis Bonaparte, was listed before them in the Almanach Impérial, and would sit at Napoléon's right hand. This was an unforgivable affront for the Bonapartes, and although Hortense and Joséphine were naturally pleased, it precipitated another family crisis. Caroline Murat was infuriated that Eugène was being honored instead of her own husband. After all, Joachim Murat had just played a key role in the war against Austria, commanding that "most beautiful cavalry," which was the terror of Europe, capturing 2,000 men, six cannon and flags, and opening the gates of Vienna. But, Caroline wailed, it was not Joachim who was receiving these grand promotions; it was Eugène de Beauharnais! In a fury she let Hortense know how angry she was, and Joachim Murat broke his sword in a fit of rage.

Napoléon was unmoved. Later he explained to Roederer, his secretary of state, why he gave preference to Joséphine's son and daughter: "I love these children (Hortense and Eugène) because they always make an effort to be agreeable; when a cannon is out of service, it is Eugène who rushes to see why it is defective; when I have to jump over a ditch, it is again he who offers his hand. Joseph's daughters don't even know I am emperor and still call me 'Consul' . . . but the little Napoléon [Hortense's son] cries out "Vive Grand-Papa le Soldat!" when he passes by the grenadiers in the garden. Yes, I truly love Hortense, because she and her brother always take my part, even against their mother, when she becomes angry over some woman. . . . If Hortense wants to speak to me [even] during the Council of State, I go right out to receive her; for Mme. Murat, I would not bother. . . ."[4]

Eugène set out for Munich on January 6, 1806, with high hopes for the future and eager to see his parents again, along with his close friends, Marshals Duroc and Bessières, and, of course, his bride-to-be. To her great disappointment, Hortense was not permitted to attend her brother's wedding, for Louis was in one of his petulant moods. The emperor had personally invited her to come and to bring Napoléon-Charles to see his uncle Eugène get married, but Hortense could not have arrived in time in any case. Joséphine consoled her daughter as best she could, but now she had to make her own preparations. A particularly sumptuous costume would be required for this momentous affair, which was to take place in the Residenz on January 13 and 14. Napoléon had already commissioned impressive jewelry for the bride's family, and he ordered his brothers and sisters to bring the bridal couple presents worth at least 15,000 to 20,000 francs, such as silver-gilt pieces for the table from the workshops of either Odiot or Biennais or a service of Sèvres porcelain.[5]

Joséphine, however, was preoccupied with Eugène's safety. He was due to arrive by January 10, but the weather was cold and snowy, and the Tyrolean passes he had to navigate were rough going and known for brigands. In fact, one of Talleyrand's messengers bearing secret dispatches had just been attacked by a band of robbers. However, enthusiasm for the forthcoming marriage was swelling, and the elector had his new title to celebrate, so Munich was in an unusually festive mood. The blue-and-white Bavarian flag flew from poles along the main routes and from the highest vantage points. Below her windows, Joséphine could see heralds, accompanied by horsemen and preceded by trumpets and drums, announcing on the street corners the elevation of Maximilien-Joseph to the rank of king of Bavaria. Napoléon had brought to Munich fifty-one guns and standards captured from the Austrians; now they were decorated with colorful flowers and ribbons, mounted on wagons pulled by horses with elaborate caparisons, and paraded through the streets.

Eugène arrived on schedule January 10 at 10 A.M., and as he and his escort rode under the entrance of the Residenz, excitement spread throughout the palace. He was led instantly to the emperor, who frowned at his cavalry mustache. When Joséphine saw him, she gave him a quick embrace and hustled him off to the court barber to have his mustache removed and his hair trimmed before he slept off the effects of his arduous journey. When Eugène finally met Auguste, he found her even lovelier than he had imagined, but with gentlemanly restraint, he treated her with tact and delicacy, for Eugène bore "all the nobility of troubadours and knights of the Middle Ages, as emblazoned upon his coat-of-arms: Honor and Fidelity."[7]

During her three-week stay at the Residenz, Joséphine had found it a delightful place, with suites of apartments representing styles from Renaissance to Rococo, as well as eight galleries of fine porcelain and paintings of such number and quality as to make it the first museum north of the Alps. The present king had not been able to afford many additions, however, and Princess Auguste, whose upbringing had been simple, was overcome by the basket full of wedding gifts ordered by the emperor. Eugène had not found time to buy his bride a suitable gift, so Joséphine came to his rescue, declaring that only jewelry would do. As it happened, her own Parisian jeweler, Etiènne Nitot, had come to Munich in hopes of finding patronage, conveniently bringing with him a resplendent diadem in a style Joséphine particularly liked. She had seen Mlle. George in a classical drama wearing a tiara of costume jewelry in this shape, so she ordered Nitot to copy it for her in real jewels. In spite of her desire to keep it, she ceded it to Eugène for his bride-to-be.

The civil ceremony took place January 13, 1806, in the Green Gallery of the Residenz (see page xv). The groom was in full-dress uniform with decorations, the bride in a simple white satin Empire gown embroidered with silver foliage, a double necklace of diamonds, a tiara (supposedly the one supplied by Joséphine), and a fresh bouquet of white flowers. Those taking part were people Eugène knew well: Talleyrand in powdered wig, his close comrades-in-arms Marshals Duroc and Bessières, chief of staff Berthier, the governor of Paris Andoche Junot,[8] the grand equerry Caulaincourt, Murat, and Eugène's Italian Guard, who came to attend their viceroy's wedding. Joséphine sat under a dais with Napoléon and the king and queen of Bavaria, and the women carefully studied the French empress's costume: a white silk gown embroidered in a gold diapered pattern with a train, the neckline *en chérusque*, a magnificent diadem, and pearl earrings.

This was a great moment in Joséphine's life, for she instinctively knew that Eugène's marriage would be happy and that it would not take long for Auguste to discover the kind of man she had married. Goethe was among the distinguished wedding guests; the great writer, who would fall under Napoléon's spell three years later at Erfurt, remarked that Joséphine's son was one of those characters who were becoming rarer all the time.

On his way to the ceremony, Eugène had passed along a corridor hung with 120 portraits of Auguste's ancestors, so now—by virtue of his marriage—Eugène became a cousin of the queens of Prussia and Sweden, as well as the czarina of Russia and the grand dukes of Baden and Hesse-Darmstadt; he would also become a nephew of the queen of England and a cousin of the queen of Württemberg. This was not the only affiliation of a member of Napoléon's family with Württemberg, for in December 1805 Talleyrand had concluded an alliance with King Frederick of Württemberg, whose daughter Catherine would become Jérome Bonaparte's bride in 1807 after his divorce from his American wife.

Throughout the wedding night, the people of Munich sang and danced despite the falling snow, and the wedding ball in the Hercules Gallery was followed by a performance of *Castor and Pollux* by Georg Joseph Vogler. It was presented in the delightful Residenz theater, another Rococo masterpiece by the Cuvillies, and Eugène and Auguste watched from the royal box lined with crimson damask. As they set out for Milan, the bridal couple appeared to be very happy, and on February 18, Auguste wrote to her father: "I have every reason to be satisfied. I was admirably received and the prince is charming with me."[9]

Joséphine and Napoléon started out for Paris on January 17, 1806, by way of Stuttgart and

Karlsruhe, having been seen to their carriage by their princely hosts. It was almost midnight on January 26 when they finally reached the Tuileries. The emperor chose this late hour for their return in order to avoid an elaborate reception that the Parisians had planned. Nevertheless, many of the houses were lighted in his honor, for the city of Paris had been in a state of euphoria ever since the battle of Auster-litz, and the popularity of the imperial couple was at its peak. In spite of the late hour, cannons boomed and rounds of artillery were discharged as the imperial carriage entered the illuminated city.

Joséphine was so tired after the long journey that she collapsed into bed, but her husband rushed up to his office, summoning his minister of finance, Martin-Michel Gaudin, to go over issues to be discussed by the Council of Finance the next morning. He examined records of the Banque de France for the rest of the night and worked with the council the following day for nine hours. When he returned to their private quarters, Joséphine could see how exhausted he was, and he even admitted that—after Austerlitz—he thought he would not be capable of many more years of "Napoléonic" warfare. She knew full well that his physical strength was due not so much to his physique as to his prodigious will power. Happily, he would remain at home with her for almost eight months, and in the evenings he would ask her to read him to sleep. The sound of her melodious Créole voice relaxed him more than anything else, and valets passing along the corridor would stop to listen as she intoned pas-sages from Plutarch's *Lives* or lines from his favorite dramatic poet, Pierre Corneille.

With her husband perpetually engaged in his study, Joséphine was arranging (from Paris) the household of the viceregal couple in Milan, the capital of their kingdom. They had been fêted all the way to Milan, where the welcome lasted a fortnight, and then they went on to Verona for ten days and Venice, where the celebrations resounded upon the marble pavement of the Piazza of San Marco, which Napoléon called "the best ballroom in Europe." The youthful charm of Eugène and his seventeen-year-old bride naturally appealed to the romantic Italians. The Vicereine Auguste was to have the Villa Bonaparte, now decorated in the latest Neoclassical style, with an enormous bust of the emperor by Canova in the anteroom of the ballroom. For the ballroom ceiling, Eugène engaged the artist Andrea Appiani (who portrayed Joséphine wearing the cameo diadem and had been at her coronation), to execute *Apollo and the Muses*. Appiani thus became Eugène's official painter, and on June 7, 1807, he would become chief painter to Napoléon in Italy. Joséphine wanted to be certain that Auguste had appropriate clothing, so she supervised the purchase of luxurious items of apparel, which began to appear in Milan just after the couple arrived home after their trip. There were robes, shawls, shoes, hats, and accessories that only Paris could provide. Joséphine insisted that the final aesthetic touch to a woman's appearance was her coiffure, so she sent Auguste a hairdresser approved by her own coiffeur, who arrived at the Villa Bonaparte early in March, fortified by a suitable *femme de chambre* who had also been hand-picked by the empress.

Another marriage (a surprising one) took place early in the new year, and it concerned the most fascinating member of Joséphine's household—the Mameluke Raza Roustam, whom Napoléon had brought back from Egypt and who was a never-ending source of unfounded scandalous gossip for the pamphleteers. They wrote that Roustam had strangled the conspirator Pichegru in prison and assassinated Admiral Villeneuve; one writer even made the preposterous charge that Roustam was the lover of both Joséphine and Napoléon.[10] Although he attended the emperor on campaign, Roustam was an entirely pacific being, holding a mirror for his master to shave, waiting upon Joséphine at the Tuileries, and serving at table. To quiet the gossip-mongers, Napoléon thought it appropriate for Roustam to have a wife, so in a Catholic ceremony on February 1, 1806, the Mameluke married Alexandrine Douville, daughter of Joséphine's first *valet de chambre.*

On March 12, Joséphine took a few days rest to accompany her husband to the château of Grignon, which Marshal Bessières had purchased after Austerlitz. Since Bessières was a close friend of Eugène's, Napoléon wrote to his stepson about their stay at Grignon, adding that he and Bessières had behaved like boys of fifteen. Méneval noticed the emperor's relief at being able to cast off, at least for a moment, the burdens of government, and Joséphine needed this respite herself before plunging into preparations for the next family wedding. In that busy March of 1806, a long, ominous shadow was cast over Joséphine's happiness. In Constant's view, it arose from the Murats' jealousy over the advantageous marriages the emperor was arranging for Joséphine's family, and they were determined to seek revenge. It was the Murats—the valet believed—who placed an attractive brunette named Eléonore Denuelle de la Plaigne in Napoléon's path. Hortense wrote that her stepfather received Eléonore surreptitiously several times and that Murat, too, saw Eléonore alone at his château of Neuilly. When Eléonore produced a son (comte Léon) on December 13, 1806, the baby was assumed to be the emperor's. The child bore a striking resemblance to Napoléon, who provided handsomely for him and his mother, although he refused to see her again. Napoléon's interest in Eléonore was not necessarily romantic, for he was troubled by the problem of succession since Joséphine had remained barren for several years. Dr. Corvisart encouraged him to test his virility by consorting with other women.[11] Although he could not be certain Léon was his son, most historians believe he was, and it is hardly coincidental that the child was given a name with two syllables of the emperor's name. In any case, another opportunity to determine his potency offered itself at the end of the year, and this time there would be no doubt.

For the moment, Joséphine had to turn her attention to another matrimonial problem. Since the court of Baden had been offended by Napoléon's snatching Auguste from under their noses, it was necessary to find a substitute for the disappointed Prince Charles of Baden. The solution was found in Joséphine's own family in the person of her niece, Stéphanie de Beauharnais, granddaughter of Aunt Fanny de Beauharnais, who had reared Stéphanie after the death of her mother. She was a student for two years at Madame Campan's school and was introduced into the consular court in January 1804, where this attractive blonde adolescent quickly gained the attention of the first consul, evoking the hatred of Caroline Murat and the jealousy of Joséphine.

*Pierre-Paul Prud'hon (1758–1823),
Stéphanie de Beauharnais (Musée Napoléon,
Arenenberg). This delicate pastel of Joséphine's
niece by the empress's favorite artist is little
known. Her marriage to Prince Charles
of Baden was celebrated with great ceremony,
and her trousseau was of unimaginable luxury.
However, Prud'hon depicts the flirtatious
Stéphanie in a simple white gown* à l'antique,
*her hair bound with ribbons embellished with
cameos on the forehead.*

Joséphine was placed in an embarrassing position, for Auguste, although happily married to Eugène, was still concerned with the fate of her rejected suitor, Prince Charles, and was taken aback when she heard that Eugène's own cousin had been chosen as Charles's bride.[12] To further complicate matters, there were the sentiments of Stéphanie herself. While staying with Joséphine at Malmaison, she had fallen in love with General Jean Rapp, a close friend of the family and highly regarded by the emperor, who had sent him to negotiate with General Mack at Ulm because of his fluent German. When her marriage to Prince Charles of Baden was proposed, Stéphanie stubbornly refused because of her attachment to Rapp, but Joséphine explained that interests of state must take precedence over affairs of the heart. However, the more her aunt objected to Rapp, the more attractive the glamorous cavalryman appeared to Stéphanie.

Napolèon usually deferred to his wife's judgment in these matters, but since Joséphine had made no progress, he turned to Hortense, trusting her to find a way around the impasse. Hortense reasoned with her cousin as follows: a liaison with Rapp would cause the good general's disgrace (since he would be acting in opposition to imperial wishes), which would seriously compromise their happiness. Hortense tried to soften her approach by praising Rapp for his undoubted qualities as a soldier, and in the end Stéphanie capitulated. The emperor adopted her on March 3, in order to make her eligible to marry a prince, a move that naturally incensed his brothers and sisters. Auguste thought it bizarre that, after Stéphanie's adoption by the emperor and her marriage to Charles of Baden, she "becomes my sister-in-law, and Charles my brother-in-law; what singular events!"[13]

Part of Stéphanie's objection to her arranged marriage may have been that she did not find her intended husband overly attractive, with his staring blue eyes, pudgy cheeks, and wispy blond hair. When the pretty young bride stood beside her bridegroom, they must have looked like decorations atop a wedding cake. To please her, Charles had cut off his military *queue* and had the barber arrange his hair in a fashionable classical style known as the "Brutus," but this only made matters worse, for Stéphanie burst into tears when she saw him and refused to have any contact with him. But the wedding went ahead and was a grand state affair, celebrated on April 7 and 8 with great pomp and magnificence, as Joséphine intended. And the reluctant Stéphanie's trousseau was superb, commensurate with Joséphine's standards. Attended by members of the imperial court, the elite of Paris aristocracy, and visiting royalty, both ceremonies took place in the Tuileries Palace. The emperor and empress accompanied the bridal couple down the grand staircase into the chapel below, and Pierre Fontaine recorded that the illuminated vestibule and gallery were decorated with the finest Gobelins tapestries from the state collections. The evening reception was worthy of the resplendent decor. Twenty-five hundred invitations had been sent out, and there were two simultaneous balls and suppers. Half the guests were invited to the Salle des Maréchaux, and the other half to the Gallery of Diana and Pavillon de Flore. Joséphine entered the Salle des Maréchaux on the emperor's arm at 9 P.M., watching from her box the quadrille headed by Hortense and the prince of Bavaria. Then they passed into the Gallery of Diana, where Caroline Murat and Marshal Duroc conducted the other quadrille. Although Joséphine would have been happy to stay all night, the emperor took her back to Saint-Cloud at 10:30. As they drove through the lighted city, she must have glanced back at the palace glowing in the night, listening to the dying strains of the orchestra playing on the garden terrace, satisfied that Eugène's and Stéphanie's marriages constituted a double triumph over the Bonaparte clan.

Constant noted, however, that the poor prince spent his entire wedding night and several nights thereafter in an armchair in front of his bride's closed door. As usual, the emperor took charge, and although he thought the situation amusing for a while, he sent them off to Karlsruhe, enjoining them to quickly put an end to the ridiculous situation. They obeyed the master's orders, and although they were never ecstatically happy, they at least became a contented couple, ancestors of Prince Rainier of Monaco, in whose family Stéphanie's name is perpetuated to this day.

Denis-Auguste-Marie Raffet (1804–1860). Dragoon of the Empress *(Ann S. K. Brown Military Collection, Providence, R.I.). The uniforms worn by Joséphine's special guard consisted of a dark green coat, white vest and pants, a brass helmet surmounted by a black horsehair plume falling down the back, and high black boots. Armed with a saber and firearms, the dragoons fought either mounted or on foot, and their reputation was formidable. When the dragoons in Spain had to be recalled to fight in the desperate campaign of France in 1814, the French people believed this was their last hope of being saved.*

As she moved from one residence to another, Joséphine was now attended by her own military escort known as the Dragoons of the Empress, one of the most impressive gifts her husband ever bestowed upon her. They were part of his own elite Imperial Guard, which functioned under the emperor's personal supervision. When the regiment was complete, Napoléon reviewed it, presented it to his wife, and appointed as its colonel in chief his intrepid twenty-eight-year-old cousin Arrighi de Casanova, who had, like Eugène, been severely wounded in the siege of Acre, and had fought at Austerlitz. It was a high honor indeed for Arrighi to command Joséphine's personal dragoons, but he deserved it. Hortense once said that of all the honors a woman could receive, military honors were the most flattering. The uniform of Joséphine's régiment was the same green as the *chasseur à cheval* coat that Napoléon preferred, plus a brass helmet trimmed with a band of panther skin, a black horsehair crest, and a red plume. The troops were quartered in the rue de Grenelle, mounted on chestnut or bay horses, and when they crossed the bridge to the Tuileries to escort Joséphine, everyone thought the Dragoons of the Empress were among the capital's most exhilarating sights.

Now Joséphine's domestic life assumed an almost monotonous regularity, especially at Saint-Cloud. She rose at nine and at ten received people soliciting favors, who must have filled the salon to overflowing. She breakfasted with Mme. de La Rochefoucauld and others at eleven, played a game of billiards after lunch, then returned to her apartments to do needlework with her ladies, perpetuating a tradition of the ancien régime. The highlight of the day was preparing her toilette for the evening, which involved selecting her gown, accessories, and jewelry for a formal dinner, concert, or reception, usually designed and organized by Isabey. Ministers were invited on Wednesdays, and on Sundays there was a family dinner. At midnight everyone retired except the empress, who played billiards with Constant, backgammon with one of the chamberlains, or entertained friends with tea and conversation. But Napoléon told her to give up this late-night activity, for the chatter could be indiscreet, and he wanted the servants to be able to retire when he did. In spite of Napoléon's desire for privacy and his need to be left alone to work, the imperial etiquette he himself imposed had to be observed when he was in residence. The formal *levée* (based on the ritual at Versailles) took place at 9 A.M., during which time those who were admitted paid their respects and no doubt asked favors. Among the ten men allowed entry into his apartment (even when he was in bed) were Talleyrand, Vivant Denon, Murat, Duroc, and his doctor, Corvisart. Joséphine had her separate apartment, again following Versailles etiquette, to which Constant would light the emperor's way. The emperor always left his valet specific instructions for Joséphine's welfare when he had to leave her for the front.

One of their favorite times of day was the hour after dinner when Joséphine poured his coffee from a Sèvres coffee pot decorated with scenes of Egypt as they talked quietly together. It was then that he went over his plans with her, discussed the qualities of the various people he depended upon, and asked her opinions. From his own letters and the testimony of Caulaincourt—who said that "she was his first confidante"—it is apparent that he appreciated her instincts and experience, which had been invaluable to his ascension, and which she projected so effectively in her formidable position.

Not only did Joséphine delight in the domestic tranquility of these few months in 1806, but she took a special interest in the emperor's vast transmogrification of Paris, which was being re-invented as the imperial seat and acquiring a new sense of space and distinction. The dome of the Pantheon was being solidified, and numerous monuments reminiscent of imperial Rome were commissioned: the Vêndome Column; the Arc du Carrousel under Joséphine's windows as a gateway into the Tuileries courtyard (for which Vivant Denon oversaw the execution of the sculptures); a model for the Arc de Triomphe de l'Étoile; and the erection of the majestic Madeleine. In 1808 the Bourse, with a sturdy sixty-six-column peristyle, would be put up by Alexandre-Théodore Brongniart, whose son, a mineralogist of real talent, had become director of the Sèvres manufactory in 1800; under his aegis the firm produced some of the most elegant pieces adorning Joséphine's dining table and her consoles at Malmaison. Thus the heart of Joséphine's Paris gradually took shape and—with the conspicuous absence of her residence, the Tuileries—it is essentially the Paris we know today. [14]

In an effort to create buffer states between France and Austria, Napoléon continued to seek fortuitous marriages for his family. Talleyrand had already concluded the arrangements for the forthcoming marriage of Jérôme Bonaparte to Catherine of Württemberg, and (as in the case of Maximilian I), Napoléon had elevated Catherine's father, the Elector Frederick, to royal rank. Caroline was somewhat appeased by the recent affronts to their dignity when she and Joachim Murat were granted the duchies of Clèves and Berg. Napoléon decided that Hortense's husband, Louis Bonaparte, should become the ruler of Holland, a decision the Dutch had to accept or be incorporated into French territory, and so on May 24, 1806, he was nominated to occupy the Dutch throne with Hortense as queen. By connecting his family with the dynastic families of Europe and distributing kingdoms among them, the emperor hoped to keep peace in the Empire and solidify it.

Napoléon then turned his attention to a reorganization of Germany, and a treaty was ratified on July 19, 1806, at Saint-Cloud, creating the Confederation of the Rhine, whereby sixteen German princes attached themselves to Napoléon as protector, with Prince Karl Theodor von Dalberg acting as prince primate. He was Joséphine's noble friend who had invited her, with Hortense and her little son, to visit him in Frankfurt the year before. Among the members of the Confederation were Bavaria, Baden, Hesse-Darmstadt, Nassau, and Berg (given to the Murats in March), and each was expected to supply a contingent of troops in case of war.

During the summer of 1806, Joséphine was concerned with matters other than the Confederation of the Rhine, one being the ongoing embellishment of the Tuileries. As usual, Pierre Fontaine consulted her about further changes in the palace, and she went with him to examine the restored ceilings. She also instructed him to deposit the arms taken from the arsenal in Vienna in the

Gallery of Diana in place of the marble statues of the great men of France.[15] On March 3 the emperor had commissioned a series of fourteen paintings depicting the main events of the great 1805 campaign, and François Gérard was assigned to execute a canvas showing the presentation of the flags to the emperor at Austerlitz. A proper place for the pictures would have to be found in the Tuileries Palace after they were shown at the Salon of the Musée Napoléon in August 1808.

In addition to the decoration of the palace, Joséphine took a lively interest in the horticultural specimens brought from the hothouses of Schönbrunn Palace. They were now flourishing in the conservatories of the Jardin des Plantes, which had been undergoing restoration and expansion since the opening of the Pont d'Austerlitz on January 1, 1806. Not only had huge hothouses been built for unusual plants, but there were also subterranean gardens destined for the culture of fragile species. A fine collection of animals from all over the world especially attracted her attention, for Joséphine was creating a small menagerie of her own at Malmaison, with flora imported from far-off lands by ships' captains eager to offer botanical and zoological gifts to the emperor's wife.

Besides supporting her husband in his adornment of their capital, Joséphine liked visiting the textile manufacturers whom Napoléon championed for assisting him in his struggle against foreign imports. Joséphine's predilection for decorating naturally drew her to the manufactory of the Oberkampf family at Jouy. On June 15, they went to see how these delectable *toiles de Jouy* were made, an event widely reported in the press. One journalist writing for the *Gazette de France* on July 6 gave details he thought worthy of circulation since "so much encouragement was given by the imperial visit to the utilitarian arts and those who cultivated them."[16] While at Jouy, the emperor bestowed the Legion d'Honneur upon M. Oberkampf, because, as he said, the manufacturer was making war on foreign industry with his products. If the emperor did his part, Joséphine certainly did hers, and her copious utilization of cotton fabrics at Malmaison would give great impetus to the industry.

Joséphine had seen Hortense off to Holland in June, but soon the new homesick queen was penning long, mournful letters. She and Louis had been greeted exultantly in Rotterdam, and she admitted being impressed by Louis's gracious response to the welcome delegation, for he truly extended himself to be agreeable to his new subjects. The citizens of this major port knew of Joséphine's love for flowers and, assuming that Queen Hortense shared her mother's taste, they offered her an elegant luncheon in a salon banked with the most exquisite floral offerings.[17]

Hortense's letters to her mother in July and August were more cheerful, filled with tidbits about people who would become a part of Joséphine's coterie when she went to Mainz to hold court in the fall. When Hortense and Louis traveled to Wiesbaden, they stayed in the palace at Mainz, where numerous princes, many from courts of the Confederation of the Rhine, came to pay their respects and give fêtes to honor the new rulers of Holland. Among the visitors was the grand duchess of Hesse-Darmstadt and Prince Charles of Nassau, whose father had gone with Bougainville on his famous voyage around the world. This connection must have instantly caught Joséphine's interest, for she was especially fond of the climbing vine with vivid mauve flowers that bore Bougainville's name, and she cultivated it in her Malmaison greenhouses, along with myosotis, hortensias (named for her daughter), and her treasured jasmine from Martinique.

By mid-August, it was already apparent to Joséphine that the summer of 1806 was going to end like that of 1805, with her husband once again taking the field. So with a heavy heart, she accompanied him to the annual celebration of his birthday on August 15. Two days earlier, Talleyrand had informed Napoléon that Prussia was unmistakably preparing for war, but the emperor appeared unruffled and accompanied Joséphine to the Salon on September 12. The next day, he directed Champagny, his minister of the interior, to have artists engrave the collection of precious stones in the library. Champagny was organizing a great industrial exposition scheduled to open on September 26, where the finest examples of decorative arts from French workshops would testify to the prosperity of the Empire, and as deeply as Joséphine regretted missing it, even this did not take precedence over the opportunity to accompany her husband. When, on September 17, Napoléon ordered his Foot Guard to be in Mainz not later than the 28th, Joséphine knew departure was imminent. The staff carriages rolled out of Paris on September 23; and Joséphine and Napoléon left Saint-Cloud the following night. The grenadiers, chasseurs, and marines had preceded them, and the cavalry and artillery were following. No other woman in history had ever found herself in such company—traveling at the heart of the most formidable army in the world with the most renowned military leader of all time at her side. Napoléon wanted her to remain in Mainz as his representative for the duration of the war, as he wrote Eugène, although the viceroy of Italy was ordered to remain in his own kingdom.[18]

By September 29 Joséphine was in Mainz, putting her household in order, while Napoléon and Bessières pored over dispatches, determining the final plan of operation for the Prussian campaign. Once again, Joséphine was to be left alone—except for Talleyrand, some officials, and her suite—and as she said good-bye to her husband again, she did not know it would be for ten long months. As harassed as he would be during the long, bloody campaign, however, he would write her at least seven letters in October, nine in November, nine in December, and this time Joséphine would be more careful about keeping up her end of the exchange.

A few hours before his departure for Jena, despite his focus on the complexities of a campaign, Napoléon wrote to Joséphine: "I am traveling from twenty to twenty-five leagues a day [roughly 59 to 63 miles]." He was rushing headlong to meet another woman—the queen of Prussia—but this time Joséphine had nothing to fear, for she had often heard him voice his disdain for this "Amazon." The Prussian ultimatum was received at Bamberg on October 7, and after reading it, the emperor turned to Berthier, his chief of staff: "We have been given a rendezvous of honor for the eighth. Never would a Frenchman miss such a thing. Since it is said that a beautiful queen wants to witness a battle, we must be courteous and march, without sleeping, upon Saxony."[19]

The Grande Armée was set into motion northward on October 8, and on the 14th the French confronted one Prussian army at Jena and a second at Auerstadt, defeating both on the same day. The battle of Jena provoked Heinrich Heine's famous line: "Napoléon breathed upon Prussia, and Prussia ceased to exist," for the proud Prussian army had been virtually destroyed. It was probably the swiftest annihilation of an army in history, accomplished within less than a month after Napoléon and Joséphine had set out from Saint-Cloud. In that fall of 1806, the French Empire was about to reach its zenith, for the peace treaties of 1805–7 came close to giving Joséphine's husband unchallenged mastery of Europe.

Joséphine benefitted personally from the Prussian disaster, for after the battle of Jena, a French military patrol found fifty paintings from the gallery of the Elector William of Hesse-Cassel stored in a forest cottage and they were sent directly to Malmaison for Joséphine's gallery, thus depriving Vivant Denon of a cache he wanted for the Louvre. Among these coveted paintings that Joséphine added to her collection were four by Claude le Lorrain and Rembrandt's *Descent from the Cross*.

The day after Jena, Napoléon had written Joséphine in Mainz to give her his own assessment of Jena-Auerstadt: "Talleyrand will show you the bulletin. Never was an army more effectively beaten or more completely destroyed. . . . Adieu, my love! A thousand loving words to Hortense, and to the grand Monsieur Napoléon [her son, Napoléon-Charles], Wholly thine, Napoléon."[20] The reference to Hortense's son pleased Joséphine, for this little boy was unusually bright and promising, and Napoléon was still seriously considering adopting him as his heir.

Hortense and her two children had joined her mother in the old imperial town of Mainz on October 12 and were installed in a town house with a view of the Cassel bridge, while Joséphine's court was set up in the Teutonic Palace. Even with the constant ebb and flow of titled individuals paying deference, Joséphine was bored and kept asking to join her husband. Talleyrand had gone to Napoléon's headquarters and reported that the empress did nothing but cry; she was immediately chided in the emperor's next letter, in which he assured her that she had every reason to be happy with Hortense and her grandchildren there and good news from the battlefront. But Joséphine wanted to see Potsdam, Frederick the Great's pavilion at Sans-Souci, and the Charlottenburg, especially the Isle of Peacocks, Queen Louise's favorite resort just outside the town. Were the gardens anything like Malmaison? She heard about the glorious entry into Berlin on October 27, where people packed the street to the rooftops watching the resplendent Mamelukes, the magnificent cuirassiers, and her husband, as he rode down Unter den Linden in his worn green uniform twenty feet ahead of his troops.

As much as the empress wanted to leave Mainz to follow her husband, however, she and Hortense had their hands full. As the French armies advanced, the families of those rulers who had fled or been deposed rushed to her quarters seeking protection. When Talleyrand left her to visit Napoléon's headquarters, she probably realized how much he had helped her disentangle the complex political relationships between various royal families. After the battle of Auerstadt, many generals and officers of Hesse-Cassel took refuge with Joséphine, who did her utmost to console them. This was no mean feat, for when the elector had allied himself with Prussia against France, he paid for his error with the disappearance of his state, which became incorporated into the new kingdom of Westphalia. The elector's daughter, the princess of Gotha, also flew to Joséphine's court, endearing herself to both the empress and Queen Hortense. Then there was the princess of Nassau and her daughters, who came to dine with Joséphine each Sunday, and her own niece, the princess of Baden (Stéphanie de Beauharnais), visiting from Mannheim.

Besides comforting distressed princes and key players in the Confederation, the wives of French officers who had attached themselves to Hortense came to be near her in Mainz to await news from their husbands at the front. When the trumpet sounded, they would all rush out to receive the latest news from the battlefront although, as Hortense said, it never even occurred to them that there would be anything but victories to announce, since the emperor had never lost a battle. Each day thousands of prisoners passed under their windows, and Joséphine and Hortense would often give them money. In one of those endearing vignettes of her mother, Hortense portrays the empress of France distributing alms to men whom her husband had just defeated. In early December, Joséphine and Hortense were invited again to Prince Dalberg's palace at Frankfurt, for almost all Germany was now allied to Napoléon by the Confederation, and Dalberg was the prince primate. In Frankfurt they were greeted with the usual elaborate receptions, concerts, masked balls, and promenades, in spite of the horrors of war just outside the windows.

Hortense found that a profitable aspect of her stay in Mainz was getting to know Talleyrand. She had seen the prince of Benevento over the years at Malmaison, with his cold, detached air, dragging his lame foot, sitting on the nearest chair without speaking to anyone, and only rarely noticing Joséphine's young daughter. To her great surprise, he sought out Hortense at Mainz and flattered her by revealing a previously hidden charm. She especially enjoyed his famous witticisms, but Hortense knew to speak with discretion, because one reason for Talleyrand's presence at Mainz was to police the salons. He would write his reports and send them off to Marshal Duroc, and the women had to be careful not to furnish any gossip that might compromise the emperor's policies.

In January 1807, Hortense and her children had to return to The Hague, and Joséphine herself was preparing to leave Mainz shortly, but the emperor was forced to continue the war, for as he wrote to Eugène, the king of Prussia, while offering France peace proposals, was negotiating with the Russian czar to fight the Grande Armée in Poland. This was not welcome news for Joséphine, and her husband continued to discourage her from joining him: "The weather is too bad, and the roads are unsure and atrocious, the distances are too great for me to permit you to come here where my business keeps me."[22] Joséphine had to return to Paris to preside again at the Tuileries, he said, for this was where he needed her most in his absence.

It was an unsettling letter, and Joséphine suspected her husband's reasons were not related entirely to travel, war, or diplomacy. In fact, two events occurred almost simultaneously at the end of 1806 that were to pose the most serious threat yet to her position. The first, as we noted, was the birth on December 13 of a son to Eléonore Denuelle de la Plaigne, the young woman with whom Napoléon had indulged in a passing affair. If he were indeed the father of this child, and if he could not adopt Napoléon-Charles, a divorce and remarriage might become more than a vague possibility. The second came on January 1, 1807, as Napoléon was leaving Putulsk for Warsaw, when he stopped to change horses at the post-station of Bronie. A small crowd of Poles had gathered there to greet the conqueror of Europe as he passed through, among them a lady whom Constant described as "a blond with blue eyes, and skin of dazzling whiteness; of medium height, with a charming and beautifully proportioned figure."[23] The comely lady at Bronie was the Polish countess Maria Walewska, and judging from the consequences of their meeting, the emperor was impressed at first sight.

10

Apogée of the Empire

Following Napoléon's instructions, Joséphine left Mainz on January 27, 1807, and traveled through Strasbourg, Lunéville, and Nancy, where she was hailed with the usual grand receptions. Her return to Paris gave an instant boost to public morale. Plunging immediately into her official duties, she received the welcome of the Municipal Corps and other officials in the throne room of the Tuileries, to which she responded with characteristic aplomb: "Accustomed as I am to sharing all the feelings of the emperor, you must not doubt the great satisfaction that I feel in finding myself once more within the walls of a city which he himself calls his good city of Paris."[1] The newspapers of their "good city" proclaimed their assurances of devotion to their sovereigns, and the *Journal de l'Empire* predicted an exciting social season, stimulated by the empress's presence: "Hardly had Her Majesty the Empress arrived in the capital than everything assumed a new face. Many brilliant fêtes are announced, which will be offered in succession by the ministers, and . . . during Carnival, it is most likely that the pleasures attending this season will be unusually lively and abundant."

The series of receptions, state dinners, special galas, and commemorative masses that Joséphine was required to attend seemed endless, especially since she would have to carry on alone for another six months. She was constantly encouraged by her husband's letters, however. Writing from Liebstadt on February 23, he praised her for attending the theaters and urged her to occupy her grand loge at the Opéra. "Grandeur has its inconveniences," he reminded her. "An empress cannot comport herself like a private individual,"[2] and she must show a cheerful spirit at court. From Osterode on March 2, he assured her that he had ordered everything she wanted for Malmaison.

Showing a cheerful spirit at court was easier said than done, for the grueling routine was wearing Joséphine down. The rules that governed every moment of her day—whether she was in Paris or abroad—were codified in *Etiquette du Palais Impérial.* The interiors of the Tuileries and the imperial châteaux were designed to accommodate this stultifying protocol, based on that enduring model, Versailles. Joséphine's apartments were divided into two parts: the Apartment of Honor and the Interior Apartment. The first (for public affairs) consisted of an antechamber, first and second salon, the salon of the empress, a dining room, and a concert room. Her interior apartment contained a bedroom, boudoir, dressing room, bathroom, and library. In 1807 she had thirty women and numerous men in attendance.

Joséphine's ceremonial life was invariably played out to the counterpoint of the military, for even when unattended by the emperor during her travels, she was received with full military honors, amid a forest of flags. When Joséphine arrived at a military post, the cavalry would meet her a few miles outside the town with a trumpet salute and then accompany her to the garrison, with half of the troops lining her route and the other half marching alongside her carriage. When she reached the town, the troops would present arms, as officers saluted, flags were dipped, and drums were beaten, while the artillery fired three salvos. Her residence was guarded by an infantry battalion with standards flying under the command of a colonel, as two mounted sentinels flanked the entrance. Her return to Paris was invariably signaled by cannon and bells, followed by official groups paying homage in her throne room.

Although she presented a serene, confident face to the public, Joséphine lived in a state of perpetual apprehension, continually plaguing Napoléon (even before leaving Mainz) to let her join him, but he laughed "at what [she] said about taking a husband in order to be with him."[3] Judging from his undated letter sent before the battle of Eylau, he had just received one of Joséphine's fractious notes, which provoked this incisive analysis of her character: "Joséphine, your heart is excellent, but your reason is weak; you feel in an extraordinary way, but you do not reason well. Enough of quarreling; I want you to be gay, happy with your lot . . . not grumbling and weeping, but have a light heart and a little joy."[4]

There was little cause for joy, however, when an official dispatch reached Paris announcing that on February 8, 1807, the emperor had fought the savage battle of Eylau against the Russians in a blinding snowstorm, the bloodiest to date. Even on this appalling battlefield, he did not forget Joséphine, and he wrote to her at 3 A.M. on February 9: "My friend, there was a great battle yesterday; victory remains with me, but I lost many men. . . . I write these . . . lines myself, though greatly fatigued, to tell you that I am well, and that I love you. Wholly thine."[5] The costly battle of Eylau became the subject of one of the most celebrated works by Joséphine's protégé Baron Gros, who paid special tribute to the compassionate care of the French surgeons for the enemy wounded, but the horror of the ghastly scene is heightened by the gruesome frozen corpses in the foreground. One of Napoléon's letters from Eylau concerned a member of Joséphine's family whom he kept under his wing, her twenty-one-year-old cousin, Maurice-Charles de Tascher, who had fought at Jena as well as at Eylau. "I have brought him to be with me with the title of *officier d'ordonnance* [aide-de-camp],"[6] he told her, two days later reassuring her that "Little Tascher is fine, but he had a real trial [at Eylau]. I shall keep him near me. . . . This young man interests me."[7]

Napoléon could not shake off his grief over so much suffering, however, and he unburdened his heart to his wife, concluding: "War is an anachronism. Victories will some day be accomplished without cannons or bayonets."[8] By early June, however, he would be maneuvering his way toward Friedland and an encounter with the Russians, for his peace overtures to both Russia and Prussia had been rejected, and, to make matters worse, England's navy was now in control of the Mediterranean.

Yet Joséphine had to remain the exemplar of confidence. She was honored as patroness of a huge ball that the emperor ordered Cambacérès to stage in the Luxembourg Palace, now the residence of Joseph and Julie Bonaparte, to celebrate Eylau. The account in *Le Moniteur* emphasized "the magnificent distribution of the apartments, the richness of their decoration, the panache of the women's parures, which rivaled their grace and beauty."[9] Laure Junot noticed that the empress no longer danced, now that she was forty-three, which left the field open to Caroline Murat since Elisa Bonaparte was in Italy and Pauline's delicate health prevented her from entertaining too often.

Although they were old friends, the relationship between Caroline and Hortense had blown hot and cold over the years, mostly because of family issues regarding succession to the throne and Napoléon's preferential treatment of Joséphine's children. However, Caroline's letters to Hortense were now warm and newsy. She also visited the empress almost daily, which indicates either that her relationship with Joséphine had improved or that Caroline thought her presence at the Tuileries would somehow please her brother. Their conversations centered around Hortense, whom both Joséphine and Caroline greatly missed after her departure for Holland, and Joséphine's conversation invariably turned to anecdotes about her four-and-one-half-year-old grandson, Napoléon-Charles, upon whom she doted.

The one subject that was off-limits to the women in Joséphine's circle was her childlessness, but the men sometimes forgot, and Laure Junot recorded one such blunder. When Andoche Junot's mother died suddenly, his father was so affected that he wanted to give up his appointment, but when the emperor heard of it, he wrote Junot a letter that Andoche imprudently read aloud to the empress: "I do not see why your father should . . . resign his employment. . . . If he is at a loss for a wife to receive company according to his duties, let him marry again."[10] Laure said her husband realized too late that the emperor's casual remark had wounded Joséphine, although she was never anything but kind to him thereafter.[11] She always sensed his instability and treated him gently, declaring that she liked him much better than the flamboyant Joachim Murat, who "smells of gunpowder half a league off and would put his Creator to the sword."[12]

In spite of the realities of war elsewhere in Europe, the social whirl in Paris never missed a beat. As the governor of Paris, Junot opened all the balls, usually accompanied by Caroline Murat,

François Gérard (1770–1837), Caroline Murat, Queen of Naples, Surrounded by Her Children (Château de Fontainebleau). Caroline is seated in the royal palace in Naples, holding the hand of her oldest child, Achille (in uniform), who would establish the American branch of the family by marrying the grand-niece of George Washington. Lucien, seated on his mother's jeweled train, wears a crimson velvet suit; Letizia is seen at the right in profile, and the youngest, Louise, advances solemnly into the room bearing flowers she has picked from the garden. Vesuvius can be seen looming in the background.

who preferred him to everyone else (if Laure Junot is to be believed). Caroline gave quadrilles at her Elysée Palace; even Pauline sometimes left her bed to host expensive soirées at her Hôtel Charost; and even the miserly Cambacérès extended himself by reaching deep into his pockets to put on one lavish dinner after another. But the luster of the season was dimmed by the queen of Holland's absence. Laure avowed that Hortense would have been queen of all the parties if only she had been in Paris.

Joséphine's feast day, St. Joseph's, fell on March 19, 1807, and for the occasion, Caroline and Pauline honored their sister-in-law with an unusual party that was centered around a play to be staged at Malmaison. The event was not prompted by any love they felt for Joséphine but, as Laure Junot pointed out, it was an excuse for yet another round of festivities, although it had required three weeks of rehearsals. Laure's own role, although small, was interesting, and she enjoyed the peculiar advantage of being coached by the famous actress Mlle. Mars. Although Pauline Borghese was awarded the coveted part of the peasant bride, the two real stars were Andoche Junot and Caroline Murat as two people madly in love. The latter's secretary had written words to accompany the music of Spontini, whose masterpiece, *La Vestale*, would make its debut late that year under Joséphine's sponsorship.

On the appointed day, the empress and her ladies rolled out of the city, bound for the château that mirrored her personality. They breakfasted in the dining room decorated with *grisaille* paintings by Louis Lafitte, looking out through the tall windows at the gardens full of spring flowers. Joséphine sat at the head of the table "with her accustomed grace, and all the simplicity of a hostess in ordinary society."[13] The play, which was meant to be serious, turned into a riotous comedy because of the amateur performances, and Laure said they all would have left were they not laughing so much. Caroline's shrill voice spoiled the effect of Junot's bass, and she proved to be no Mlle. Mars, despite assiduous prompting. The amusement lasted far into the night, followed by the usual cold collation in the white tent, so by the time Joséphine's carriage drew up to the entrance to the Tuileries, dawn was breaking over the Seine.

These diversions helped to allay Joséphine's fears about her husband's safety, but she sometimes gave way to her emotions, provoking the emperor's impatient response: "Why so many tears? . . . If you want to remain dear to me, show some character and strength of spirit. . . . An empress must show courage."[14] Eugène's notes of warning from Milan implored his mother not to irritate the emperor with her complaints and advised her to avoid unnecessary expenditures, a plea that likely fell on deaf ears, as Eugène well knew.

One evening in March, Cambacérès lumbered into Joséphine's salon and solemnly handed her a letter from the emperor written in his own hand—in handwriting so illegible that she had to give it to Junot to decipher, for he was accustomed to Napoléon's scrawl. The emperor gave her the location of his winter quarters, which (Junot thought) appeared to be between the Vistula and Passargue Rivers, a spot that her attendant found on a map. This was hardly reassuring, for it meant that

François Gérard (1700–1837), Countess Walewska (Musée de l'Armée). Maria Walewska (1786–1817) was married at eighteen to the sixty-eight-year-old Polish nobleman Athanase Walewski, who promoted Maria's liaison with Napoléon as a way to advance the political interests of Poland. When Maria came to live in Paris in 1810, her love affair with the emperor was apparently over, although a son had been born of their union and Napoléon continued to be generous to her. Her black dress is reputedly mourning garb, symbolizing her country's loss of its freedom.

her husband—whom she had not seen in six months—was 1,250 miles away from Paris, and once again in a precarious position, with Russians on the Danube and Austrians threatening his flank.

With Napoléon away, Joséphine, who would shortly be forty-four, feared losing her hold over him. When they were together, she always managed to cajole him into giving her almost anything, and he was contented in her presence. But a snowball of gossip had been gathering momentum in her salon at Mainz, and in Paris the Polish ladies were now bragging that the emperor had taken a mistress from their own country—a reference to Countess Maria Walewska. Rumor also had it that Marshal Murat was urging his commander-in-chief to obtain a divorce. Eugène's letters to his mother admitted that he, too, had heard these rumors from both Paris and Munich, and he hastened to assure her that she was welcome to come to Italy to live with them should the emperor be obliged to remarry in the interests of France.

When Joséphine wrote to her husband hinting at rumors of a mistress, he simply disavowed them: "Put no faith in the evil rumors that may be spread about. Never doubt my feelings toward you and have no uneasiness."[15] And again: "I don't understand what you say about women who are corresponding with me. I love only my little Joséphine, kindly, sulky, and capricious. . . . She is always adorable . . . except when she is suspicious."[16] Napoléon was, of course, being a good deal less than candid. On April 1 he had established his headquarters at the beautiful East Prussian château of Finkenstein, a far cry from the dreary farmhouses and damp, drafty sheds that had sheltered him during the cold wet marches of recent months. Now, seated before a roaring fire with the Countess Maria Walewska beside him, he was enjoying some semblance of the domestic life he had shared with Joséphine. Maria came from a family ennobled since 1574, was an ardent patriot, modest, intelligent, and religious. She had tried to ignore the emperor's advances, but she was advised by her countrymen, including her own husband, Count Athanase Walewski to sacrifice her own interests to that of the state. But Napoléon's letters to Joséphine described the decor rather than the company—"many fine mantles . . . handsomer than Bessières' [at Grignon]. This is very agreeable since I rise often during the night. I love to see a fire."[17] Joséphine was hardly interested in architectural details at this point, nor did she need to be told how much he liked fires, for when he was home, she saw to it that a fire was kept burning almost year round to accommodate his sensitivity to cold. Had Joséphine realized that the countess was often at his fireside, she would have worried even more, for this was not a brief nocturnal visit from the adventuress Mlle. George or a fleeting affair with an Eléonore de la Plaigne.

One bit of good news lightened that spring for Joséphine—Auguste's first pregnancy—so she shipped an elaborate layette to Milan, where on March 14, the bells of the city rang and the guns discharged to announce the birth of a daughter to the viceroy and vicereine. The glad tidings were taken by Italian noblemen to Joséphine at Malmaison, to Hortense at her palace in The Hague, and to the Wittelsbachs at the Residenz in Munich, where King Maximilian wept for joy. Auguste received an affectionate letter of congratulations from the emperor, who told Eugène on March 27 their daughter could only be named Joséphine. Eugène was happy, of course, but he still missed Paris and his regiment. Joséphine knew he needed a lift, so she asked an old friend, Stanislas de Girardin, a member of the Legislative Corps, to visit Eugène at his country house in Monza, just outside Milan. She knew this horseman would instantly endear himself to Eugène, who was pleased to show off his impeccably kept stables. Eugène whisked his visitor off in a light carriage drawn by six Neopolitan horses to see his Persian stallion, which Girardin declared "the most beautiful horse I have ever seen." Eugène confessed to his compatriot that "I was never ambitious ... and my present situation seems like a dream; but . . . I miss my independence in Paris. So far as the emperor is concerned, there is only one word for me: obey. He ordered me not to think of myself as French and I try, but . . . I find consolation in the memory of my country. . . . I married a princess, but it is not by her rank that I am impressed; I love her beauty, her heart, and her virtues."[18]

Like the others, Eugène knew that obedience was the order of the day wherever the eagles flew. It was unlawful in Italy (and Germany) to criticize the emperor in spite of his various faults—

vanity, arrogance, and impetuosity. But Eugène also recognized his stepfather as an uncommon genius of extraordinary intellectual superiority, energy, and unbounded imagination. Napoléon's interest in Italy was personal: it was the land of his ancestors, and Italian was his native tongue. With his stepson as viceroy, the peninsula was being transformed, and Eugène—although his heart was with the army—could at least derive satisfaction from that. For the first time since the Lombard invasions, Italy was being governed by a centralized administration, albeit a French one; the foundations of a modern Italy were being laid, and the most capable Italians were enthusiastically enlisting in this innovative administration. Even Joséphine's friend, the writer Réné de Chateaubriand, whose attitude toward the emperor was ambivalent, conceded: "These new monarchies of a military dynasty brought life into a country that had been distinguished by the dying languor of an old race. . . . We brought to Rome the germ of administration. Napoléon is great because he restored, enlightened, and administered Italy in a superior way."[19]

In Girardin's opinion, the viceroy inspired the greatest confidence and was in every branch of his domain a remarkable administrator to whom Italy should be deeply grateful. But both he and Auguste were disappointed that their projected visit to Paris was again delayed. She wrote to her brother Ludwig: "You know Eugène submerges himself in work. . . . [He] never complains and tries to appear happy . . . and has taught me to ride."[20] Yet in the privacy of a wooded grove (ironically called the "Vale of Tears") at their country house, they could, without being seen by their court, shed tears for their beloved France and for Bavaria.

In early May, Joséphine suffered a crushing blow. During the night of May 4, after a short illness, her precious grandson Napoléon-Charles died of diphtheria in The Hague. Not only was this an intolerable personal loss, but it also constituted the greatest threat yet to her marriage. Hortense had been keeping vigil by her son's bed night and day, refusing to believe that he would not recover. But when she realized Napoléon-Charles was gone, she went into a state of shock and seemingly lost her reason. Caroline Murat received special permission to leave Paris that night to comfort her heartbroken friend, and Joséphine went straight to the Palace of Laeken near Brussels, where Louis was bringing Hortense, Caroline, and two of their former school friends to join her. Laeken was as far as Joséphine or Caroline could travel without express permission from the emperor, who in any case wanted the Belgians to see the empress. "Your presence," Napoléon wrote his grieving wife, "will give pleasure to the Belgian people."[21] By May 19, Hortense had sufficiently recovered to accompany her mother and Caroline back to Paris, and after a suitable interval, she set off to the Pyrenees for convalescence, where in the Vignemale her "gracious manners and benevolence [made Hortense] positively adored by the inhabitants of this district," as Laure Junot effusively recorded.[22]

For Joséphine, the summer of 1807 was a series of trials. After hearing of Napoléon-Charles's death, Napoléon apparently would not even contemplate adopting Hortense's second son.

Since the dead child was the only would-be heir he had ever considered, a divorce now appeared unavoidable. And to make matters worse, Joséphine sustained another loss, her mother's death in Martinique, on June 2.

For Napoléon, on the other hand, the summer was a succession of triumphs. As the threat from Russia became ever more menacing, it was necessary to besiege the strategic city of Danzig, which finally surrendered on May 27 after a nine-week siege, and then he maneuvered toward Friedland, where the Russians had retreated. As the two armies engaged, the French suffered enormous losses and found themselves in a critical situation. At this point, as he was on the verge of being overwhelmed by the Russian cavalry, General Sénarmont displayed a stroke of genius by changing the position of his gunners in the very face of the enemy, which managed to disperse them. Finally, at about 10:30 P.M., the long day's struggle was over. The victory marked the crowning moment of the Polish campaign and greatly redeemed the bloody battle of Eylau, which had gained little for France.

Then followed Napoléon's first interview with Czar Alexander, who realized that the French ruler now stood at the zenith of his power, with only England left in his path. The historic encounter took place at Tilsit, on a raft on the Niemen River (the requisite neutral territory), upon which the French engineers had erected a fine military pavilion. Napoléon's aim was to offer Alexander peace without humiliation in order to gain an alliance against England, and never had he sought peace as fervently as he did now. Joséphine received the full details of the meeting on July 7, along with the emperor's highly confidential letter of the same date, in which he wrote to her of another important event: "The queen of Prussia dined yesterday with me . . . [desiring that I] make some concessions to her husband: although I was polite, I held to my politics. . . . When you read this letter, the peace with Prussia and Russia will be concluded, and Jérôme made King of Wesphalia. . . . This news is for you alone."[23] The peace was signed on July 9, 1807.

Joséphine knew she had no reason to be jealous of the Prussian queen, for Napoléon had already assured her that Louise's charms were lost upon him, although she was said to be a beautiful woman, the most popular princess in the history of Prussia. Besides, Joséphine was busy receiving many noteworthy visitors eager to taste the delights of Paris. Instructions kept pouring in to her from the emperor to keep Fontaine and his architects moving ahead with the various construction projects. Although the emperor could govern France even from the field, governing his wife was another matter, as comte Nicolas-François Mollien, the minister of the treasury, knew first hand. Earlier that spring, Joséphine had run up such huge debts, unbeknownst to her husband, that she asked one of her jewelers, Edmé-Marie Foncier, for a loan, for which she deposited with him jewelry of equal value as collateral. She even begged help from Hortense, and when her creditors became ever more insistent, she turned first to the discreet Mollien and then to Ferdinando Marescalchi, the Italian minister of foreign affairs. Eugène counseled him to act in concert with Mollien to find a solution to his mother's dilemma. When Napoléon finally discovered the magnitude of Joséphine's debts, he took extreme measures, placing all her monetary affairs under Mollien's supervision. Although he was responsible for the complicated finances of the Empire, Mollien's efforts to manage Joséphine's spending constituted one of his more formidable tasks. The long-suffering minister was finally honored posthumously when the Louvre's glass pyramid was completed with the dedication of the Pavillon Mollien, and no one more richly deserved it.

During June and July, Joséphine stayed at Saint-Cloud, where she was caring for Hortense's second son, Napoléon-Louis, while her distraught daughter continued to take the waters at Cauterets. On June 11 Joséphine reported to Hortense that "your son is in perfect health and amuses me greatly. He is so sweet. I find that he has all the manners of the poor child whom we mourn."[24] Early on the morning of July 27, the cannons of the Invalides announced the emperor had finally returned to his capital after an absence of ten months. He arrived sooner than expected and immediately pushed on for Saint-Cloud. He had written his wife a letter reminiscent of those he composed during the first Italian campaign: "One of these beautiful nights, I shall burst into Saint-Cloud like a jealous husband. I forewarn you of it. It will give me the most intense pleasure to see you. Entirely thine, Napoléon."[25] When they did meet again, nothing seemed to have changed, and the old flame was rekindled, as she reported to Eugène. Although Eugène was not summoned to France to pay his respects to the emperor, the ever-resourceful Hortense assured her brother that the omission was not personal. She thoughtfully added that the emperor never ceased to appreciate Eugène's services. If Napoléon had conquered Italy, she said, it was the viceroy who, by his tact, was insuring its tranquility.[26]

On the day of the emperor's arrival at Saint-Cloud, he and Joséphine were joined by the arch-chancellor, Cambacérès, for dinner. With all Europe (except England) at his feet, it might now be said that—in this year 1807—no one since Charlemagne, not even Caesar himself, had ever wielded such power. Yet as she studied him, Joséphine noticed that he had changed, and not necessarily for the better. He had put on weight, was even more authoritative, and would not tolerate contradiction. His staff also noted that this overbearing manner had become particularly marked after Tilsit. He was even abrupt with Hortense, toward whom he was usually indulgent, warning her that he would no longer tolerate her continued mourning, for it bordered on self-pity. Joséphine tried to mollify his harshness, and in the end Hortense admitted it was for her own good. Her brief reconciliation with Louis following their child's death had resulted in another pregnancy, but neither of Hortense's other two sons would ever replace Napoléon-Charles in the emperor's heart.

As Joséphine reigned over the grand ball on August 16 that celebrated the emperor's birthday, he was detained by pressing matters, one of them being a conference with Jean-Baptiste Champagny, former minister of the interior who had just been named minister of foreign affairs, replacing Talleyrand, whom Napoléon had begun to distrust. Like other officials, Champagny had been obliged to cope with Joséphine's demands, such as when she took advantage of her husband's absence to acquire objects for her beloved Malmaison. The docile, honest Champagny dared not displease his master, so when Joséphine insisted that four marble columns Pierre Fontaine had earmarked for the museum be rerouted to Malmaison, Champagny gave in. After all, as Joséphine told the compliant minister, Fontaine had no real use for them, and they would be just right for her gallery and as supports for the pediment of the Temple of Love in her garden.

At the end of that summer, Joséphine immersed herself in plans for yet another state wedding, the marriage of her youngest brother-in-law, Jérôme Bonaparte, which was to be celebrated at the Tuileries on August 22.[27] This was one of her happier assignments, for she had always appreciated Jérôme's kindness to her. He was considerably younger than his siblings and had not been part of the Bonaparte-de Beauharnais conflict; as he grew older, he made a habit of sending her thoughtful gifts, such as some exquisite shawls from Breslau that he had dispatched while in command of the Bavarian corps in Prussia. The bride chosen for the debonair Jérôme was Princess Catherine of Württemberg, and the marriage would unite yet another family member to a European dynasty. The bridegroom had no say in the matter, of course, but from Napoléon's point of view, it was a perfect alliance because of Catherine's relationship to most of Europe's crowned heads, including her cousin Czar Alexander. Jérôme and Catherine were to rule over the kingdom of Westphalia, which had been formed from Prussian provinces on the left bank of the Elbe and the former electorate of Hesse-Cassel.

Catherine was intelligent, kind, and reasonably attractive, but the critical Laure Junot found her hopelessly old-fashioned by French standards: "Her gown was of white moiré, but a bluish white, which was out of fashion at the time . . . trimmed . . . with a very badly worked silver embroidery. . . . It was a very tight frock, with a little train exactly resembling the round tail of a beaver, and tight flat sleeves, compressing the arm above the elbow like a bandage after blood-letting. . . . She wore round her neck two rows of very fine pearls, to which was suspended the portrait of the Prince [Jérôme] set in diamonds; [the jeweler] had made it of dimensions capable of carrying the greatest possible number of jewels, but . . . much too large to be ornamental, as it dangled from the neck of the princess and inflicted heavy blows at every movement."[28] Catherine's ill-fitting dress must have painfully contrasted with Joséphine's elegant costume created by Leroy, which was handsomely set off by her famous black pearls.

After Austerlitz, Napoléon had promoted Catherine's father, the Elector Frederick, to the rank of king, in recognition of his troops' services during the war with Austria. The new king of Württemberg was extremely corpulent, and Constant was shocked when he saw him, noting that his skin was stretched so tightly that it would surely burst. The king's dining table had a half-moon cut out to accommodate his pendulous abdomen, and chairs were specially designed to support his ponderous weight.

Francis-Joseph Kinson (1770–1839), Jérôme Bonaparte and His Wife, Catherine of Württemberg (Château de Versailles). Jérôme and Catherine are sitting on a terrace at their château near Kamel. Since Prussia was threatening France, Jérôme's marriage to the daughter of the elector Frederick was highly advantageous for Napoléon. Catherine produced two children; their daughter Mathilde married Prince Demidoff in 1840, and their son, Prince Jérôme-Napoléon, is the ancestor of the present imperial house.

Meanwhile, Hortense finished her pilgrimage through the south of France and reached Saint-Cloud on the evening of August 27. Her memoirs give glimpses of her mother's life at this time. It was Joséphine's custom at Saint-Cloud to drive out with her husband in the afternoon. Although they enjoyed these few private moments, the emperor often insisted that Hortense join them in the carriage and steered their conversations toward topics calculated to cheer her up. Once he tried to distract her with an account of his interview with the czar, delivering his opinion of the queen of Prussia: "She is beautiful, amiable, but a little affected, and not at all worthy of my Joséphine," whereupon, he turned to the empress and gave her a kiss.

An anecdote recorded by Hortense provides a rare glimpse of Napoléon at play. One day, after they had finished dinner, he told Hortense to put on something informal because he was taking her to the Saint-Cloud fair, which was held in the vast park surrounding the château. Joséphine was indisposed with a headache, so she stayed behind. The party set off on foot, Hortense on the arm of the emperor and General Bertrand beside them. They avoided the crowds, because the emperor did not want to be recognized, and he managed to escape notice. At one point, however, the mass of humanity was so dense that he feared for his pregnant stepdaughter's safety, so he pulled her into the nearest exhibition tent without paying the admission fee. Bertrand was responsible for buying tickets, since neither Napoléon nor Hortense ever carried money, but he had not seen where they went.

The tent they had entered contained a display of wax figures representing the famous interview at Tilsit and included Napoléon, the czar, and (unaccountably) members of the imperial family. Only a few people were in the tent, so the proprietor waxed eloquent to his captive audience, identifying each figure in turn and explaining their relationships to the emperor and empress. Hortense and her stepfather edged their way to the door, because General Bertrand was nowhere in sight and the moment was coming when the manager would ask for their tickets. But he continued to rhapsodize about the remarkable resemblance of the wax figures to their real-life counterparts: Empress Joséphine was exactly as she looked when she appeared on the Tuileries balcony or in her box at the Opéra; the queen of Holland was especially true to life, a fact he could verify, having seen her once himself. The emperor became increasingly uneasy, so Hortense decided to move outside into full view in hopes that Bertrand would spot her and come to their rescue. After having searched high and low, he finally found Hortense and duly paid their admission fees. The trio slipped out of the tent and linked arms as they haltingly navigated the dark allées of the Saint-Cloud gardens, laughing all the way home to the château, where they were saluted by puzzled guards. The exhausted Bertrand went right up to his room, but Hortense and Napoléon rushed to Joséphine's apartment and regaled her with a recital of their amusing adventure.[29]

Hortense was relieved to be back in Paris, and Laure Junot was equally elated: "[Hortense] brought back to us the charming parties where the most distinguished artists of France came to bring their tributes to a princess whose proficiency in the arts enabled her so perfectly to appreciate them.

There, at a round table, sat Gérard [portraitist of the imperial family] with his immortal pencil; Isabey [Joséphine's First Painter] . . . after working long upon a design for an album, ended by sketching the room we were in with such fidelity that its most trifling articles of furniture might be recognized."[30]

September 1807 began with news that jolted Europe. Because Denmark had joined Napoléon's blockade of English goods, a fleet of English ships mercilessly bombarded Copenhagen for five days, without declaring war, a vivid reminder that the much-desired but tenuous peace hung in the balance. Napoléon's blockade, which was designed to bankrupt England and thus end the hostilities, did not please the commercial and manufacturing classes because the merchandise he banned—sugar, coffee, tea, cloth, and machinery—was so in demand that smuggling began to be organized on a grand scale. Joséphine herself was guilty in a relatively modest way, for she could not resist having plant cuttings brought in from Kew for her precious greenhouse at Malmaison, and she rationalized that a cashmere shawl or two wouldn't really make that much difference.

When the theater season opened in September, Joséphine and Napoléon went as often as possible, attending the Opéra on September 4 for a presentation of *Les Prétendues*, which was ushered in by a sonorous rolling of drums. On September 19, the imperial pair witnessed a performance of *Cinna* by their friend Talma at the Théâtre Français, where they were again met with tumultuous fanfare and loud cheers. The possibility of seeing the emperor and empress always attracted huge crowds, and all the loges facing the imperial box were rented well in advance of a performance, including the seats in the uppermost balcony.

Following long-established royal custom, the court left Paris on September 21 for its fall sojourn at Fontainebleau, where they stayed until November 16. Hortense and her son followed by boat because of her delicate condition, as she was now nearly six months pregnant. As Napoléon and Joséphine were passing the hospice of Mont-au-Pierreux, the empress noticed an apparently destitute old priest and pointed him out to the emperor. He motioned the aged man to come closer and listened closely to his account of his situation, after which he doubled the priest's pension.

Having been renovated for the pope's visit, Fontainebleau was in a state of absolute splendor, which proved a worthy setting for elaborate parties, which never ceased to amaze Laure Junot: "No language can convey a clear idea of the magnificence, the magical luxury . . . the diamonds, jewels and flowers that gave splendor to the fêtes."[31] The principal attraction, however, was hunting, for Napoléon had revived this royal ritual (hunting was never merely a sport for French royalty). Joséphine followed the hunt in a carriage with her ladies, whose costumes were described by the observant Mme. Junot:

> When the mornings were fine . . . we went out hunting and breakfasted in the forest.
> The ladies wore a uniform of chamois cashmere, with collars and trimmings of green

cloth embroidered with silver, and a hat of black velvet, with a large plume of white feathers. Nothing could be more exhilarating than the sight of seven or eight open carriages whirling rapidly through the alleys of that magnificent forest, filled with ladies in this elegant costume, their waving plumes blending harmoniously with the autumnal foliage; the emperor and his . . . suite darting like a flight of arrows past them in pursuit of a stag. . . . The gentlemen's hunting uniform was of green cloth, turned up with amaranth velvet, and laced *à la Brandenbourg* on the breast and pockets with gold and silver.[32]

Hortense said that those who didn't care to hunt or were indisposed like herself found an alternative in the physics lectures of Professor Jacques-César Charles, protagonist of aeronautical science, although Joséphine herself would not have attended. She preferred the concerts and plays that enlivened her apartment in the evening, and she was busy planning for the arrival of German princes seeking favors for their small states. These gentlemen especially desired admission to Joséphine's own salon, knowing her to be unswervingly sympathetic, and she received them as kindly as at her court in Mainz.

What should have been a restful interlude was marred by furtive murmurs about the dissolution of Joséphine's marriage. Once, when Laure Junot came to pay her respects, the empress told her that "they will never be satisfied until they have driven me from the throne . . . they are inveterate against me." By "they," she meant not only the Bonaparte family but also a faction in the government that was urging the emperor to obtain a divorce. At Fontainebleau everyone seemed to notice the emperor's distracted manner and his solitary rides into the dense forests, accompanied only by his equerry Jardin. Napoléon said little, and his silence was more alarming than words. Laure believed that "the death of the young prince of Holland had evidently overthrown all of his projects."[33]

In July 1807 Joseph Fouché, the minister of police, boldly suggested to Joséphine that a divorce was needed for the good of France, but she replied that the emperor would have to make that decision. On November 19, Fouché even published a bulletin setting forth two opposing views: on the one hand were those who rallied around the empress, citing her popularity, claiming she was the emperor's talisman, and fearing that their separation would mark the end of his good fortune. On the other hand, the imperial family unanimously favored a divorce, along with others in Paris, including Fouché himself. In spite of these insults, Joséphine responded as usual, sending gifts to Mme. Fouché (it wasn't *her* fault), holding their little girl during her baptism, and even supporting Fouché when Napoléon decided to replace him.[34]

A happy diversion came for Joséphine on October 14 with the opening of a special exhibition at the museum featuring works of art acquired during the 1806–7 campaign. Vivant Denon had been hard at work. There were fifty statues, eighty busts, forty-five bronzes, and many old master paintings, mostly of the Flemish school. Joséphine was eager to see the exhibition, for her own gallery was rich in canvases by Dutch and Flemish artists, and her consoles were adorned with fine antique bronzes.

In November the emperor set out to visit Eugène, but Joséphine was not allowed to go, because of expected bad weather (in fact, Napoléon encountered a raging storm in the Mont-Cenis Pass and barely escaped into a cave). She was disappointed not to be able to see Eugène, Auguste, and her new namesake, the baby Joséphine, but Napoléon tried to make it up to her by allowing her to send a handsome present to Auguste. She wished to commission a flower—the hortensia—executed in diamonds. The Paris jewelers wanted a fortune for the piece, and since the emperor thought them all robbers, he asked Eugène to investigate its cost in Milan.

The occasion Joséphine would have enjoyed most on this Italian trip was the ceremony on December 20, 1807, in which Eugène was named prince of Venice and heir-presumptive to the throne of Italy. The baby Joséphine was given the title countess of Bologna, as well as a handsome endowment, for Napoléon continued to provide liberally for Joséphine's family. While in Venice, Eugène timidly remarked that the local population regretted its lost liberty, but Napoléon countered arrogantly that the last doge would have "considered it an honor to become a French senator," at which the incredulous Eugène could only smile nervously.[35] In the emperor's view, Italy should be organized along the lines of the French imperial model, and bringing Venice under French control marked an important stage in the unification of the kingdom of Italy.

Back in Paris, Joséphine frequently visited Hortense, who spent most of her time now on a chaise longue, although her condition did not preclude her from giving her usual soirées in the Hôtel de Lannoy, which were attended by many of the German princes who had been at Fontainebleau. Those who had lost their territory were playing upon the emotions of Joséphine and Hortense, and these intimate evening parties attracted them more than the official balls and receptions. The emperor's return on January 1, 1808, would put an end to all this, Hortense said, for he asked her if there weren't enough nice Frenchmen she could invite instead of strangers who had no real concern for them personally.

By far the most exciting event came on November 25, when the Imperial Guard made its official return from a victorious campaign. The ceremony was conducted by Marshal Bessières, followed by the eagles of the different corps: fusiliers, grenadiers, mounted troops, Mamelukes, and dragoons—all hailed by 30,000 spectators. The guard was welcomed by Frochot, prefect of the Seine, who attached a wreath of silver leaves tied with a blue ribbon to the eagle of each corps as a gift from the city of Paris. When the guard reached the Tuileries, passing under the Arc du Carrousel (still covered with scaffolding), it was an exceptionally stirring moment for Joséphine. For there was young Arrighi, prancing at the head of one surviving squadron of the empress's dragoons, which she had christened only the past year. In the evening, she looked out at the damp Tuileries gardens glowing with light, where tents lined both sides of the *grande allée* for the feast given by the municipality to welcome the guard home.

A fête followed on December 19 at the Ecole Militaire, honoring the anniversary of the coronation, a rich illumination that set the Invalides aglow and the entire Champ de Mars blazing with decorations. Joséphine and her entourage arrived, followed by the great dignitaries, ministers, and high authorities, as the officers of the guard did the honors. She watched the grenadiers and chasseurs execute various maneuvers followed by a ballet, a glorious fireworks display, and a ball that stretched far into the night. In the sunset of the year 1807, Paris was in the mood for celebration, the prosperity of the country portending a glorious new year, but Joséphine could not rejoice. She was the subject of a police bulletin of December 4, reporting outrage over the prospect of a divorce on the part of some Parisiènnes of the Faubourg Saint-Germain, even though the Faubourg was the center of pro-Bourbon sentiment.[36] Antoine Hamelin's wife was accused of having repeated confidences supposedly received from the empress herself, and other women claimed it was the emperor who was sterile. Although the movement was intended to support Joséphine, it was all acutely embarrassing for her.

There was yet another reason for Joséphine's discomfiture: on October 12, the emperor had relieved Andoche Junot of his duties as governor of Paris and sent him to command troops in Portugal in an attempt to bring the Iberian peninsula into his blockade of England, which could be enforced only if he controlled the entire Atlantic coastline. This now seemed impossible without force, so the prospect of another war loomed. Although viewed by history as a warmonger, peace was a priority for Napoléon at this time, for it signified prosperity and gave him time to continue his improvements in the capital and the provinces. But members of the Spanish royal family were squabbling among themselves, which provided the emperor with exactly the opportunity he needed. Joséphine was ordered to accompany the emperor to meet this strange family, for (as Constant saw it) his master depended upon her "exquisite perception of what was suitable . . . and her sound, infallible judgment" to help him unravel this tangled affair.[37]

When they heard that the empress of France was coming, the women of the Spanish and Portuguese courts were thrilled. Laure Junot had gone through Spain in 1805, and the first thing the queen asked her was what the empress Joséphine was like. What kind of clothes does she choose? Does she wear rouge? Any artificial flowers? So Laure described Joséphine's delicate coloring and beautiful chestnut hair, and in her best public relations manner, assured the Spanish queen that the empress dressed "in the most elegant and tasteful style. We take her as a model in all that relates to dress, not merely because she is our Sovereign, but because her exquisite taste prompts her to wear everything that is most graceful and becoming."[38]

When the Junots reached Queluz, they were again greeted with questions about their empress. As Andoche Junot entered, wearing his full-dress uniform of colonel-general of the hussars and a heron plume in his shako—an extravagant gift from Joséphine—the Spanish queen's daughter, the princess of Brazil, asked about Joséphine: Was she really as handsome as people said? Laure Junot immediately produced a miniature of the empress painted by Isabey on ivory, which satisfied their curiosity.

Napoléon's military involvement in Spain was poisonous from the start. After marching in dangerous sub-zero weather over the Sierra de Guadarrama, only to face an unremittingly hostile people, even his men openly expressed their bitter resentment. Joséphine's encounter with the Spanish rulers would be among the most unsettling of her life, and it was into this charged atmosphere that she stepped in the spring of 1808.

11

The Tide Turns

The year 1808 opened with the Invalides cannon booming a welcome to the emperor as his carriage rolled into Paris from Italy. Barely recovered from the journey, he whisked Joséphine off on January 4 to the atelier of his first painter, Jacques-Louis David. The occasion was the unveiling of the long-awaited painting of their coronation, a vast canvas containing numerous portraits that had required four years to complete. Were there nothing else to insure Joséphine's enduring fame, this painting would suffice, being a pictorial record of her finest hour. Constant reported their mutual delight, and the emperor told David that what most pleased him was his choice of the crowning of Joséphine as the central focus.

During Napoléon's absence, Joséphine had kept her eye on the continuing work at the various royal residences. She examined Pierre Fontaine's designs for her new bedchamber, checked the progress of the new Tuileries theater, and no doubt looked over the novel settings Fontaine was designing for the Italian operas that would be presented every few days during the first part of the winter season. As noted, Joséphine had brought Fontaine's diverse gifts into the service of the emperor, and he was, along with Charles Percier, among her most felicitous discoveries. One of Fontaine's responsibilities was to design provisional architecture for the public fêtes, including the setting for the coronation that appears in David's painting.

The usual court functions took place at Saint-Cloud during the winter of 1807–8, and according to Laure Junot, one of the greatest attractions of the imperial court that winter was "the collection of beautiful women who graced it," but she said that this could easily be accounted for because "almost all of the French generals and the superior officers of the Imperial Guard had married for love."[1] The emperor's sisters had to stage one ball each week: Pauline on Wednesdays and Caroline on Fridays. Caroline was a resourceful hostess; on March 4 she gave for Mardi Gras a masked ball that both Joséphine and Napoléon attended. He liked to don a mask and work his way incognito among the guests, while the painter Isabey impersonated him.

Hortense, still in Paris awaiting the birth of her third child, gave her parties on Mondays, and Caroline asked her to present one of her trademark quadrilles. The theme that Hortense chose, the Vestal Virgin, was greatly in vogue, its popularity owing to the success of Spontini's opera by that name. Hortense danced beautifully, like her father and brother, and could not resist participating in the quadrille herself, which Caroline thought contributed enormously to the Carnival spirit "since the Vestal Virgin was eight months pregnant."[2]

The Tuileries theater was inaugurated on January 9, 1808, and Laure called it a seasonal high point, for all Europe (except England) had sent representatives of their courts to honor the imperial couple—Russia, Austria, Poland, Denmark, Spain, Italy, and princes of the Confederation of the Rhine. These dignitaries made an impressive cast in their colorful uniforms splashed with a rainbow of decorations as they followed the sovereigns from the throne room of the Tuileries to the presentation in the theater. The audience's pleasure in the concert was enhanced by the theater's splendid Neoclassical decor by Percier and Fontaine. The emperor's box faced the empress's, with crimson hangings backed by mirrors that could be arranged to reflect either the audience or the spectacle. This space was calculated to show off the gowns of Joséphine and her attendants, and Constant praised Fontaine's ingenuity in "distributing the boxes to make the splendid dresses of the ladies appear to the utmost advantage."[3] Fontaine was appalled, however, by the fact that the women on this cold January evening were "almost naked, their breasts, arms, and shoulders uncovered, [since] the mode and *bon ton* of the court wanted it thus."[4] Fontaine meant, of course, that the women were following Joséphine's example in spite of Napoléon's disapproval.

Despite the distractions at the court that winter, Joséphine knew that the appointment on February 20, 1808, of Joachim Murat to commander of the French army stationed in Spain meant that the emperor was preparing to make a move toward the Spanish peninsula. Murat was officially sent to Madrid as the leader of friendly troops of an allied power, but Napoléon was concerned that the British navy continued to use Spanish ports and he needed to establish a foothold in the country. The opportunity presented itself in the form of a struggle within the Spanish royal family. Crown Prince Ferdinand was at odds with his parents, the well-intentioned but indecisive King Charles IV, whose education "had been defective, and no attempt had been made to remedy it in later years,"[5] and the queen, Maria Luisa of Parma, who was more ambitious and determined than her husband. The queen ruled the country through her lover, the minister Manuel Godoy, of whom Ambassador de Beauharnais wrote in 1807: "'Fearful, timid, excessively ignorant, greedy to a supreme degree, insatiable, in possession of all the gold of the two Spains . . . his unique talent in administration is to be profoundly corrupt. . . . Subtle, adroit, his principles are not to have any, his motive is gold and dishonesty his politics."[6] The crown prince was said to have possessed only three virtues: "he despised his father, loathed his mother, and detested Godoy."[7]

Francisco de Goya (1746–1828),
Ferdinand VII in Royal Cloak *(Prado).*
Ferdinand's portrait in royal robes was not
commissioned by the sitter because an
antipathy existed between himself and the
artist, who served as court painter for
Ferdinand's father. During the eventful days
of 1808, Ferdinand became king briefly
after his father's abdication on March 19,
but then forfeited the throne himself at
Bayonne. He wears the great collar of the
Order of the Golden Fleece and the sash
of the Order of Charles III.

Ferdinand was eager for Napoléon to recognize him as the king of Spain and to give him a Bonaparte princess as his wife, but the emperor had no such intentions. He hoped that Ferdinand, who had been imprisoned by his father for treason in October 1807, would head a faction to overthrow Godoy and perhaps his father as well. After the French troops arrived under Murat's command in mid-March, Ferdinand, who had been released in January, was supported by a popular uprising that led to Charles's abdication in Ferdinand's favor and the temporary imprisonment of Godoy. Napoléon's ultimate plan, however, was to oust the Bourbon family altogether and replace them with a king of his own choosing, and he decided to capitalize upon the weaknesses of the royal family and make them the unwitting instruments of their own downfall.

Joséphine, however, was too concerned with the political ramifications of the Spanish affair to consider its military implications. Another family wedding was being arranged to strengthen ties through the Empire, and the bride-to-be was yet another relative of Joséphine's, also named Stéphanie: her cousin Stéphanie de Tascher de la Pagerie. Joséphine's brother-in-law, François de Beauharnais, was the French ambassador to Spain, and since Crown Prince Ferdinand had just become eligible through the death of his wife, de Beauharnais suggested that Ferdinand make a formal request for Stéphanie's hand, and so he did, unaware of Napoléon's plans for his future. The Spanish court was not alone in seeking a liaison with Stéphanie de Tascher, for according to Hortense, Prince William of Württemberg also wished to marry her. But Napoléon rejected the offers of both Spain and Württemberg, declaring that Stéphanie's husband should be Duke Prosper-Louis of Arenberg, because it would mean an alliance with Belgium, of which the duke of Arenberg was prince sovereign. The duke's family was also in favor of this marriage. The bride-to-be, however, was opposed to all of these suitors, for the simple reason that she—like Stéphanie de Beauharnais before her—had fallen under the spell of the irresistible General Rapp. Improbable as it seems, Joséphine was confronted with the same problem she had faced in the spring of 1806 when she had to convince the first Stéphanie to forget her infatuation with Jean Rapp and marry Prince Charles of Baden. Neither case was simple, for Rapp had been like a family member since consular days and was highly valued by Napoléon for his fluent German and diplomatic gifts, which made him indispensable to France's advance posts on the Baltic. But Rapp already had a wife, and besides, as Joséphine pointed out, a marriage to Rapp (even if he were divorced) would be a misalliance for a member of the de Tascher de la Pagerie family. And so Joséphine set about planning a wedding for Stéphanie and the duke of Arenberg, which took place in Hortense's spacious town house on February 1. The emperor gave Stéphanie a large dowry on the condition that she buy a house in Paris, but Stéphanie had a mind of her own. Although she went through the ceremony, she refused to live with the duke of Arenberg, and in 1816 the marriage was finally annulled.

Joséphine's situation seemed to improve during the early months of 1808, for her husband could not make up his mind to leave her, despite the urging of the Bonapartes, who kept tormenting him. He loved Joséphine, she knew him better than anyone, she adapted herself so perfectly to his needs, and the thought of losing the singular ambiance she brought to their daily life was more than he could bear. One day in March, while she waited with her ladies for him to appear for the usual evening gathering in the salon, a valet summoned her, whispering that the emperor was ill. When she entered, he burst into tears, took her into his arms, and kept repeating: "Oh, my poor Joséphine, I simply cannot let you go!"[8] Comforted by the contempt he had shown for his family's attitude, Joséphine would "transform her trip to Bayonne [with him] that summer of 1808 into a veritable personal triumph, conquering the populace by her grace and smile, and submitting entirely to the caprices of her husband."[9]

The trip to Bayonne, a town in southwest France on the Spanish border, was ostensibly planned as a tour of the departments in that region, although Napoléon's real intention was to meet with the Spanish royal family. These plans were formalized in early March, and by month's end, the Saint-Cloud courtyard was cluttered with baggage-wagons, carriages, chests, portmanteaux, and trunks. The emperor, who would be away for four-and-a-half months, left on April 2, and Joséphine was to follow him in a few days. Shortly before Napoléon's departure, Hortense (near the end of her pregnancy) entered his salon to wish him good-bye just as her mother was leaving the room. Hortense found him in deep thought, and he confided to her his torment at being torn between his desire for an heir and the pain of separation from the woman so dear to him. Suddenly, he looked at his stepdaughter and exclaimed: "If only I could see your mother in your state!"[10] It was never to be, but at least Joséphine was going with him to the Spanish border, and as he became immersed in the challenge awaiting him there, any thought of divorce would be postponed for a while. Since Joséphine wanted to give Pierre Fontaine final instructions about decorating her apartment, she did not leave until April 5, although she was reluctant to leave Hortense so near delivery. The emperor reached Bayonne on April 14, but Joséphine was detained en route by an official visit to the beautiful city of Bordeaux, for which the emperor had ordered a new urban ensemble, hospital, market, and housing for the indigent.

In Bayonne—which Laure Junot described as a "pleasant little town in the Spanish style"—Napoléon was dealing with the issue of where he might lodge the French court for three months, as well as the Spaniards who would descend upon them at the end of April. He arranged to purchase and refurbish the château de Marrac, and he looked forward to Joséphine's arrival so that she could take over the preparations. Through the French ambassador to Spain, Ferdinand had pleaded with Napoléon to recognize him as king of Spain, in light of the abdication of his father. The emperor summoned Ferdinand to Bayonne, where he arrived on April 20, unaware that he was walking into a trap, for his parents had been invited to visit Bayonne on April 30, preceded by Godoy on April 26.

On April 23 came good news: the birth of Hortense's third son on the night of April 20, and the emperor spoke of his great satisfaction, ordering salvos along the length of the Spanish frontier. In Paris, the unsmiling Cambacérès had lumbered into Hortense's room to witness the birth of Charles-Louis-Napoléon, his legal duty as arch-chancellor. Talleyrand was obliged to be there too, but he was so heavily powdered that she almost suffocated when he drew near to offer his compliments. Joséphine was still in Bordeaux when she received word of her new grandson, and the letter with her marching orders arrived about the same time, telling her to leave the city on April 26 in order to reach Bayonne the following day. The ever-vigilant Constant watched as Joséphine's carriage pulled up at the château de Marrac on April 27, and the valet reported their meeting: "His Majesty received her with much tenderness and showed great solicitude for the fatigue she must have experienced, since the roads were so rough, and badly washed by rains. In the evening the town and château were illuminated."[11]

Joséphine's first sight of the Spanish king and queen and their son was shocking, as she related to Hortense several times.[12] She felt sorry for the ineffectual Charles, stout and crippled with gout as he was, and the character of Queen Maria Luisa was "written on her face," as Napoléon put it. The secretary Méneval believed that Napoléon hoped to establish in Spain "one of the fundamental bases of the repose and security of Europe,"[13] but if he was counting on any help from Spanish royalty, he was sadly mistaken, for after their first meeting, it was apparent that any regeneration of Spain under such rulers was patently impossible.[14] Méneval testified that when they met, the deposed king tried to attack his son with a cane and María Luisa had to be restrained from plunging her talons into Ferdinand's eyes.

Despite the trying circumstances, Joséphine tendered the visitors such an amiable reception that Charles IV was moved to tears by this touching consideration from his powerful ally. Although still recovering from her journey, Joséphine invited the Spanish rulers to dinner at Marrac, and her dilemma as hostess can only be imagined, for seated at the table were Charles IV, his wife, and her paramour, Godoy. Ferdinand was apparently missing from the dinner party, for we are told that he was called into the room afterwards, at which point his father insisted upon retaining the crown.

Before anything could be resolved, news from Madrid changed the whole picture, for on May 2 Spaniards rose up in arms against the French because of what they perceived as the abduction of the royal family. Many French troops were massacred in the streets, and Murat took reprisals the following day, the infamous day immortalized in Goya's *Third of May*. In an effort to restore order, the emperor, who finally secured the abdication of both Charles and Ferdinand, gave Joseph Bonaparte the crown of Spain on June 7. Joseph had been the king of Naples since March 1806, and in his place Napoléon made Joachim Murat the new king of Naples. This made Caroline Bonaparte the queen she had always wanted to be, but both Murat and his wife regretted losing the coveted throne of Spain to Joseph, who was reluctant to leave his château at Mortefontaine and did not arrive in Madrid as king of Spain until July 20. He soon found his position there untenable and on August 9 wrote to the emperor that he was "an object of terror and execration," being regarded by the Spaniards as an invader, which in fact he was.

Although Talleyrand is said to have disapproved of the Spanish venture from the outset, he became a victim of it in a curious way. As the new vice grand elector, he was ordered to house the three Spanish princes, including the sullen Ferdinand, who were sent to stay in Talleyrand's château of Valençay, where he was to be their unwilling host for six long years. It was "a neat stroke of Napoléon's malice, because the Spaniards' various unintellectual hobbies caused a certain amount of damage to the estate."[15] The former Spanish king, queen, and Godoy were exiled to Fontainebleau, then to Compiègne, and finally to Marseilles.

Insofar as Joséphine's relationship with her husband was concerned, the stay in Bayonne was exceedingly rewarding, as she had written to Eugène on May 31: "I am with the emperor; each day seems to make him increasingly more amiable and more perfect for me."[16] But the sunny atmosphere clouded when she learned that her lady-in-waiting Mme. de Montmorency had written to her mother in Paris, assuring her that divorce could not be far away, for it was general knowledge that a costly diadem for the new empress had just been ordered from a Paris jeweler.

Jean-Baptiste Joseph Wicar (1762–1834), Joseph Bonaparte (Château de Versailles). Joseph Bonaparte was valued as a skilled negotiator, so Napoléon made him king of Naples in March 1806 and then king of Spain in April 1808. A true "amateur" of the arts, Joseph probably commissioned this portrait by David's pupil Wicar, who was director of the Academy of St. Luke in Naples and owner of an incomparable collection of ancient drawings and wax models. The Athena statue is a flattering reference to Joseph's sagacity, and he proved to be a generous supporter of the arts during his exile in America.

Joséphine left Marrac with her husband on July 21 to tour the western provinces of France, but they were fraught with anxiety all the way, as distressing bulletins arrived from the Spanish front at each stop. On August 1, they reached Bordeaux, which Lucie de la Tour du Pin reported was "very much taken up with the affairs of Spain, since several refugees from that country had already arrived there."[17] When news of the humiliating capitulation of General Dupont before the Spanish insurgents arrived the next day, the emperor was so upset that he decided they should push on quickly to Paris to allay fears in the capital.

Lucie—who always managed to be in the right place at the right time wearing the right costume—noted that even during their brief stop in Bordeaux, protocol was scrupulously observed, which meant that Mme. d'Arberg must have gone along, for she knew better than anyone the usage of courts. Lucie was always amazed that "the emperor, with all Spain and all Europe on his hands . . . still had time to dictate the empress's order of the day, in the most minute detail, even which ensembles she was to wear."[18] Yet the pleasurable aspects of the tour (the tender intimacy with her husband and his constant attentions) were drawing to a close, and Joséphine's apprehension steadily mounted as they neared Paris. What she needed most was a trustworthy soul with whom to discuss her personal affairs, so she opted for Lucie's husband, the marquis de la Tour du Pin. "Accustomed to the adulation of some, the deception of others, [Joséphine] found great relief in talking with my husband," wrote Lucie, "and she opened her heart to him on a subject [the divorce] which she had not dared to broach to any person of her entourage."[19] Joséphine confided to him her belief that Talleyrand was to blame for urging such an action upon the emperor, but what she did not know was that Talleyrand had already discussed such a prospect with Lucie herself in Paris.

By August 14, Joséphine and Napoléon were back again at Saint-Cloud, greeted by Hortense with her new baby, whom they saw for the first time. As usual, Joséphine fretted over Hortense's health and unhappy marriage (the reconciliation after the death of Napoléon-Charles had been brief), so she insisted that Hortense and her two children come for a long visit. The very next day, Joséphine had to stage the annual diplomatic reception in honor of the emperor's birthday, and Napoléon took advantage of the presence of Prince Metternich, ambassador from Austria, to query him confidentially as to the Austrians' real political designs, for he was concerned about the fragile Austrian situation. Napoléon could hardly have expected a candid answer, because Metternich, who suspected that Napoléon intended to liquidate the Austrian Empire—doing to the Habsburgs what he had done to the Bourbons—was hoping for an Austrian alliance with Russia. But outwardly the relationship was a cordial one, since Joséphine invariably received the Metternichs with courtesy.

After the customary celebration in Paris, which culminated with rockets swishing through the night sky over the Seine, the imperial couple toured the Tuileries Palace with Pierre Fontaine and M. de Fleurieu, now governor of Paris, to see the final renovation, including the new staircase for the museum. When Napoléon asked why the triumphal Arc du Carrousel being constructed at the entrance to the Tuileries was still covered, he was told that the statue of himself in a chariot designed for the top of the arch was not finished.[20] He was very upset, saying that the chariot would remain empty because the arch was built to glorify his army and not himself. Joséphine surely tried to placate him, begging him to consider the feelings of the architect and of Vivant Denon, whose well-intentioned idea it had been. Afterward, they moved to the Tuileries balcony to hear the concert given by the Conservatory of Music, returning to Saint-Cloud the same evening.

Life at the Tuileries now resumed its regular pace. In the mornings, as the emperor worked in his study, Joséphine embroidered with her ladies in one of the salons, although she was often summoned to another salon to meet with an endless stream of petitioners who wished an audience with her. According to Constant, "the empress was extremely generous and bestowed much in alms. . . . Many émigrés lived solely on her benefactions; she also kept up a very active correspondence with the Sisters of Charity, who nursed the sick, and she sent them a multitude of things. Her valets were ordered to go in every direction, carrying to the needy the assistance of her inexhaustible benevolence. . . . All these gifts . . . so widely diffused, received an inestimable value from the grace with which they were offered, and the good judgment with which they were distributed."[21]

Hortense, however, found all this rather dull (despite the joy of a Paris without Louis), and life with her parents at the Tuileries Palace was too confining for the twenty-five-year-old queen of Holland, who was, according to Laure Junot, the animating spirit of every party she attended. Furthermore, Hortense often had to try to defend her mother against the emperor's entirely warranted charges of prodigality. Joséphine always dreaded the end-of-the-year accounting, but after his initial wrath, he always forgave his penitent wife, warning her to be more careful in the future. She was trying to be the model of circumspect domesticity during these days at Saint-Cloud, remaining at her husband's beck and call. He often summoned her for a chat on the balcony overlooking the magnificent gardens and cascades or for an afternoon trip in the carriage. In the evenings, the three dined together alone (in the absence of state functions), after which Joséphine played whist, a game that Hortense thought a colossal bore. Napoléon sought his study, dictating to several secretaries simultaneously on various topics. Once, when asked how he could possibly manage this, he succinctly replied, "I know how to compartmentalize."

Devoted daughter though she was, Hortense was not quite as chaste as her memoirs imply, although she admits to an infatuation with Comte Charles de Flahaut even before 1804, the year they doubtlessly became intimate.[22] Her closest friends lived double (if not triple) lives as well. Caroline Murat, who delighted in attracting other women's husbands or lovers, threw herself shamelessly at Andoche Junot and also set her cap for the interesting Prince Metternich, who was himself infatuated with Laure Junot. But Caroline left the field open to others when she departed in September for Naples, where she played the role of dominant queen to Murat's passive king.

Laure Junot remained in Paris, flirting with Metternich in the grotto of the Folie de Saint-James, while her husband was in Portugal. Court gossip had it that the flamboyant Junot was consoling himself away from Laure by maintaining what might be called a virtual seraglio. Nor did the Junots adhere to the emperor's embargo on British goods even while in Paris, always managing to devise ingenious ways to secure imported luxuries despite the blockade that had been decreed in November 1806, closing all ports on the continent to British commerce. Although no excuses can be made for Hortense and her circle, they were certainly no more decadent than the society attached to most European courts of the time; owing to the political and cultural hegemony of France, however, they were the most visible.

On the beautiful evening of August 21, 1808, the empress and emperor left Saint-Cloud for Paris to view one of the most impressive presentations ever offered the crown of France, a gift from Czar Alexander, with whom Napoléon had recently signed the peace treaty at Tilsit and would shortly meet at Erfurt. The Russian ruler had sent four carriages laden with cases that had arrived on June 24, and they contained two malachite tables of medium size, an enormous malachite vase in the form of a cup, another with a gray jasper base, and two drums of malachite columns matching the tables and vase. When Fontaine saw them, he decided they should immediately be mounted with the rich gilt bronzes that were a speciality of French craftsmen, and this must have been accomplished in record time. After a Mass and a reception for the diplomatic corps, Napoléon and Joséphine moved into the Gallery of Diana, where the Russian ambassador, Alexandre Kourakine, made the formal presentation.

For Joséphine, that August was filled with both pleasure and responsibility, for she had to intervene yet again in the arrangement of a marriage that her husband greatly desired—that of his favorite aide-de-camp, General Henri-Gatien Bertrand. This time Joséphine agreed with Napoléon's choice of bride for Bertrand, Fanny Dillon, who happened to be another of Joséphine's relatives and the sister of Mme. de la Tour du Pin. Although Bertrand was in love with Fanny, she cared for someone else, so Joséphine was asked to resolve the problem, a formidable challenge. Fanny was enamored of the Italian prince Alphonse Pignatelli, a match that pleased her arrogant sister, Lucie, "for I should have preferred to have my sister called Pignatelli rather than Bertrand."[23]

Although Joséphine could hardly rejoice in the dénouement, her problem was nevertheless resolved by the hand of Providence. Poor Prince Pignatelli died suddenly of consumption, leaving Joséphine free to receive the marquis de la Tour du Pin as spokesman for Fanny's interests. The two had a long conversation in the empress's alcove, which Talleyrand claimed was overheard by Napoléon, and when the emperor himself suddenly appeared and persisted in favor of General Bertrand, Fanny acceded. Lucie described her sister as "extremely frivolous, with the fantasy of a Créole like her mother," and it may have been this aspect of Fanny's personality that appealed to Napoléon, for she no doubt reminded him of the young Joséphine. In any case, he ordered Fanny to accompany the empress during the court's week-long sojourn to Fontainebleau, even paying for the expensive wardrobe Fanny was required to wear in Joséphine's company.

Anonymous artist, Henriette Lucie Dillon, Marquise de la Tour du Pin *(1770–1853). Lucie was a distant relative of Joséphine's and, curiously, the step-daughter of Mme. de Longpré, a mistress of Joséphine's first husband, Alexandre de Beauharnais. Lucie had been a* dame du palais *to Marie-Antoinette, and her husband was governor of Versailles, so her memoirs of the former régime and the Empire are valuable, though tinged with an air of superiority. Like Talleyrand, she went briefly into exile in America, where she coped ingeniously with her deprivations in the "wilderness."*

The final wedding plans had to be made very quickly because the emperor had ordained that the marriage take place before he had to leave for an important conference at Erfurt on September 22. Although, as Lucie reported, the emperor found time to regulate the smallest details of Bertrand's marriage, the burden fell upon Joséphine and Hortense, at whose summer home, the château of Saint-Leu just outside Paris, both the religious ceremony and festivities were to take place on September 17.

A long line of carriages emblazoned with coats-of-arms filed along the road to Saint-Leu as all the dignitaries of the court set out on September 16 to attend the soirée at Hortense's château the night before the marriage The ceremony took place the next day at 3:30, followed by an elaborate meal, then a dance. Many of Hortense's Paris friends were in attendance, but Lucie noticed that Hortense (who always liked to dance) appeared to be distracted and was not in the best frame of mind. The reason was that Joséphine had been ordered, as usual, to select a gift of jewelry for the bride, and for Fanny, it had to be emeralds surrounded by diamonds. When the emperor saw the pieces, however, he found them not grand enough for Bertrand's wife, so he turned to Hortense for the solution. As it happened, his stepdaughter owned a similar parure, so Hortense had to sacrifice her own exquisite ensemble of emeralds and diamonds to Fanny Bertrand. Perhaps Hortense contented herself with the fact that her sapphire-and-diamond parure complemented her delicate blonde beauty more effectively than emeralds anyway.

Less than a week after the Bertrands' wedding, the emperor prepared to leave for the large European congress at Erfurt, where he would meet Czar Alexander again, but Joséphine would not be going. Nor was Eugène, for "even though he punctually executes my orders," his stepfather said, "he does not have the art of persuasion."[24] But Talleyrand did, and despite his reservations about the crafty prince of Benevento, Napoléon realized that he was the only diplomat with the necessary knowledge and skill to execute his plans. The emperor's aim was to fortify his relationship with Russia by ceding Moldavia and Wallachia to the czar, shutting Austria out of the Balkans. Then, he hoped, with himself as emperor of the West, and Alexander as emperor of the East, England would be brought to her knees by the embargo. Talleyrand, however, had suggested to his master than Austria could be France's ally against England, but apparently Napoléon turned a deaf ear.

Just before his departure, Napoléon took Joséphine out to Rueil for their last days together at Malmaison. This final visit must have been heart-wrenching for her, for she knew that her days as empress were numbered, and the château was haunted by memories of their happy years there during the Consulate. She must have remembered how Hortense, Eugène, Isabey, and the promising young officers delighted in presenting impromptu theatricals on the stage of the little theater, or how they played games on the clipped green English turf. Napoléon's secretary Méneval reported that the gathering at Malmaison all played prisoner's base one more time and that Joséphine herself had entered into the revelry. "It was in the evening; and footmen bore lighted torches, and followed the players when they went beyond the reach of the light. The emperor fell once while he was trying to catch the empress and was taken prisoner; but he soon broke bounds and began to run again . . . and carried off Joséphine in spite of the protests of the other players."[25]

Hortense said that her mother wept bitterly as her stepfather was leaving, for she had heard rumors that the czar's sister, the Grand Duchess Catherine, was under consideration as the new empress of France, and Joséphine was afraid the subject would be broached when Alexander and Napoléon met again. He guessed why Joséphine was crying and assured her that it was only a political interview, unrelated to any sort of family alliance,[26] but this was hardly comforting to Joséphine, who knew better than anyone that every "family alliance" was motivated by purely political reasons. Nor could she be happy that Talleyrand was going, for he had made peace with his former rival, Fouché, and the pair were now the most vocal proponents of the emperor's divorce, believing that the only way for Napoléon to establish his position was by making a royal marriage. Napoléon agreed but was still reluctant to pay the personal cost of having to relinquish his Joséphine.

Reports that reached Joséphine about Erfurt only heightened her disappointment at being left behind, for besides Alexander and his brother, the Grand Duke Constantine, there were present many notables whom she had received in past years, such as the kings of Bavaria, Württemberg, Saxony, and Wesphalia. She could clearly envision the two palaces set up for the meeting, furnished with magnificent tapestries, bronzes, furniture, and porcelain, because the Garde Meuble had arranged the same luxurious settings for her courts in Mainz and Strasbourg—French showmanship in the decorative arts at its best. What Joséphine especially regretted missing was the performance of that fine interpreter of classical tragedy Catherine Duchenois, whose debut in *Phèdre* at the Théâtre Français in 1802 Joséphine herself had sponsored.

The Congress of Erfurt turned out to be part theater, part conference, and mostly intrigue. The theater was provided by the Comédie Française, and the conference consisted of Napoléon's and Alexander's ostensibly amicable talks by day. The intrigue took the form of Talleyrand's late-evening meetings with the czar over cups of strong tea in the salon of the Princess von Thurn und Taxis. Although in his memoirs he did not admit to betraying the emperor, it is believed that Talleyrand, working on behalf of Austria, told the czar about Napoléon's true motives and recommended that Russia stand by Austria, against Napoléon's wishes. After his final conversation with the czar, Napoléon remained silent for a long time, knowing he had obtained nothing and suspecting that he had been duped, for "nothing is sadder than a *fête manquée*."[27] Although Napoléon would never see Alexander again (except on the battlefield), the czar and his brother Constantine would enter Joséphine's life six years later in a singularly curious manner.

The misgivings that Joséphine expressed to her husband proved to be fully justified, for at Erfurt Napoléon had finally confided to Talleyrand his torment over having to give up his wife, even as he knew he must ally himself to a princess from one of the great European houses in order to found a dynasty. Napoléon also opened himself up to Armand Caulaincourt, his ambassador to the czar, but he was less abrupt than with Talleyrand for he knew that Caulaincourt was very close to Joséphine: "I love Joséphine . . . never will I be happier [than with her]. . . . This act will be a sacrifice for me. My family, Talleyrand, Fouché, all the men of state ask it of me in the name of France."[28]

Anxiety was also the temper of life in Paris, especially in Joséphine's circle at the Tuileries. Life appeared to go on as usual, with complimentary speeches from Prefect Frochot delivered to a corps of the Grande Armée and recurrent banquets staged for the troops in the Tivoli Gardens. But Joséphine was well aware of the columns of French troops marching through the city all month long on their way to the Spanish front. The solemn mood was somewhat dispelled, however, with the opening of the Salon of 1808, which attracted visitors from far and wide. Vivant Denon had already sent an enthusiastic note to Duroc, grand marshal of the palace, detailing what was to be expected: "The Salon fixed for October 14 this year will be the most impressive there has ever been . . . by [the artists's] great talents. Everyone will place His Majesty's reign in the front rank in the arts, as it is in warfare, science, and literature."[29]

Antoine Gros (1771–1835), Napoléon Visiting the Salon of 1808 *(Château de Versailles). At the Salon of 1808, more than 600 works were exhibited, including canvases by at least six of Joséphine's protégés: Prud'hon, Boilly, Gros, Girodet, Elisabeth Chaudet, and Gérard. Her favorite, Prud'hon, and Baron Gros were especially honored. In this unfinished painting Joséphine stands at the right, robed in an ermine-trimmed* redingote; *Hortense is beside her, wearing a tiara, and Napoléon-Louis is looking up at his grandmother.*

Joséphine went to the exhibition several times, for among the paintings on display were David's dazzling coronation painting, Gros's troubling *Battle of Eylau,* and Horace Vernet's dramatic *Austerlitz,* which portrayed General Rapp presenting prisoners to the emperor. Joséphine herself had lent two major works of sculpture to the exhibition: Canova's *Hebe* and Cartellier's *Modesty.* The artists were always gratified to see the empress there, for her interest in their work was genuine, as proved by her generous patronage and encouragement, and she always made a point of speaking to each artist in turn, "with the grace that was so familiar to those who knew her," as the Paris journals reported.[30] Napoléon returned to Paris late on October 19, and on October 23, he accompanied Joséphine to the Salon, where he honored Baron Gros with his own cross of the Legion d'Honneur.

Joséphine's reunion with her husband was another of those brief interludes, for he remained only ten days at Saint-Cloud before setting out again on October 29 for Bayonne, a stopping point on his way to Spain. Constant noted that he had the greatest difficulty dissuading Joséphine from going with him, but he did allow her and Hortense to accompany him as far as Rambouillet, where they spent the night before his departure the next day. As he was leaving, Hortense saw her mother more dispirited than usual, and she asked Napoléon point blank: "Won't you ever stop going to war?" He appeared to be taken aback, and after a long pause he responded: "Do you think I do it for my amusement? Surely you know I prefer to remain quietly in a good bed, to have a good dinner . . . rather than suffer the privations that await me. . . . I can do other things besides fight, but I go out of necessity to my duties to France; it is not I who dispose events; I obey them."[31]

Napoléon insisted that the reason he could not take Joséphine was that he needed her to remain in the capital during his absence, and he urged her to appear in public whenever possible to maintain a climate of optimism. His final injunction was followed by a letter of November 26 ordering her to be back in the Tuileries by December 21 and to have a concert performed in the theater there every eight days; the message concluded with his affectionate greetings to her, Hortense, and "M. Napoléon" (Hortense's second son).[32]

So once again, Joséphine showed herself at the Opéra and Comédie Française, frequented the salons, and participated in public events such as the reception for students from the École Polytechnique. The sculpture salon in the Musée Napoléon attracted huge crowds eager to see the masterpieces that had been transported at great expense from the Villa Borghese in Rome by Pauline's husband, Prince Camillo Borghese. Napoléon had bought this distinguished collection of Borghese antiquities the previous year (1807), and there were 523 pieces—among them statues, busts, herms, 170 bas-reliefs, sarcophagi, and vases, all of which afforded wonderful models for the student artists.

At the end of December, Joséphine entertained the Russian ambassador, Alexandre Kourakine, who had presented the sumptuous malachite gifts from the czar on August 21. On December 21, the emperor had written from Spain advising her that Kourakine was granted permission to call on her and the imperial family, and that she was to keep the eminent visitor amused.[33] This assignment would have challenged even Joséphine's ingenuity, for the elegant Kourakine was renowned for his magnificent dinner parties, and his knowledge of the art of the table carried such weight that he was able to introduce into highest social circles *service à la russe*, which replaced the time-honored *service à la française*. In the French tradition, food was already placed upon the table in silver or silver-gilt terrines and other covered serving pieces when the guests arrived; Kourakine's innovation, which decreased the number of ornamental tureens and used bouquets of flowers and fruit compotes as decoration, represented an almost complete break with the past and signified the beginning of modern table settings.

Joséphine entertained the urbane ambassador by taking him to see her heated glass conservatory with its tropical trees in bloom and its beds filled with fragrant jasmine, lobelias, gardenias, bougainvilla, amaryllis, and other exotica that Kourakine had probably never seen. Then she conducted him around her art gallery, for many Russian intellectuals (including the immensely rich Count Stroganoff) were drawn to Western European art. Little did Joséphine dream that many of the paintings and the masterpieces of sculpture she was showing to Kourakine would some day form part of the treasures of the Hermitage Museum in Saint Petersburg.

Joséphine was also occupied with her ongoing struggle with Pierre Fontaine. Her own taste was for relative simplicity, whereas Fontaine was basically committed to the rich decoration of imperial Rome. She was disappointed with his decoration of her apartments at the Tuileries, and the architect recorded their meeting in his journal: "She said that we had not conformed to her command and instead of the lovely things she had ordered, we had overdone the paneling and ceilings with ornaments that were too heavy and out of style. . . . I asked her pardon, being persuaded that I would find refuge in her goodness rather than in her reason."[34]

Earlier in December, at the same time that Joséphine was involved in the annual series of parties commemorating the coronation, Napoléon had arrived in Madrid and summoned the junta to lay down its arms. Madrid capitulated on December 4, but a month later, on January 2, Napoléon made the sudden and ultimately disastrous decision to leave Spain after receiving a certain mail bag from his postal commissioner, Antoine Lavalette. Had he stayed in Spain, the English would most likely have relinquished their interests in the country and never made another attempt there. This decision is one of the greatest riddles of Napoléon's career, for it gave the Spanish renewed courage, and the ongoing rivalries among French generals did the rest.

But why did Napoléon leave the field at such a critical moment, and what was in the bag other than the usual dispatches from the foreign minister, Champagny? There was a report confirming that his own sister Caroline and her husband, Joachim Murat, were working with Talleyrand and Fouché to bring about the divorce, but there was a third item, a letter from the king of Bavaria reporting a serious military threat from Austria. At the end of 1808, Joséphine had written her husband from Paris that the court believed a confrontation with Austria was imminent, but he reassured her, candidly confiding to her some details of his plan. "If [Austria makes war] I have 150,000 men in Germany, and as many on the Rhine, and 400,000 Germans to respond. . . . Russia will not separate from me. They are crazy in Paris; all goes well."[35] Apparently, his confidence had been shaken by the latest news from home, for Napoléon set out from Valladolid on January 17 at full tilt, traveling so fast that his retinue couldn't keep up with him. Relays of horses had been sent on ahead, and at one stage he covered ninety miles in six hours. The emperor was headed for Paris.

12

Flight of the Island Bird

$\mathcal{O}$ ne conspicuous personality who remained a constant fixture in Joséphine's life was Arch-Chancellor Jean-Jacques Cambacérès, whom Isser Woloch regarded as one of Napoléon's "three iron men."[1] In various crises, Joséphine had confided in this eminent jurist who had so greatly assisted in her husband's rise to power, and Napoléon—in gratitude for Cambacérès's services—had named him duke of Parma in March 1808, with the proper "gratifications." This had enabled him to buy the fine Hôtel de Roquelaure on the Boulevard Saint-Germain and to acquire superb furnishings from the Mobilier National. Here the arch-chancellor led the life of a *grand seigneur*, offering dinner parties each Tuesday and Saturday for sixteen to eighteen people. Since his table was reputedly the best in Paris, his friends sent him rare delicacies from every corner of the Empire to titillate the palates of his guests.

To celebrate the New Year 1809, Camabacérès gave a special party to honor his friend the Empress Joséphine. Although both setting and cuisine were calculated to delight the most epicurean tastes, the party fell rather flat. None of his dinners was ever truly convivial, since the arch-chancellor rarely smiled, but Laure Junot reported that this one "surpassed all its predecessors in dullness," for throughout the meal the host maintained a glacial silence that discouraged any sort of levity on the part of his guests. Contributing to the dismal atmosphere was the dark, gloomy house itself, for the eccentric Cambacérès could not often bring himself to buy the quantity of expensive white wax candles required to illuminate such a fashionable establishment.

The sobriety of the evening was heightened as well by Joséphine's pensive air, for the guests were speaking guardedly about rumors of war with Austria, and Prince Metternich, who had just arrived from Vienna, was unusually constrained despite his habitual courtesy. Laure Junot thought this was a reaction to his cool reception at the Tuileries, where the Metternichs had not been invited to dine with Joséphine, or even with Caroline or Pauline, probably as a result of instructions the emperor had conveyed through Denon. Laure thought this imprudent gesture contributed to Metternich's becoming an irreconcilable enemy of France, but this is hardly possible since war with Austria was already in the offing, and Metternich had never been a friend of Napoléon's. Hortense had overruled her stepfather, however, and stood her ground, inviting Princess Metternich to join her own circle, for neither she nor Joséphine saw any reason to offend the Metternichs personally.[2]

While awaiting the emperor's return from Spain, Joséphine continued to handle delicate matters concerning military personnel and their families. One concerned a soldier whose entire life was dedicated to the cause of the emperor, General Charles Lefèbvre, who was now with the army in Spain. Napoléon's letter to Joséphine of December 31, 1808, had told her that "Lefèbvre was taken . . . his horse was injured and drowned. . . . The current carried [Lefèbvre] down the river, where he was made prisoner by the English. Console his wife."[3] Joséphine must have summoned Mme. Lefèbvre and broken the news immediately, although she could offer little consolation. The poor woman would have to wait four years to see her husband again. General Lefèbvre finally managed to escape in 1812, just in time for him to participate in the ill-fated Russian campaign.

During her husband's nine-week absence, Joséphine had received fourteen letters from him, entrusting to her military information that would today be called classified and assuring her of his devotion. To be sure, these were no longer the impassioned notes he had feverishly penned from the battlefields of Italy, but his faithful correspondence proves that the woman in whom he confided never ceased to occupy a major place in his mind and heart. This casts Joséphine in an entirely different light from that of the frivolous sentimentalist portrayed by some of her biographers, and Napoléon's confidence in her meant that he not only honored her intelligence but he also trusted her discretion. This did not, of course, dispel the vexing problem of the succession and the inevitable divorce, but Joséphine could console herself that this was a matter of politics and was unrelated to her husband's unquestioned affection for her. In addition to masterminding the selection of a new empress, Talleyrand, working with Fouché, the minister of police, was also said to be secretly drawing up a list of people to replace the emperor in case he failed to return from Spain. None of the emperor's brothers was acceptable, so their choice lay between Joachim Murat and Eugène de Beauharnais, who wielded a strong claim as the emperor's adopted son. Talleyrand and Fouché seemed to favor Murat because of his malleability, whereas Eugène was known to be incorruptible.

Joséphine, always prey to random gossip, was told that "Murat had boasted he would run Eugène through with his sword if he stood in his way to the throne."[4] True or not, her letter of January 2, 1809, reminded Eugène that the Bonaparte "family detests my own, in spite of the fact that I have done nothing but good toward them. . . . I am keeping completely silent about all this, and in my position, one is often obliged to live with enemies, but it is always good to know who they are."[5] Her summary of the situation was accurate (with certain exceptions), although when she married Bonaparte, Joséphine had no idea she was stepping onto a battlefield where no truce would be declared. It was a war she could never win, being so greatly outnumbered, in spite of her husband's unwavering affection and support for members of her own family. Joséphine had attempted to ameliorate the relationship between the two families, caring for young Jérôme when he was Eugène's comrade in his Saint-Germain *pension*, and paying Madame Mère deferential respect. But it had not been easy for this dignified Corsican matron to accept Bonaparte's marriage to a former demi-mondaine, nor could she approve of Joséphine's extravagance, for this thrifty, realistic woman set aside large sums of money during the height of the Empire, believing the Bonapartes' prosperity to be ephemeral and suspecting that one day she would have several ex-kings and ex-queens on her hands.

On the morning of January 23, 1809, a thunder of artillery suddenly announced the emperor's return to Paris, and at 8 A.M. his carriage drew up in front of the Tuileries. Fontaine noted in his memoirs that Napoléon would never have been expected at that hour under normal circumstances, and the empress had been obliged to rise quickly to properly receive her husband. His sudden reappearance in Paris had caught her completely off guard, for she had just been reading bulletins from the army in Spain that were reassuring soldiers' families that all was well. He must have given her only a fleeting embrace, for according to Louis Bausset, prefect of the palace and Napoléon's chamberlain, the emperor plunged immediately into his work "without a moment of repose."[6] He then toured the newly refurbished apartments, followed by a breathless Fontaine, who now had to endure the emperor's criticisms of the decor and furnishings after he had just finished placating the empress.[7] The next day, Napoléon and Joséphine received city officials with the usual formalities, and on January 27—after he had called in Fouché and reprimanded him severely for scheming behind his back with Talleyrand—they went off to the Opéra.

Dealing with Talleyrand was a different matter, for Napoléon could not forgive him for his duplicity, especially after he had declared to one and all that he had tried to dissuade his master from going to Spain, hypocritically lamenting the folly of an intervention he himself had publicly supported.[8] Napoléon's relationship with Talleyrand was already strained in any case, but the manner in which he confronted Talleyrand on January 28, was so dramatic that it would be discussed for weeks in the salons of Paris and Europe. The emperor summoned the privy council and in front of everyone erupted violently against Talleyrand, accusing him of being a thief, liar, and traitor.[9] He dismissed Talleyrand from his post as grand chamberlain, although he did retain his titles as vice grand elector and prince of Benevento.

Joséphine probably suspected that the particularly memorable social season over which she now presided would be her last, and Laure Junot thought that "nothing could even approach the court . . . in this winter of 1808–9, for it had become to a supreme degree both beautiful and brilliant."[10] The season began with a glamorous ball at the house of Champagny, the minister of foreign affairs, and not to be outdone, the Italian minister, Ferdinando Marescalchi, staged a masked ball on

February 8 for which he embellished his Paris mansion with orange trees, exotic flowering shrubs, and pots of fresh flowers blooming out of season. The imperial couple was so impressed by Marescalchi's decorations that they remained in the rooms for more than an hour, Napoléon stopping at intervals to address his customary words to the ladies, as Joséphine stood smiling beside him. Even the parsimonious Cambacérès offered another party—a masked ball on February 14 to honor the emperor and empress.

This endless round of parties required Joséphine to appear in a wide array of gowns and jewels in order to proclaim the prosperity of the French crown. As the most conspicuous woman on any occasion, she could not wear the same gown twice, and her closet brimmed with 673 dresses in velvet or silk and 33 in cashmere. It may have been at this time that Napoléon gave her an extravagant parure worth more than 100,000 francs, consisting of a diadem, necklace, comb, plaque for her belt, earrings, and bracelet; if so, it was one of his farewell gifts to his wife, whose fate he knew was sealed.

Joséphine's reputation for prodigality derived, in large part, from her inability to resist the trinkets offered by the tradesmen who crowded her rooms and from whom she bought perfumes, boxes, bonbons, a tree of singing birds, and the mechanical toys that delighted her grandchildren. But we have also seen her equal extravagance in giving to the destitute, which also contributed to her chronic indebtedness. At the beginning of the year, however, she tried once again to turn over a new leaf as she assured Eugène in her letter of January 2: "As for my debts, I have found a new means of order and economy upon which I am counting a great deal; this begins with the new year."[11] In spite of her efforts to reform, she was still able to extract almost anything from Napoléon himself, as he later confessed to Caulaincourt: "It does me good to see a happy face; but I am compelled to defend myself against this natural disposition, lest advantage be taken of it. I found that out more than once with Joséphine, who was always begging me for things, and could even cry me into granting what I ought to have refused her."[12]

As Napoléon and Joséphine were attending a performance of *Andromache* in the Tuileries theater on the evening of April 23, a telegraph was handed to Napoléon informing him that Archduke Charles, Austria's most competent commander, had entered Bavaria on April 9, crossing the Inn River without any declaration of war. The imperial couple quickly slipped out of the theater at the end of the third act. Napoléon decided he must leave for the front within four days, and this time he decided that Joséphine should go with him, so she immediately summoned her ladies to prepare for the journey, and at 4:30 A.M. on April 13, their carriage stole away from the palace under cover of darkness. The emperor wanted Joséphine to reestablish her court in the imperial palace at Strasbourg during the campaign, and he left instructions for Hortense and her children to join her mother, for he knew his stepdaughter would be an immense asset at court.

As for Eugène, none of this came as a surprise. Napoléon had expected an advance by the Austrians for some time and had already dispatched his campaign plan, telling Eugène to prepare

Albrecht Adam (1786-1862), La Cavalleria del Regno d'Italia (Bibliothèque Marmottan). This aquatint by Adam (whom Eugène engaged as his painter in Vienna in 1809) portrays the viceroy reviewing his cavalry— three regiments of dragoons and four of chasseurs à cheval—in the square in front of the Sforza Palace in Milan. Prince Eugène, with cavalry mustache, is mounted on a gray horse in the foreground.

defenses behind the Adige River. The young viceroy assured the emperor that the Army of Italy would be in fighting form by April 1 and expressed his joy that the moment had come "since for so long I have been of so little use to you."[13] It was a mercy, however, that Eugène had no idea of what the next three years held in store, for this war with Austria would be far more serious than previous conflicts. This time Napoléon had to deal with a rebellious Spain buttressed by England, which was forwarding substantial subsidies to Austria, with whom England signed a treaty on April 12.

Before Eugène received orders from Napoléon to move toward the town of Pordenone, near Venice, the Archduke John of Austria (brother of Archduke Charles) made a declaration of war to the Italian advance posts with the objective of recapturing territories that had once belonged to Austria and to incite a general insurrection against the French. The Austrians advanced in three columns, and at Sacile on April 16 came Eugène's first pitched battle as commander-in-chief of the Army of Italy. Facing Archduke John's superior force of cavalry, Eugène's own cavalry arrived too late to help his troops, and his men were thrown back, fortunately not pursued by the Austrians. Napoléon was highly displeased and threatened to send Murat from Naples so that Eugène would operate under his orders, the one thing the viceroy could not tolerate. His old protector, Marshal Duroc, consoled him by saying that one battle lost was nothing, but he urged Eugène by all means to keep the emperor precisely informed of the situation in Italy.

When she heard about Eugène's setback at Sacile, Joséphine shared her son's humiliation and sent him a firm but philosophical letter from Strasbourg on April 28: "The unhappiness you have just experienced I understand very well, but it did not crush me. It is in painful moments that we must be armed with courage and I count greatly on yours. Reverses are the tests of brave souls. A success can repair this disadvantage. I hope that you will find such an opportunity shortly, and that you will seize it without recklessly exposing yourself, unless you wish to make me really unhappy. In all these matters, follow exactly what the emperor prescribes."[14] She hoped her husband would realize that Eugène had been outnumbered, but she feared that her son would become so despondent that he might get himself wounded or killed.

Joséphine and Hortense followed the campaign by consulting the map as dispatches came in, and they received first-hand information from the capital as well, because Champagny had stopped off to see them at Strasbourg on his way to join the emperor. The foreign minister reported that the ministers in Paris believed Eugène would again be deployed, placing the Austrian army in an unfavorable position, wedged between two forces.[15] News also came to them directly from headquarters, for Napoléon, in an amazingly detailed letter sent on April 29, gave Joséphine the exact position of his army and the sector in which Marshal Lefèbvre was to be stationed. She immediately wrote to Eugène: "The direction of [Lefèbvre's] division it seems to me, according to the map, will threaten the enemy you have in mind and prepare for him a total defeat which will perhaps help your position. For I hope you will take your revenge [against Austria], and I desire it, without exposing yourself too much. . . . I also hope the emperor is not as grieved as you think. . . . He tells me that all goes according to his wishes, that the Austrians were beaten in a thunderclap [the victory at Landshut April 21]. . . . I believe that by now he has received your news. . . . My dear son, don't be too hard on yourself. Steadfastness of soul in times of misfortune is more honorable than victory."[16]

The stunning series of events that took place between April 13 (the date of their departure from Paris) and April 22 (Napoléon's victory against Archduke Charles at Eckmühl) enabled Eugène to take the offensive on the last day of the month. This 1809 campaign against Austria, however, marked the beginning of Napoléon's "difficult" victories. His subordinates committed errors when not under his personal supervision; his army was no longer at its peak and was made up of many raw recruits; his desire to seek a decisive battle was less acute; and he now faced an enemy who had learned their battle tricks from him. For Eugène, the news that tipped the scales was the fall of Ratisbon on April 23, and when he heard of it, he ordered salvos fired up and down his lines outside Verona. Joséphine must have written her husband expressing concern over his fatigue and his constant exposure to danger, for on May 6 he tried to reassure her: "I received your letter. The ball [that hit him at Ratisbon]. . . did not wound me; it only grazed my Achilles tendon . . . .You are wrong to worry."[17] Constant said the emperor would give orders before each battle that if he were wounded, it should be concealed from the troops insofar as possible; if he were killed, it was not to be made known until afterwards.[18]

Eugène's own role now became clear—to block Archduke John's retreat toward Vicenza. Although the Austrians offered stiff resistance, Eugène and General Macdonald threw them back to the other side of the Piave River. The bombardment of Vienna began on May 11, and on May 13 the city capitulated. Joséphine wrote to congratulate her son the next day: "I am so glad you have taken fresh courage; I learned by a telegram of the success you won on the eighth of this month [at the Piave]. . . . I know how much you want to please the emperor, and I urge you to write him frequently and give him all the small details about all the operations of the Army of Italy. . . . Give me your news. I spend painful days awaiting it . . . and I only get bits from your sister, who receives them from M. Lavalette."[19]

After the battle at the Piave, the mass of the Austrian army marched north, where they were met by French artillery and were forced beyond the Drave River to Klagenfurt. When Eugène arrived at Klagenfurt on May 21, he received orders to rejoin the Grande Armée, and in the ensuing engagement at the town of Sankt-Michel, Eugène commanded General Durutte's division in person, winning a victory of real importance. He sent his aide-de-camp to announce it to the emperor, who summoned him to come at once. When Eugène arrived, Napoléon greeted him with open arms, proclaiming before all his assembled generals: "It is not only courage that animates [Eugène], it is also his heart!"[20] He was so delighted that he wrote Joséphine an enthusiastic letter on May 27, reporting Eugène's contribution: "I am sending a page to tell you that Eugène has joined me with his army [at Ebersdorf]; he has perfectly fulfilled the task that I have given him; he has almost entirely destroyed the enemy army which was before him. I also send you my proclamation to the Army of Italy."[21] Part of it ran as follows: "Ebersdorf, 28 May, 1809. The viceroy has demonstrated during this campaign a sang-froid and an eye that are characteristic of a grand captain." Napoléon's postscript to Joséphine asks her to arrange to have this proclamation printed at Strasbourg in both French and German, and to dispatch a copy to Paris, i.e., to arch-chancellor Cambacérès. To the immense relief of his mother, sister, and wife, Eugène had now more than redeemed himself, for his setback at Sacile was now entirely forgotten.

Yet not everything went Napoléon's way. On May 22, at the village of Essling, near Vienna, Napoléon had 60,000 men on the left bank of the Danube. He sent his old friend Marshal Lannes to attack the Austrians when the bridge across the river gave way because of rising water, so the French were trapped and had to retreat. Napoléon was defeated by natural forces rather than the Austrians, who nevertheless claimed a victory against the invincible emperor. Marshal Lannes was killed in the battle, which was a grievous personal loss for Napoléon. It is said that when he went to Lannes's side, the dying man entreated his master to make peace and to limit his conquests.

Meanwhile, numerous distinguished refugees had been flocking to Joséphine in Strasbourg, and Hortense gives a vivid picture of the haven Joséphine provided for royalty in flight.[22] Catherine, queen of Westphalia, arrived on April 29 with her large retinue, for her husband, Jérôme Bonaparte, had sent her to Joséphine from their capital at Kassel. The king and queen of Westphalia had set up a palatial establishment there, greatly vexing the emperor, who urged his brothers and sisters to live more frugal lives. Catherine regretted that she had not yet borne Jérôme a child, for she adored her pleasure-seeking husband and closed her eyes to his philandering. Nor did Jérôme adequately defend his territory—another frustrating example of the Bonaparte brothers' limitations, which plagued Napoléon throughout his career.

Another refugee was her niece Stéphanie de Beauharnais, whose flirtatious manner Joséphine had not always appreciated. But she took the princess of Baden under her wing, although her meeting with Catherine must have been awkward, for Stéphanie was one of Jérôme's amorous conquests. Her presence in Strasbourg attracted another famous visitor, Baroness Julianne von Krüdener, former wife of the Russian ambassador to Venice, a well-known writer, and a friend of Germaine de Staël.

The outcome of Essling had produced severe repercussions throughout Europe. Eugène had been sent to safeguard Vienna; more troops were being raised in Austria and Germany; and resistance was hardening in Spain. Napoléon was so agitated by these developments that he fell ill, for it was obvious that he was facing yet another campaign. But Joséphine, who went with Hortense to Plombières in mid-June, was concerned about her husband for other reasons. Although Plombières was supposed to be relaxing, she was tormented by what she was hearing from Vienna. On the eve of the siege of Vienna, May 10, Napoléon had moved into Schönbrunn, a Habsburg château, where he would remain until October 16, and he was joined there by the Polish countess Maria Walewska, although she did not stay in the château but in a house nearby. It was during this period that Maria became pregnant, and by the time Napoléon reached Fontainebleau on October 26, he knew that she was carrying his child, who would be born on May 4, 1810. Hortense called this interlude one of the most agonizing in Joséphine's life, reporting that the countess's presence at Schönbrunn drove her mother almost to despair.[23]

Joséphine well knew that this was not like his other affairs, the details of which he often related to her in a perfunctory manner, just as he shared with her his most far-reaching military plans. Caulaincourt wrote years earlier that Joséphine was Napoléon's first confidante and that she had, "on the very night, full particulars of the conquest of Mme. Duchatel."[24] Joséphine's reaction to her husband's astonishing forthrightness has not been recorded, but this unusual candor must have convinced her that he attached no significance to these brief encounters. The liaison with Maria Walewska was not a passing affair, however, and Joséphine knew it.

There was some welcome news at Plombières, however, for the emperor's letter of June 19 proudly reported that Eugène had won a victory on June 14 at Raab in Hungary, where the French were able to rout the Austrians. The young de Tascher (Joséphine's relative in whom the emperor had taken a special interest) was there as well, and he carried the news of the Army of Italy's achievement back to Milan. Napoléon's warm letter to his wife concluded with the affectionate words: "You know my sentiments for Joséphine; they are invariable."[25]

On June 30, a week after the siege of Raab had ended, Eugène dined quietly with his step-father and Marshals Davout and Bernadotte. The emperor was in a reflective mood that evening, try-ing to forget his strenuous preparations for the coming conflict, and the talk turned to one of his favorite subjects—literature. Suddenly he declared: "If Corneille were alive, I would make him a prince,"[26] and Eugène (who shared Napoléon's delight in the theater) was amused by this vicarious addition to his celebrated "aristocracy of merit." Eugène was about to play an important role in another major contest of the Empire—the battle of Wagram, which was fought from July 4 through July 6, 1809, northeast of Vienna across the Danube. Years later, on St. Helena, Napoléon would say that his stepson had largely contributed to the happy outcome of this legendary event, in which Eugène had to face Archduke Charles himself. Wagram was another of those hard-won victories, in which the cavalry had to assume the role traditionally played by the infantry, who were altogether missing or defeated.[27] Hortense would also play an indirect role in the battle of Wagram, for the most popular battle song was her "Partant pour la Syrie," which would become a veritable national anthem during the reign of her youngest son some decades later.

After the signing of the Franco-Austrian armistice on July 12, Eugène was invited to Vienna on July 22, where he stayed with his suite of eighty people for three months in the palace of Duke Albert of Saxony, while his army was quartered outside the capital. Vienna was returning to normal, and the viceroy attended the theater and visited museums, porcelain factories, and military establishments. Count Adriani, marshal to the court of Duke Albert, could not say enough in praise of Eugène's patrician manners, his noble comportment, his punctuality in paying bills, and his gen-erosity. A great attraction in Vienna at that time was the inventor Johann Maelzel, who made extraordinary mechanical dolls and ingenious toys, which Eugène bought to send to his children in Milan and to Hortense's two boys. A sad sign of the times was that Maelzel's other inventions included folding stretchers and prostheses, which were in great demand, as the surgeon Dominique Larrey and his assistants were still hard at work in his hospital at Rennweg, amputating arms and legs.

For Eugène, the most rewarding aspect of his stay in Vienna was the reunion with his old friends Bessières and Duroc, because the trio had not been together for five years. It was especially good to have Bessières there, for he had been wounded at Wagram, having been borne unconscious from the field on a stretcher, so that his men had thought him dead.[28] On Sundays Eugène and Duroc went riding, in civilian clothing, for if they went out in uniforms on the Bastion, as he told Auguste, they would be instantly recognized and followed by a crowd. Auguste was hoping her husband would return to Milan, but Eugène was expected to remain at Schönbrunn for the celebration of Napoléon's birthday on August 15.

There was a parade, a gala dinner given by the soldiers, a banquet and ball for the officers, a review of the guard with master drummers of the fusiliers beating "Aux Champs" and other airs, and a proper drum roll for the emperor. Joséphine was represented by the presence of her master of the horse, General Raymond de Saint-Sulpice, a brilliant cuirassier commander, who was named colonel of the empress's Dragoons of the Guard, replacing Arrighi, who was now duke of Parma. The festivities ended with fireworks watched from the terrace, illuminations in the city, waltzes, and cries of "Vive l'Empereur!" echoing far into the night.

Side by side with this official life, the emperor continued to lead a secret one, and Eugène knew that almost every evening Constant would go to a villa in the park to fetch Countess Walewska, who was admitted to the castle through a private entrance. As unpleasant as this was for Joséphine's son, he must have been relieved at least that the countess never appeared in public with the emperor and that she was entirely discreet and genuinely devoted to his stepfather. Eugène even began to take heart, for he reasoned that if the countess satisfied the emperor, there might not be any more talk of divorce. But when Maria found herself pregnant, proving Napoléon capable of producing a child, Eugène knew there was no hope for his mother.

By mid-August, Joséphine was ready to leave Plombières, but when she returned to Malmaison, she found it sadly empty, so Hortense sent her two children to stay with their grandmother. Hortense was supposed to join them but was delayed, and Madame Mère reproached Hortense when she arrived, saying that her mother needed her. Laetitia Bonaparte even tried to assuage her son's anger when Joséphine displeased him by imprudently receiving tradesmen and fortune-tellers. At Malmaison Joséphine was always cheered by the wonders of her conservatory, for during the past campaign, the emperor had sent her eight hundred plants and a wide variety of seeds from Schönbrunn. She had wanted for many years to buy the adjoining property of Bois-Préau, and the emperor's letter of September 23 from Schönbrunn authorized her to do so, for he was in good spirits and in a generous mood. Knowing her penchant for garden follies and interesting landscape features to embellish her English garden, he added a touch of humor to his letter of authorization: "Once you have bought it, however, don't destroy the building in order to make several rock formations!"[29]

Joséphine undoubtedly went to see the circular panorama put up by two Americans, Joel Barlow and the inventor Robert Fulton, on the boulevard des Capucines. It was painted with views of Paris, the English evacuation of Toulon, the camp on the Iron Coast, the interview at Tilsit between Napoléon and Czar Alexander, and the famous battle of Wagram in July. Even the artist Jacques-Louis David admired the exhibition and sent his pupils to have a look.

Napoléon's letters to his wife during October revealed him in good humor as he prepared to return to France, and on October 14 he told her a peace had been signed between Champagny and Metternich that very day at Schönbrunn. The guns of each town saluted the Treaty of Vienna, and at the Tuileries, the imperial standard was raised as the ceremonial battery fired 101 guns. On October 21, Napoléon wrote to Joséphine in a tone that resembled his youthful zeal: she would have only twenty-four hours' notice of his arrival, they would have a celebration when they met, and he was impatiently awaiting their reunion. When he arrived without warning at the gates of Fontainebleau at 10 A.M. on October 26, however, there was no one to greet him at the château except a courier, the grand marshal, and the gatekeeper. Thoroughly vexed, he stalked about, demanding to know why the empress had not come and repeatedly glancing at his watch. She did not appear until 6 P.M., by which time he was too angry to even meet her, and Constant said this was the first time he had ever seen Napoléon act this way. Putting on his most imperious manner, he greeted Joséphine icily, and then—seeing how deeply he had hurt her—he relented and took her into his arms. The valet noted that Joséphine's dress at dinner, made of white satin edged with swan's down, and her hair coiffed with blue flowers and a diadem of silver wheat ears, were exceedingly becoming, and the evening ended with the emperor in excellent humor.[30]

During their two weeks' stay at Fontainebleau, a constrained air pervaded the palace, for Napoléon had now made his decision to repudiate Joséphine "pour epouser un ventre" (to marry a uterus), a crass phrase he used in private. It was his way of saying that he was making a political marriage, and in Vienna on November 29, Metternich suggested the Austrian archduchess Marie-Louise (daughter of Emperor Francis I of Austria) to fulfill Napoléon's aims. The fact that Joséphine was barren and forty-four years old was sufficient grounds for divorce, but Kircheisen believes there was an even deeper motive for Napoléon's action. He attributes it to the transformation of the emperor's character that began to surface in 1807 after his meeting with the czar at Tilsit, and which became even more pronounced after the Treaty of Vienna was signed in October. Living in royal palaces was not enough, nor were the making and breaking of rulers. What Napoléon wanted now was the daughter of a king as his wife to provide a tradition and legitimacy to his dynasty.[31] His marriage to a Habsburg would be the culmination of his decade-long policy of "amalgamation." And so the following year Napoléon would have his Habsburg princess, and future security in the form of children with "ancient" as well as "new" blood. It was believed that the young Marie-Louise of Austria could provide both.

Hortense was hurt by the emperor's behavior during their stay in Fontainebleau, for he acted as if his wife did not exist. For the first time, instead of taking his customary drives with Joséphine, he took in his carriage only his sister, Pauline Borghese, to whose quarters he would repair each evening. This was so unusual that Hortense believed he dreaded the coming event and was trying to harden himself, or else he was pretending it would not actually take place: "His will was firm, but his heart still hesitated. He was forcing himself to think of other things. Also, perhaps, he was trying to find a way to prepare my mother."[32]

One day, after a tearful interview with Joséphine, Napoléon asked Hortense to come into the room. He was visibly upset by his wife's grief, but he told his stepdaughter that since the French people wanted the divorce, he could not resist. Hortense replied: "Do not be surprised by my mother's tears. You would be even more stunned if she did not cry, after a union of fifteen years. . . . But she will submit . . . and we shall all go, carrying with us the memory of your kindness toward us." After Hortense's speech, the emperor's face completely changed, and he began to weep, begging her and Eugène not to abandon him, for they would always remain his children.[33]

They returned to the Tuileries on November 14, and their reestablishment in Paris signaled the beginning of celebrations to commemorate the victories and Treaty of Vienna, as well as the annual coronation fêtes. It was the last time Joséphine would play the role of empress, and she must have done so with the utmost difficulty, for the divorce was no longer a secret. Yet she appeared at all the assemblies, remarkably self-controlled, wearing the crown she knew would soon rest upon another's head. The Bonapartes, Hortense noted bitterly, made no effort to conceal their satisfaction,[34] for they were about to have their revenge upon the seductive "bird of the islands" who had held their eagle so long in her grasp.

The king of Saxony had already arrived on November 13, followed, to Hortense's discomfiture, by her husband, Louis. Joseph had been called from Spain, Elisa from Italy, Jérôme from Westphalia. In fact, the entire clan was assembling to savor this triumph of the Bonapartes over the de Beauharnais family and to recognize the Treaty of Vienna. The princes of the Confederation of the Rhine would all be coming to celebrate the peace, so Joséphine would have to face this greatest crisis of her life in the presence of an exalted company. On November 16, Prefect Frochot and the magistrates presented their respects, two days later Joséphine attended the Opéra, and on November 19 the imperial couple occupied their usual loge at the Théâtre Français as if nothing had changed. But when the emperor received the diplomatic corps on November 26 and then reviewed the troops in the Tuileries courtyard, his dispirited expression was apparent to all.

The moment that Napoléon and Joséphine had both been dreading came after dinner on November 30, 1809. Constant recalled that the couple sat silently without touching their food, the only sound being made by the emperor striking his knife mechanically against his glass. When they went into the salon, he closed the door against the staff, and after a short time the empress could be heard shrieking: "No, you will not do it! You would not kill me!" and fell into a dead faint, whereupon Napoléon opened the door and summoned Baron de Bausset, prefect of the palace. At this point, a potentially tragic scene turned into a farce, if Bausset is to be believed. The emperor asked the portly prefect if he could lift Joséphine and carry her up the narrow staircase to her room while he himself held the candle. Bausset managed to convey the unconscious empress across the room, but when he prepared to ascend with his burden, he needed help. So Napoléon called the watchman at his study door to take his candle, and he himself relieved Bausset of Joséphine's legs, as Bausset started backward up the stairs with his arms under hers. At this point, the prefect's sword fell down between his legs and almost catapulted all three of them down the stairs. As he disengaged it and tried to swing it out of the way, he hit the empress accidentally on the shoulder with the hilt. According to his own words, Joséphine whispered to him that the sword had hurt her and that he was holding her too tightly. Then she resumed her faint. Although some have contested this alleged bit of hypocrisy on Joséphine's part, all agree that Dr. Corvisart and Hortense were summoned as soon as the empress was laid upon her bed.[35]

Eugène had received a terse message from his stepfather summoning him to Paris with his suite by December 5, but he was given no reason. At Nemours, the viceroy's outriders noticed his sister's coach, so Eugène entered and learned the bad news from Hortense. As they continued to Paris, she told Eugène that his success in the last war had greatly ameliorated his prestige in the army. Joséphine had not seen her son since his marriage in Munich, and Eugène dreaded meeting his mother and stepfather. When Napoléon told him his decision was for the good of France, Eugène said it would be best if all of them were banished, whereupon the emperor became very agitated, recalling all that Eugène had done for him: "You must not abandon me, I need you."[36] Joséphine, too, would live nearby, retaining her title and dignity so that everyone would know she had been sacrificed to the necessities of state. She would receive Malmaison as her country house, the Elysée Palace as her Paris residence, the château of Navarre, and all her debts would be paid, for her husband intended that Joséphine's forfeiture for the good of France bring her honor, not banishment.

The first two weeks of December 1809 were exquisite torture for her, as European royalty (whom she had so often entertained as empress) arrived to commemorate the victories and peace. The king of Württemberg appeared on December 1, and the king and queen of Bavaria on December 21. Joséphine received them at the Tuileries with a magnificent show, and for the remainder of the month, the city was almost nightly a theater of grandiose fêtes. In addition, the sessions of the Legislative Body had just reopened, and Constant (deeply moved by the empress's suffering) said that the divorce being proclaimed at this busiest time made her plight even more pitiable, for "it was necessary . . . that the empress should be present on all these occasions, and attend all these festivities under the eyes of an immense crowd of people, at a time when solitude alone would have in any degree alleviated her sorrow."[37]

Surely, one of her most grievous trials was her last attendance at the coronation commemoration on December 3. Five years earlier she had received her crown from the emperor himself, and in thirteen days she would set it down. Somehow she summoned enough courage to leave the Tuileries for Notre Dame at 10 A.M. amid salvos of artillery and to take her official place in the tribunes of the choir, along with Madame Mère and the (now triumphant) imperial family, the kings of Württemberg and Saxony, and Queen Catherine of Westphalia. They did not return to the Tuileries until almost 5 P.M., where a lavish banquet was held, after which the guests passed into the Gallery of Diana. Joséphine had to sit right in front of her husband, "magnificently dressed in a robe blazing with diamonds, but her face expressed even more suffering than in the morning."[38]

Joséphine's last public appearance came on the evening of December 5—her final reign over the great, famous, noble, and royal—but she presented herself with admirable dignity and courage, as those who attended the celebrations affirmed. During the day, the city of Paris offered a large fête in honor of the Austrian peace and the emperor's return, but he did not want Joséphine to appear at this particular event, which would have required her to be ceremoniously accompanied by twenty-four of the first ladies of Paris. His reason, as he told Laure Junot, was to insinuate into the festivities the first hint that the divorce had been decided.[39] Joséphine was allowed to appear at the evening affair, however, "where she displayed her accustomed grace and kind consideration."[40] Followed only by her lady-of-honor and two ladies of the palace, at 5:30 P.M. she entered the throne room of the Hôtel de Ville, which was resplendent with flowers and sparkling with candles.

Then came the sound of guns announcing the emperor, who was accompanied by Caroline and Jérôme, always sympathetic toward Joséphine. Prefect Frochot pontificated as usual, and after presenting decorations of the Légion d'Honneur, Napoléon left the room, followed by Joséphine, then the kings and queens, for a dinner in the Salon of Victories. Sitting in the places of honor normally reserved for them, the sovereigns heard a concert presented by the choir of the Conservatory of Music, and the evening ended with a great, showy ball. Although Joséphine was normally among the last to leave a party, her husband took her away early, at 11:30, no doubt out of consideration for her emotional and mental fatigue. Those in attendance understood his gesture, and as much as the people of Paris loved Joséphine, they knew that the emperor and the Empire needed a successor.[41]

The dreaded day of the Family Council in the throne room of the Tuileries came on the evening of December 14, 1809, in a blaze of splendor, with everyone arrayed in court dress and jewels. Although her husband abhorred exposing Joséphine to yet another unpleasant encounter with the Bonapartes, they did have to be present to witness the Act of Renunciation.[42] Talleyrand attended in his capacity as vice grand elector, and of course Cambacérès, as arch-chancellor of the Empire. Eugène and Hortense stood as representatives of the de Beauharnais family, and Joséphine, in a simple white robe with no jewelry, although pale, was surprisingly calm, and far less agitated than either of her children. Napoléon began to read the speech provided him, but then he put it aside and improvised his own, which he pronounced with choking voice, speaking of the terrible cost of having to renounce the woman who "has adorned fifteen years of my life, and the memory of this will remain forever stamped on my heart. She was crowned by my hand. I desire that she shall keep the rank and title of crowned empress, but above all, that she shall never doubt my feelings and that she shall have me always as her best and dearest friend."[43]

Then Joséphine's turn came, but she likewise modified the language of the prepared declaration. Masson, rarely generous in his remarks about Joséphine, nevertheless praised her admirable conduct on this agonizing occasion: "The words which she spoke were apt and noble, and it was she who chose them; once more she gave proof of that tact which was one of her virtues and one of her charms."[44] She could not finish it, however, and she handed it over to Regnault de Saint-Jean d'Angély, secretary of state, to complete the reading. Even the Bonapartes appeared to be moved as Joséphine surrendered her husband and her throne. Hortense later tried to console her mother by reminding her that the last queen (Marie Antoinette) to leave the Tuileries was on her way to the scaffold, whereas Joséphine would be going to Malmaison. Eugène tried an amusing story to cheer his mother up, but Mlle. d'Avrillion reported that it fell rather flat.

Joséphine left the Tuileries for the last time the next day in wind and gloom, under a steady downpour. Constant said that all those without specific duties to perform assembled in the vestibule "to see once more this dethroned empress whom all hearts followed in her exile. . . . A concert of inexpressible lamentations arose as this adored woman crossed . . . to her carriage." But he was incensed by the absence of those many who had experienced the empress's largesse first-hand.[45] It was a noisy, confused equipage that jostled away from the palace that cold Saturday afternoon of December 16, and once again, a scene that should have been poignant bordered on the burlesque. Joséphine, heavily veiled, embarked with Hortense in a court carriage, trailed by a string of other vehicles loaded with furniture, caged birds, a talkative parrot, sundry trunks of clothing, and bandboxes by the dozens. It was Mlle. d'Avrillion's lot to share a carriage with a brace of Alsatian dogs her mistress had bought in Strasbourg, the female of which had just produced a litter of whining pups.

As devastating as it was to leave the emperor, Joséphine could be grateful for his magnanimity. She retired with no liabilities, a splendid income, a town house, and two country houses, although the château of Navarre would require some time to put into shape. If it was any consolation, Napoléon found the Tuileries insupportable after her departure, for only two hours after her carriage drove away, he left for Trianon, where he spent eight days "in an unaccustomed state of ennui," according to Méneval.[46] The emperor told his secretary he would not see anyone, not even his ministers, and the very day after Joséphine's arrival at Malmaison, he rode out to see her. Hortense described his holding her mother's hand and walking through the château, talking with her and trying to encourage her. The same evening he wrote assurances of his enduring and tender friendship, urging her not to give way to melancholy.[47] This was followed up with daily letters, in which he complained of his solitude and of how much he missed her company.

On December 25, Joséphine and Hortense were summoned to dine with him at Trianon, but the queen of Holland said it was the saddest dinner she had ever attended, with her stepfather wiping

tears from his eyes. When he returned to the capital on December 27, Napoléon wrote to Joséphine: "I was very sad to see the Tuileries again; this great palace appears so empty and I feel isolated."[48]

He was not alone in finding the old royal residence depressing after the dismissal of his "incomparable Joséphine," and Laure Junot later recalled the grandeur of the court as it had been under her aegis: "The emperor's wish was that his court should be brilliant. . . . I well remember the truly fantastic appearance of the *Salle des Maréchaux* on the night of a grand concert when it was lined with three rows of ladies on either side, radiant in youth and beauty, decked with flowers, jewels, and waving plumes. Behind them came officers of the household, then generals, senators, counselors of state and foreign diplomats, all clothed in rich costumes and wearing the decorations and orders which Europe offered us on bended knee."[49] Over it all, Joséphine had reigned with inimitable charm and the "exquisite politeness and . . . wide acquaintance with society" that had always been invaluable assets to her husband.[50]

Only two years after Joséphine's removal, unmistakable signs of the once-powerful French Empire's dissolution would appear. Despite the Austrian marriage and arrival of the long-awaited heir in 1811, the ever-widening cracks in the giant edifice would become ever more apparent. In 1812 would come the catastrophic Russian campaign, and in 1813 the withdrawal of French troops from Spain. In a remarkably short time after Joséphine's retirement, the far-flung Empire would be like "the still-ticking watch on the arm of a dead soldier" (Jean Cocteau), and in a few months more, the finely tuned timepiece would run down.

13

Joséphine in Retreat

*G*radually Joséphine adjusted to her new life at Malmaison, although Bonaparte rarely strayed from her thoughts. She often mentioned him in letters to her children, and when she knew there was to be a hunt in the forest of Saint-Germain, she rushed to the window to watch the emperor's coach as it passed. He continued to be concerned for her welfare, writing her frequently and satisfying her wishes with unqualified generosity: "I set aside 100,000 francs . . . for extra expenses at Malmaison. You may now plant whatever you wish. . . . I ordered that your ruby parure be paid for as well. . . . You will find, in the safe at Malmaison, 500 to 600,000 francs; you may use it to have your silverware made and for your linens. I have ordered [Sèvres] to make a very beautiful porcelain service."[1] Not only was the technical virtuosity of Sèvres placed at Josephine's service, but that of several Paris manufactories as well, among them Dagoty, Dihl and Guérhard, and Nast, which most likely made the bust of Joséphine at Malmaison.

On January 2, Joséphine invited the wife of Prince Metternich to visit Malmaison, and, surprisingly, told the princess that she would like to see an Austrian archduchess mount the French throne.[2] She may have thought that by championing the Austrian marriage, she might be asked to serve as consultant for the eighteen-year-old Archduchess Marie-Louise (a post that went to Hortense). In any event, Joséphine assured Princess Metternich she would do her utmost to insure the future happiness of Napoléon and his new bride.

On February 2, the emperor sent Eugène to visit Prince Karl Phillipp zu Schwarzenberg, the new Austrian ambassador to France, and to propose the marriage, an offer that was immediately accepted. On March 5, Marshal Berthier arrived in Vienna as the emperor's "ambassadeur extraordinaire," and officially asked for Marie-Louise's hand on March 8 in a ceremony at the Hofburg. Her father, Francis I, gave his consent and accepted a miniature of Napoléon encircled in gold and sixteen large diamonds. The following day, the princess renounced her rights to succession to the

had occasionally to be sacrificed to the Minotaur: others spoke about the "sacrifice of Iphigenia." Such witticisms at her expense made it more difficult for Marie-Louise, who needed some polishing herself, according to Metternich. Hortense heard that Metternich had advised the Austrian court that the shy, gauche archduchess could benefit from some dancing lessons before she confronted the Parisians and recommended she should not attempt to perform in public. As Austrian ambassador, Metternich had spent enough winters in Paris to observe the standards set by Joséphine, Hortense, and the Bonaparte princesses at their seasonal balls.

As April 1, the day fixed for the ceremony, approached, the emperor wanted to make certain that Joséphine would not even be near the capital, so on March 28 she set out for Evreux, some fifty miles west of Paris, to the château of Navarre, which Napoléon had purchased for her on March 8. Her household was now greatly diminished, but her entourage remained an impressive one. Her carriage bore her coat-of-arms with the imperial crown and mantle sewn with golden bees, and when she drove into Evreux, she was ceremoniously received by the prefect, the mayor, the National Guard, the local clergy, and a band that included a choir from the cathedral.

When the newspapers arrived from Paris, Joséphine eagerly pored over accounts of the wedding in which her own family had played major roles. The new empress's train was carried by the queens of Holland (Hortense), Spain (Julie Bonaparte), and Westphalia (Catherine). Eugène's wife, Auguste, and Stéphanie de Beauharnais, the grand duchess of Baden, walked in front, carrying tapers and insignia on cushions, while Stéphanie's father, comte Claude de Beauharnais, served as knight of honor to Marie-Louise. Eugène sent his mother amusing anecdotes about the exiled Spanish royal family, who competed with each other in adulation of the emperor. At the banquet they gave for the bridal party, the former King Ferdinand loudly cheered every time the emperor's name was mentioned. Joséphine must have smiled at Eugène's letter, remembering their bizarre behavior at the dinner she had tendered them in Bayonne. The viceroy also told his mother that, thanks to the emperor, he was making another advantageous marriage for one of her relatives: his aide-de-camp, Louis de Tascher de la Pagerie to Princess Amélie-Thérèse de la Leyen. Young de Tascher's career began to soar, and when Joséphine's grandson (Hortense's third son) Louis-Napolèon, whose childhood nickname was "Oui-Oui," ascended the throne as Napoléon III, Louis de Tascher would become senator and grand master of the household to Napoléon III's wife, the glamorous Empress Eugénie.

Although Joséphine complained that not one door or window would close tightly in the château of Navarre, the gardens were so splendid she forgot these discomforts, writing to Hortense on April 3: "One ought to live at Navarre in . . . May, June, July, and even the beginning of August; it is then the most enchanting place there is."[11] This first spring after the divorce, however, she would return to Malmaison in mid-May, for she complained that Bonaparte had always summoned her away just when her double hyacinths and tulips from Holland were about to bloom, and this year she was determined to see them flower.

Joséphine's relative Maurice de Tascher visited her at Navarre in May, arriving just as the gardens were unveiling their early spring beauty. Joséphine took him through the Garden of Hebe, which was ornamented with flowers, rare trees, and classical statuary. She also showed him the English garden, which was punctuated with numerous follies—a Chinese *gloriette*, rock formation with cascades, and a Temple of Love much like the one that adorned Joséphine's gardens at Malmaison. Maurice thought Joséphine entirely worthy of the setting, still beautiful and seductive despite her forty-five years (forty-seven, actually).

She regretted not being in Paris to say good-bye to Hortense, who had agreed to rejoin Louis Bonaparte in The Hague for a final attempt at reconciliation. Although Hortense's letters are full of complaints about her husband's coldness, his lack of response to her anecdotes, and his gravity, Louis must be seen as a tragic figure, as much the victim of political necessity as Hortense herself. He sincerely tried to be a good king and studied Dutch in order to be able to communicate with his subjects, but he had no real autonomy in Holland, being torn between serving the politics of the Empire and the interests of his own kingdom. Lucie de la Tour du Pin succinctly summed up Louis's dilemma: "The iron hand of Napoléon prevented [Louis] from carrying out his policy for the good of the country. He left in Holland a very honorable record, as I know from King William himself."[12]

Hortense's reunion with Louis in April 1810 was ill-fated, and Joséphine was soon bombarded by her daughter's mournful letters. By early June, Hortense was ready to leave The Hague, and when Joséphine wrote to ask Napoléon's permission for Hortense to leave Holland, she took the opportunity to request that her daughter be released from her marriage. Napoléon responded by going out to Malmaison himself to see her, and Joséphine wrote to Hortense from Malmaison on June 14: "Yesterday I had a day of happiness; the emperor came to see me. His presence made me happy even though it renewed my pain. . . . All the time he stayed with me I had the courage to keep back my tears. . . . He was so good and kind . . . and I hope he was able to read in my heart all the tenderness and devotion with which I am suffused. I spoke to him of your position, and he listened with interest. It is his opinion that you should not remain in Holland, the king not having conducted himself as he should; your health and the effort you have made were a sacrifice; you have proved to both the emperor and his family how much you wanted to do something that was agreeable to them. . . . As for your son [the younger], the emperor will give the order that he is not to leave France. . . . I shall be traveling incognito under the name of Mme. d'Arberg; you may send letters . . . by Lavalette. Your son is with me at the moment . . . doing well; he is pink and white."[13]

This letter reveals a great deal about Napoléon's continued respect for Joséphine's wishes: he listened to her observations on Hortense's marriage; he concurred with her view that Hortense and Louis should no longer live together; and he agreed to allow her younger grandson to remain in France, with Joséphine nearby. Although Hortense was not given an official divorce, she was permitted to live peacefully in Paris or in her château at Saint-Leu, to retain her title as queen of Holland, and to be entitled to her own household with sixteen officers. Joséphine was relieved her daughter's long agony was past, and Eugène must have heaved a sigh of relief, for almost every post carried a catalogue of his sister's trials and tribulations. It was a trying time for Louis as well, for Napoléon had greatly undermined his confidence with his criticism, so on the the night of July 1, Louis slipped out of his palace and fled to Bohemia. Napoléon learned of it on July 6, named Lebrun lieutenant general, and by a decree of July 9, Holland was annexed to France.

That summer Joséphine traveled to Aix-les-Bains with her usual train of attendants, including the artist recommended by Hortense, Count Lancelot-Théodore Turpin de Crissé. He painted informative watercolors of Joséphine's peregrinations in Savoy, and at least three of his works hung in her gallery at Malmaison. Eugène and Auguste remained in Paris, attending the last parties celebrating the wedding, which almost cost them their lives. The concluding fête was a splendid ball for 1,500 people given by Prince Schwarzenberg in honor of the new empress on July 1, in a ballroom adjoining the embassy. Eugène opened the ball with Princess Pauline Borghese, but within minutes a candle somehow ignited the gauze draperies, and the entire wooden structure instantly became a roaring inferno. Eugène found Auguste and they escaped through a door hidden behind a curtain. Marie-Louise sat almost immobilized upon the stage until she was rescued by Metternich. Catherine of Westphalia just missed being trampled to death as she rushed about looking for her husband, Jérôme Bonaparte.

One of Hortense's friends, Mme. Durosnel, was trapped in the fire before being rescued and suffered such severe burns that she remained dreadfully disfigured. Prince Schwarzenberg's sister-in-law was struck by a heavy chandelier when the ceiling collapsed; she fell through the floor, and her body was identified by the jewelry she had been wearing. The mother of Amélie de la Leyden, Louis de Tascher's bride, was so badly burned while searching for her daughter that her tiara melted on her head and she died shortly afterward. Later in July, Louis de Tascher would visit Joséphine at Aix with Amélie, who was still mourning her mother's horrible death.

Joséphine found life at Aix an agreeable way to pass the summer, for she was the center of attention there; her carriage with its imperial liveries stirred the townspeople as she passed through the streets on her way to Geneva, and in early September, she made an excursion to La Secheron in the parish of Petit Sacconex to meet Eugène on his way back to Milan. First, she wanted to hear about the fatal ball that had taken the lives of so many friends, and then she poured out her domestic woes on her patient and forbearing son. Her favorite parrot had died at Malmaison—probably the same one that squawked as they tried to stuff him into a carriage when his mistress left the Tuileries. It was a sad loss to her household, for the bird spoke Spanish, knew several songs, and was able to accompany himself as he danced. She also told Eugène that she had almost drowned during an excursion on Lake Bourget in June, an experience that provoked the emperor to jest with her in his letter of June 10: "For an inhabitant of the Isles of the Ocean, to die in a lake would be a real catastrophe!"[14]

As Hortense and Julie Bonaparte traveled together that summer to see Joséphine in Aix, their carriage was passing a small village near Geneva, when Hortense suddenly noticed two horsemen rapidly approaching, and instead of passing, they stopped alongside her carriage. One she saw to be her mother's equerry, the comte de Pourtalès, and the other she suddenly recognized as the man she had been in love with for years: Auguste-Charles de Flahaut, who happened to be staying at Aix that summer. In May 1809, Charles had been made a colonel, and in August a baron, although he was not yet twenty-five. Napoléon keenly appreciated his ability, and Charles's rapid advancement became a notable success story in the army. Joséphine had known Charles since his youth, for his mother, Mme. de Souza, was an old friend. It was, of course, Joséphine who had sent Pourtalès and Flahaut to escort Hortense and Julie to her house that day, and she must certainly have guessed its consequences. In her memoirs, Hortense describes the strong emotion provoked by the sudden reappearance of Charles de Flahaut, whom she claimed not to have seen for years, while admitting she had never forgotten him.[15] Whatever feelings had existed between the two were suddenly rekindled, and from this time on, Charles de Flahaut played a major (albeit surreptitious) role in Hortense's life.

When the court returned to Fontainebleau in the fall, the emperor ordered Hortense to join him because he needed her to teach Marie-Louise some French social graces and to help put the shy Austrian princess at ease: "Draw with her. Play some music. You will give her pleasure. She would not dare to ask you to do it herself."[16] Hortense knew better than to insinuate herself into Marie-Louise's household without being invited, but the emperor insisted she be there, and soon Marie-Louise herself asked Hortense to stay. One day she told Hortense about a message she had received from Prince Metternich before she left Austria: "Pauline is the most beautiful person in the world; the queen of Naples the wittiest; but the queen of Holland is the only one with whom [you] could form an intimate relationship."[17]

At the behest of both the emperor and the new empress, Hortense remained a fixture at court, doing whatever she could to liven things up and introduce a little gaiety into the imperial salon by inventing drawing-room diversions and creating a decorous artistic atmosphere. It was not easy, however, for Marie-Louise was incapable of playing the role in which Joséphine had shone so conspicuously. This became evident on an occasion recorded by Lucie de la Tour du Pin, who had been invited to an imperial dinner on April 2 following the marriage. The emperor needed a woman of distinguished family to present the ladies to Marie-Louise, so he had asked Lucie to do the honors. As each woman came along the line, Lucie was astounded that Marie-Louise did not address one personal word to any of them; she could hardly believe that a Habsburg princess (and grandniece of Marie-Antoinette at that) could be so maladroit, for not even the illustrious names of the duchesse d'Arenberg or comtesse de Mérode meant anything at all to her.[18]

The comtesse de Boigne's appraisal of the new empress was even more forthright: "Marie-Louise . . . was somewhat too red. Notwithstanding her dress and precious stones, she seemed very vulgar and entirely without distinction."[19] Obviously, the whole tenor of life at the Tuileries was going to be different, and soon it was whispered about that the new empress was much less satisfactory than the old one. Childish, vacillating Marie-Louise was easily influenced by those around her, but hers was not an enviable lot, for she undoubtedly hated the patriotic duty imposed upon her by her family, who had forced her to marry Bonaparte. She had been pleasantly surprised, however, to find him anything but the monster she expected, and she admitted that he treated her with tenderness and respect, but she also discovered—as had many other foreigners—that French social standards were not easily met.

In mid-September, Joséphine heard from Napoléon that Marie-Louise was pregnant, and as her waist expanded, Napoléon remarked to Hortense: "If it is a girl, she will be a little bride for your son Napoléon, because she must not marry outside the family nor France."[20] It was clear that he wanted Joséphine to be in Italy with Eugène, or at least no nearer Paris than Navarre, until after the child's birth, and Claire de Rémusat wrote cautiously to Joséphine that, although the emperor wanted her and the new empress to meet, the time was not yet propitious. Claire, who may have thought it prudent to distance herself from Joséphine at this point, would soon be moving in secretly royalist circles with her old friend Talleyrand, who, as Crane Brinton put it, found it necessary "to change his principles if he were to retain his power. He changed them simply, as one would change clothes, and for so public a performance, with amazingly little loss of dignity."[21]

There also existed the real possibility of provoking Marie-Louise's jealousy, which would only be exacerbated by Joséphine's return to Paris. So Joséphine headed for Navarre, but via Malmaison, where she was authorized to spend twenty-four hours. General Bertrand was among her callers, and he told her how greatly honored he would be if Prince Eugène would serve as godfather to his and Fanny's child.[22] Others gathered about Joséphine with grievances about the new order, with stories of Marie-Louise's real or imagined ineptitude, and her fear of encountering Joséphine. On November 14 Joséphine was still at Malmaison, so Cambacérès was dispatched to hasten her departure as the new empress's pregnancy advanced. Joséphine had also stopped at the Elysée Palace as she passed through Paris, so the following year the emperor took it away, giving her instead the palace of Laeken, which was ten miles from Brussels, leaving Joséphine with no Paris residence for the first time since 1796. She seems not to have been concerned, however, for Malmaison remained hers, and—as she told Hortense—"at Navarre . . . I shall have the pleasure of seeing you sometimes."[23]

Eugène had returned to Italy, making a tour of his realm accompanied by his Mameluke Petrus, as his stepfather was by Roustam, for it was considered appropriate that the combatants of the Battle of the Pyramids and the campaign in Syria be followed by Mamelukes. Eugène also reported to his mother on the marriage of Auguste's brother, Prince Ludwig, in Munich. The attendant festivities were such a success that they became an annual event known as the Oktoberfest. The viceroy's sword bearer, Count Caprara, called on Joséphine on December 18 at Navarre, bring-

Jean-Baptiste Isabey (1767–1855),
Marie-Louise and the King of Rome
(private collection). After Napoléon went
into exile in 1815, his son was given the
title duc de Reichstadt, and taken to
Schönbrunn Castle—virtually a golden
cage—where he was much loved by his
grandfather, Emperor Francis I, and rather
neglected by his mother, Marie-Louise.
In 1830 the name of Napoléon II was
proposed as the king of Poland or Belgium,
but Metternich opposed it. The young man
died of complications from being chilled
when he was only twenty-one and—like his
father—was entombed in the Invalides.

ing official news of the birth of Eugène's son. As the emperor had been urging her to do, Auguste had borne a son after two daughters, and Joséphine tactfully appended to her letter of congratulations a note of reassurance—that Eugène had been perfectly happy with two girls.

The year 1811 began quietly for Joséphine at Navarre, but imperial protocol demanded a certain degree of ceremony, such as two footmen standing behind her chair at meals and one behind the chairs of guests. Passing into her salon after dinner, Joséphine would sit by her fireplace working on a piece of tapestry, a genteel pursuit for ladies of the ancien régime that obviated the necessity for the hostess to rise when guests entered the room. At 2 P.M. her chamberlain read aloud from novels, memoirs, or the latest novelties from Paris, such as Chateaubriand's just-published *Itinerary from Paris to Jerusalem*, a recitation of his adventures in the Near East.[24] This celebrated author had formed part of Joséphine's circle in Aix-les-Bains the previous summer, when witty Charles de Flahaut had enlivened her evening gatherings by singing romances to the assembled company. Not everyone in Joséphine's household at Navarre contributed to its ambiance, however, for Stéphanie de Tascher d'Arenberg, who came for an extended visit, proved more liability than asset, with her nervous disposition and proclivity for fainting fits. Stéphanie's marriage continued to be unhappy, but she would finally be liberated from it in 1817.

As the birth of Marie-Louise's baby drew near, Eugène was required to return to Paris in order to witness the birth, along with Hortense and the other courtiers. The labor was so long and difficult that the doctors became pessimistic, and about 7 A.M. on March 20, the emperor told them their duty was to save his wife. As they waited, Hortense pondered the consequences: if it were a girl, the child would become her future daughter-in-law (according to the emperor) and if it were a boy, her own sons would fall behind in the line of succession. The child's gender would become clear to all France when the guns were discharged, for according to a monarchical tradition taken over by the Empire, 21 guns denoted the birth of a princess, 101 guns for a prince.

Just after 8 A.M., the bells of Paris sounded the first carillon, followed by those of every church in France. When the twenty-second gun sounded, the populace went wild, but Hortense, who stood beside the emperor as he emerged from his wife's room, said that while all the court was congratulating him, Napoléon's face was clouded with sorrow. He drew Hortense aside, whispering that he could never forget Marie-Louise's ordeal. Hortense was impressed that the great emperor forgot ambition, grandeur, and his future (at long last seemingly secure) in the midst of his personal grief.

Joséphine was preparing to celebrate by giving a ball for the people of Evreux as Napoléon's letter arrived, telling her that his son was big and healthy and that he was very satisfied with Eugène. This abrupt switch from his newborn heir to his stepson may seem inappropriate, but it must be remembered that Napoléon, by his own account, never ceased to regard Eugène as his first son. Eugène had noticed, from the moment he reached Paris, that everything possible was done to make his visit agreeable: Marie-Louise showed him real solicitude, inquiring about the ailment that had kept Auguste in Milan, and the emperor invited him to shoot at Marly and to hunt at Saint-Cloud, Saint-Germain, and Fontainebleau, just as if nothing had changed. The two men spent long hours together, and Eugène wrote Auguste that his stepfather reiterated his pleasure in Eugène's services. "For two weeks," he wrote his wife, "my best friends have secretly advised me that the emperor considers me the only [man] of his family in whom he is able to place his complete confidence, and is meditating a decree that would charge me with the government of France each time he is obliged to be absent."[25] Eugène hoped the political horizon was clearing and that the "talk of war would simply go up in smoke."

This was intended to reassure Auguste, but in May Caulaincourt was recalled as ambassador to Russia. As the relationship between France and the czar rapidly deteriorated, Caulaincourt advised Napoléon that war would be the worst possible thing for France, for it would bring the nation down with him and Europe would rise against him. Although the emperor's advisers had to be discreet, there was another compelling reason why they advised against the Russian campaign: Napoléon was no longer the man he had been. He was only forty-three, but according to Kircheisen, he was "physically worn out. . . . His body had long ceased to possess the recuperative powers of earlier days, though during the years that followed he still frequently endured the most extraordinary hardships. . . . His good fortune had spoiled him, for up to the present all his activities had been crowned with success."[26]

What Eugène heard and saw at the Tuileries was at once disturbing and encouraging. Disturbing, because Caulaincourt's observations seemed to make sense; encouraging because it surely meant that Eugène would again serve with the Army of Italy under the emperor's banners. But as much as he longed to return to the field, this campaign appeared to be unlike any of the others, and as always, he dreaded the pain his departure would inflict upon his mother, sister, and Auguste. Moreover, the imperial armies—like the commander himself—were no longer what they had been, not hardened veterans, but increasingly green recruits.

During the summer of 1811, Hortense complained of not feeling well, but this was not her usual malaise. While Eugène was in Paris, she gave him some very distressing news, that she was expecting Charles de Flahaut's child in mid-September. This presented a dilemma because the emperor wanted Hortense to represent Caroline at the imperial christening on June 9, but her couturier Leroy must have devised gowns that cleverly concealed her figure, for she reports having appeared as commanded.[27] The pregnancy would have to remain secret, so Eugène was called upon and, as always, he found a solution. He announced in Milan that his sister would be paying him a visit in September, and under the pretext of having to inspect the work he had ordered at the Simplon Pass, he went to meet her and returned without her (September 16–24). During these few days, his whereabouts (and Flahaut's) were hazy, but the dates coincided with Hortense's brief stop at Saint-Maurice-en-Valais, where her child was born, and her brother and her lover must have been at her side.

During their mother's absence, Hortense's boys lived with their governess in the Pavilion of Italy in the park of Saint-Cloud. They usually lunched with the emperor, and since his meals were customarily served on a small table, there was hardly room for them, but they squeezed up close to him anyway. Oui-Oui never forgot those days with the emperor and those with his grandmother at Malmaison and Navarre. When he became Napoléon III, he would recall that his grandmother spoiled him in every conceivable way. She would even allow him to cut sugarcane in the hothouse, so that he could suck the juice from the stems just as she had done as a child in Martinique. Joséphine wrote to Hortense from Malmaison on September 3: "you may be certain [the boys] will be the object of all my attention. I am well provided with toys; I shall give playthings to them when they want; but as far as candy is concerned, don't worry, for they won't have it."[28] Her postscript sends greetings to Adèle de Broc, indicating that Hortense's best friend, a talented artist, was with her during her secret confinement.

Napoléon must have known the identity of Hortense's child's father, for in May 1812 he would abruptly send Flahaut off to inspect the Austrian army that Prince Schwarzenberg was going to command in Russia, and then he dispatched Flahaut to Warsaw. These tedious missions were probably intended to humble Charles de Flahaut, and worse still he would eventually participate in the fateful invasion of Russia, an assignment that only the bravest and most fortunate would survive. Charles Auguste de Morny, the child born to Charles and Hortense, never lived with either parent and was reared by Charles's mother. He grew up to become the celebrated duc de Morny, the indispensable president of the Legislative Corps during the reign of his half-brother, Napoléon III. So Joséphine herself unwittingly made a major contribution to the Second Empire by having sent Charles de Flahaut to meet Hortense on the road to Aix-les-Bains that summer's day in 1810.

Hortense now tried to live as quietly as possible, staying at home and drawing with Adèle de Broc. She went to see her mother whenever possible but found the crowd thronging Malmaison too tiring. The fact that Joséphine could no longer confer favors seemed to make no difference to the young and talented who sought entry into her circle, and Hortense contrasted Marie-Louise's dull, formal evenings at the Tuileries with the gaiety and ambiance of Malmaison.[29] France's most illustrious families brought their children to see Joséphine, and in October 1811, a scion of the de La Rochefoucauld family was baptized at Malmaison.[30] The baby, Joseph-Eugène, was baptized on October 20, with Joséphine as godmother and Prince Eugène as godfather in absentia, represented by Hortense's older son.

During the early spring of 1812, Joséphine showed her guests around the gardens as they came to life, a park that Alexandre de Laborde thought rivaled the Jardin des Plantes in Paris. The luxuriant specimens of wisteria, Chinese peonies, camellias, and jasmine in her conservatory excited visiting horticulturists such as the Prussian ambassador, Baron Alexander von Humboldt, who had recently returned with his friend Aimé Bonpland from a five-year exploratory voyage in America. Bonpland, a distinguished scholar and Joséphine's official botanist and devoted friend, would publish the following year (1813) his *Description des plantes rares cultivées à Malmaison et à Navarre.*

It was probably at this time that Joséphine's desire to see the emperor's child was honored. Their meeting had to appear accidental (in deference to Marie-Louise), so the governess, Mme. de Montesquiou, took the baby to the lovely eighteenth-century pavilion of Bagatelle in the Bois de Boulogne on the very day that Joséphine just happened to be driving over from Malmaison, and where Napoléon just happened to be accompanying his son's carriage on horseback. Joséphine wept and kept embracing the small boy who was "the crown of her sacrifice."[31] According to Hortense, her mother said to him: "Ah, dear child. You will know some day how much you have cost me."[32]

Many historians think it strange that Joséphine should have subjected herself to the pain of seeing the child she herself could never produce. But she actually invited this opportunity and even asked the Countess Walewska and her son, Alexandre, to Malmaison. Joséphine welcomed the countess and offered cookies and toys to little Alexandre, as she did with her own grandchildren. The countess must have enjoyed Joséphine's hospitality, for she continued her visits until the empress's death. Joséphine had even forgiven the emotional damage caused by Mme. Duchatel's brief liaison with the emperor in 1804, and she took the former lady-in-waiting back into her good graces. Another offender who had created a stir in 1807 was Mme. Gazzani, but Joséphine retained her as a reader. Joséphine had her weaknesses, like everyone else, but she apparently did not hold a grudge and extended impartial generosity even to women who had hurt her in the past.

Although France appeared to be at peace, Eugène knew better, for his stepfather was urging him to step up operations, and Eugène described the preparations as being on the scale of Alexander the Great's expeditions into India and Persia. On February 22, he refused to accept the kingdom of Poland, which was about to be offered to him, saying "I would not be able to bear being so far from the emperor. I have only one ambition: to live and die as close to him as possible. . . . This overrides any other, for I do not desire a throne."[33] The viceroy's troops would be accompanied by special ambulances equipped with mechanisms to grind the grain during the marches, thanks again to the ingenious mechanic Maelzel. By February 24, Eugène's commitment was certain, and Hortense knew what lay ahead, but it was Carnival season, and the balls and fêtes "seemed to obliterate any thoughts of the most formidable expedition that had ever been seen . . . which was being prepared in silence."[34] Everyone abandoned himself to pleasure, and "never had Carnival been as brilliant as that of the winter of 1812."[35] The balls Hortense gave in her house on the rue Cerutti were even more enticing than ever, and her marvelous costumes dazzled the emperor, but his personal librarian, Antoine-Alexandre Barbier—over at the Tuileries—was assembling all the books he could find on the topography of Russia.

In March another distinguished officer, General Michel Pacthod, who was greatly attached to Eugène, called on Joséphine on his way to Milan, so she gave him a letter for her son: "I am taking advantage, dear Eugène, of General Pacthod's departure to respond to your last letter. I see with real sadness that you will not come here [to Malmaison] before reporting to the army.[36] . . . You would have served as intermediary with the emperor [and] have asked what I should do, and where I should live during his absence. I agree . . . that I should not stay too close to Paris. . . . He assured me [in his last letter] that his feelings for me have never changed and I know he will approve of my conduct. . . . I cannot finish . . . without speaking of General Pacthod, who is taking this to you. He interests me because of his attachment to you and his desire to be under your orders. It would be good of you to take care of him."[37]

The rupture between Napoléon and Czar Alexander had been inevitable. Although the emperor had needed Alexander to keep an eye on Austria while he was engaged in Spain, the cordial relationship they had enjoyed at Tilsit in July 1808 had deteriorated rapidly. The meeting at Erfurt had left Napoléon dispirited, and the czar, having refused to stand against Austria, had shown himself openly hostile to France by April 1809. After Napoléon's difficult victory at Wagram in July, things went from bad to worse, with Russia opening her ports to English ships in 1811; by April 1812 the Grande Armée was on the banks of the Oder and Davout's advance corps were pushing toward the Vistula. Now faced with a French invasion, Alexander resolved to stand firm.

breathe. Eugène, Duroc, Murat, and Armand de Caulaincourt came separately to beg the emperor to leave the Kremlin while he could, claiming the building was mined, and Napoléon was finally persuaded when it was learned the arsenal was aflame. By September 19, the scene had become utterly surrealistic, according to de Ségur's account: the French camped in the fields, sitting on silk-upholstered sofas, wrapped in cashmere shawls and rarest Siberian furs, eating half-cooked horseflesh from magnificent silver dishes. Finally, on October 18, when it became apparent that the czar was not going to ask for peace, and with a merciless northern winter encroaching, the emperor gave orders to set the Grande Armée into motion for the retreat the following day. It was an event for which "history can show no parallel . . . the most powerful leader of his time invading a foreign country with an army of half a million . . . occupying its ancient capital and then, still undefeated, forced to . . . [make] a retreat which reduces his magnificent army to a few miserable remnants!"[46]

On October 24, Eugène was attacked at Malo-Jaroslavetz, but he and his men were able to drive the Russians back. The emperor narrowly escaped being taken by Cossacks and was so proud of Eugène that he published his unqualified praise for his stepson on November 18 in *Le Journal de l'Empire*: "The brilliant affair at Malo-Jaroslavetz accords the greatest honor to the corps of the viceroy. This prince showed himself to be the worthy pupil of the great captain under whom he learned the art of warfare, and he deployed all the valor of a young warrior [combined with] the consummate experience of an old general. . . . This prince animated and inspired everyone by his presence, made his dispositions calmly, and executed them with vigor. . . . His horse was killed under him."[47] When he surveyed the field where 8,000 Russians and 6,000 French had fallen, Napoléon announced: "The glory of this wonderful day belongs altogether to Prince Eugène,"[48] and it was true that the viceroy had won a victory in grand style.

Joséphine received a precious letter from Eugène and forwarded it to Hortense, saying she had "passed from the most acute anxiety to a great joy. At least my son is alive!"[45] She also read with maternal pride about Eugène's conduct and the emperor's praise in the bulletin of the Grande Armée of November 19. Charles de Flahaut, who had also been at Malo-Jaroslavetz, sent his mother, Mme. de Souza, a report of the glorious victory whereby Eugène, with Marshal Davout, had repulsed a furious Russian attack in savage combat.[49]

By September 30, Joséphine had left Aix to spend three weeks near Geneva in the small château of Prégny-la-Tour, which she had bought during her sojourn through Switzerland in late October 1810. Genevans were intrigued by the aura that surrounded her personage and by her distinguished following. The costume she wore to a ball was greatly admired: a silver-embroidered gown of pink crêpe, cut low to show off her necklace of large pearls worth some 100,000 francs, and bands of silver linked through the marvelous elaborations of her chestnut hair achieved by her hairdresser. She left Prégny on October 21, taking home a Swiss shepherd and shepherdess to live in a rustic building in her park and to care for her Swiss cattle.

Antoine Gros (1771–1835), The Burning of Moscow *(Musée du Louvre). This drawing was made for a painting that Gros never executed, although it could have been one of his most effective works. The scene is set against a wide panorama of Moscow in flames, as Napoléon appears to be immobilized by the horrible spectacle and Murat stands beside him, glancing anxiously over his shoulder. Frenzied women appeal to French soldiers, one of whom is helping an old man at the right. At the far left, another soldier carries an old man, a motif Gros probably borrowed from* Le Déluge *(1805) by his friend Anne-Louis Girodet.*

Joséphine arrived at Malmaison on October 27 at an upsetting moment, for on the night of October 22, the mad General Malet had escaped from an asylum, seized the minister of police, and tried to take over the government (for which he was subsequently executed). When Joséphine learned of this, she wrote Eugène on October 27: "I am even more affected by [the conspiracy] because nothing prepared me for it, because all along my route there was the greatest tranquility. . . . If I had been able to detect the least danger to the King of Rome [Napoléon's baby son] and the empress, I do not know what I could have done but very certainly I would have followed my first impulse: I would have gone, with my daughter, to be with them."[50] It is a fascinating letter from at least two points of view, but hardly surprising since Joséphine was warm-hearted in even the most trying circumstances. Firstly, it evokes the improbable image of two defenseless women going to the aid of an equally defenseless Marie-Louise and her eighteen-month-old son. Secondly, the letter displays Joséphine's remarkable intuition. Incredible as it may seem, Marie-Louise was "in a highly vulnerable position, for—in the melee surrounding the tumultuous affair—no one had even thought of

Roustam and a Polish officer and had reached Paris the previous night. Caulaincourt came immediately to see Hortense with an account of Eugène's heroic performance on the fateful retreat. Joséphine heard more about Eugène's behavior through Mme. de Souza, who brought Hortense a letter from Charles de Flahaut, which centered mainly on Eugène: "He has won esteem, respect, and devotion on every side."[55] Other tributes to the viceroy came from Laure Junot, Napoléon's secretary Baron Fain, and all the Paris newspapers.

As the momentous year of 1812 drew to a close, Joséphine was in a state of perpetual alarm, and when the emperor's name was mentioned, she grew pale, blaming fate for having deprived him of her own consoling presence. Then there was Eugène, who faced the formidable task of pulling together the remains of the Grande Armée, which had lost its cavalry during the terrible Russian winter. Reports trickled through about the imminent desertion of the emperor's allies—first the Prussians, then the princes and princesses of the Confederation who, one by one, would soon abandon their emperor.

The one bright spot for her during that dark winter was the presence of Hortense, who, as confidante to both Marie-Louise and Napoléon, often dined with them at the Tuileries. The queen of Holland thought one compelling reason for the emperor's hasty return on December 18 was to revive sagging spirits, and it was hoped that the approaching Carnival would work its yearly magic by shifting attention away from the recent catastrophe. Although Hortense noted that the mood during Carnival was more serious, the annual balls and receptions were staged in the capital just as if an army of half a million men had not just perished. As 1813 dawned, not even the frenzied preparations to defend the capital against as imminent invasion of enemy troops were enough to alter "French gaiety," Hortense wrote. "Other nations are serious and grave; misfortune does not take them by surprise; they calculate all the odds and find energy in reflection. The French find theirs in merriment. At the very moment when the capital is threatened and all fortunes compromised, they still laugh, and try to save their precious possessions from the Cossacks as if they were at a party in the country. The theaters remained open until the very last moment."[56] Years later, Victor Hugo made a similar observation about the people of Paris: when things go badly for her, Paris dons a mask, and instead of a shroud, she puts on a domino.

14

Swan Song

January 1, 1813, fell on a Friday, something few people would have noticed, but Joséphine, always prey to Créole superstitions, remarked that the first day of the year 1813 falling on Friday was "a sign of great misfortunes."[1] Although they may have smiled at her gloomy predictions at the time, her friends must have looked back later with anything but a smile. For the year 1813 would witness the last full year of both Joséphine's life and Napoléon's reign, as his dominion in Europe slipped away.

In January Talleyrand would make overtures to the royalists who awaited the fall of "the Usurper." In May Eugène would see his stepfather for the last time after the battle of Lützen, and the deaths of Bessières and Duroc would leave him bereft of two beloved friends and comrades. In June Napoléon was to give up Spain, committing on June 4 perhaps the gravest error of his career by signing a peace treaty with Russia and Prussia. And by year's end, Murat and others would desert Napoléon as the Allies stood poised to cross the Rhine. To be sure, Napoléon would claim a few victories on the battlefield, but by the end of this depressing year, it was obvious to one and all that the days of the once mighty French Empire were numbered.

Joséphine had returned home from Prégny on October 25, 1812, and proceeded to make Malmaison once again the resort of fashionable people, including many who were prominent in political and military spheres, as the emperor wished her to do. One visitor was Eugène's close friend Marshal Oudinot, duc de Reggio, a valiant hero of the Russian retreat, whose wife left a description of their warm reception: "After having made me sit beside her on her sofa, she [Joséphine] addressed to me the . . . kind and affectionate questions that put heart into a timid young woman whom she wished to encourage. She was holding a spray of white camellia, a new product of her magnificent hothouses. She gave it to me with infinite grace. . . . Soon afterwards, the empress rose and went to find the marshal, who was engaged in conversation at the end of the room. She had not seen him for two years. He complimented her on her appearance of good health.

'Yes,' she replied with a sweet, resigned air and melancholy smile, 'that is my compensation for being no longer the reigning empress!'"[2]

Mme. de Chastenay found a welcome at Malmaison, too, and marveled at the wondrous enchantment of the conservatory: "I never went [there] without having that truly amiable lady conduct me personally to see the flowers in her hothouse, which one might call the Palace of Flora. She knew all the rare plants, was interested in their reproduction, and understood perfectly how this was done. Botany owes to her in large part the popularity that it acquired at this time in France. From all parts of Europe she was sent objects of incalculable value. Following her example, the beautiful ladies who had access to the court embroidered only marvelous flowers and even learned their names and classifications. The luxury of plants, which [Joséphine] now encouraged, had turned the flower market into a sort of museum."[3]

After the emperor's return from Russia at the end of 1812, social life resumed at the Tuileries, but its regeneration required the charismatic presence of Napoléon himself, because Marie-Louise was unable to please, even with Hortense's able assistance. Although Joséphine was very well informed of both political and military affairs, she was physically removed from court, whereas Hortense remained at its epicenter. Early in the new year, she was astonished to receive a visit from the Austrian ambassador, Prince Schwarzenberg, who explained that he had come to see Queen Hortense because she knew Napoléon's character so well. The object of the visit was to ascertain whether her stepfather truly wanted peace (as the prince claimed Austria did), and he hoped the queen of Holland could persuade the emperor of this, possibly enlisting the help of Prince Eugène.[4] Charles de Flahaut was in Paris from March 12 through the 24th, picking up instructions for Eugène, although this could hardly have been the only reason for his visit, for even Hortense admitted in her memoirs at this time that Flauhaut's love for her was now general knowledge.

The relationship with Austria was now strained beyond repair, and a major new threat arose when the czar signed an accord with the Prussian king, Frederick William III, who declared war on France on March 17. Napoléon arrived at Erfurt on April 25 with his new army for his final campaign into Germany, and was joined by Eugène and his corps near Lützen on May 1, where they met the Russians and Prussians. It was a terrible day, for the viceroy lost one of his most cherished friends and Napoléon his finest cavalry commander when Bessières was struck in the breast by a cannon ball and died instantly. The battle of Lützen on May 2 sent the enemy into retreat, so the French marched on Dresden, where Eugene's corps upset Miloradovitch on May 7. Eugène was granted a leave, because the emperor needed him to build another Italian army and protect his kingdom against probable Austrian aggression, and so Eugène and his stepfather said farewell on May 12, neither realizing that it was to be their last.

That month Malmaison was darkened by grief, for when Joséphine heard of Bessières's death, followed by that of Marshal Duroc on May 22, she was so intensely stricken that she became ill. Duroc, whom Joséphine had seen daily as grand marshal of the palace, was fatally wounded in Silesia just after having fought beside Eugène at Lützen. In Joséphine's letter of condolence to Mme. Duroc, she spoke of their long friendship, Duroc's excellent qualities, and his undying devotion to the emperor. Joséphine knew how cruelly Eugène was affected by losing his two oldest comrades-in-arms in the same campaign, but she was relieved that he was now returning to Auguste and his children in Milan.

At the end of May Joséphine was off to Saint-Leu to collect her two grandsons for their stay at Malmaison while Hortense and Adèle de Broc were in Aix-en-Savoie. Joséphine's reports to Hortense about Napoléon-Louis and Oui-Oui begin on June 11: "Don't worry for a moment about your children [who] are in perfect health. Their skin is white and pink. . . . Since they came, they have not had the slightest problem. I am enchanted to have them near me, they are charming."[5] Now that they were older (Napoléon-Louis was nine and Louis-Napoléon five), they must have been fascinated by the army officers who came to pay their respects to their grandmother, sometimes straight from the battlefield. General Marcognet arrived on June 14 on his way to serve under their uncle Eugène, so Joséphine gave him a letter for her son: "My life is always the same, seeing to my gallery and plants. My garden—the most beautiful thing possible—is even more frequented by the Parisians than my salon, because at the moment of this writing, they say there are at least thirty people promenading in the garden."[6]

Many people came for the sheer pleasure of touring this showplace with the empress herself, the gardens open to visitors, the conservatory to horticulturists and enthusiasts of botany, the gallery to art lovers, the farm to those interested in husbandry. All of it delighted her grandchildren: setting sail in the barque on the lake with their governess; racing over the ornamental bridges and throwing bread to the black swans; playing on rainy days in the tropical forest of the giant glass conservatory; cuddling the newborn lambs in the sheepfold; watching the cows being milked and butter being churned in the warm, inviting dairy; and giggling at Paulus Potter's *Vache Qui Pisse* in the art gallery.

On June 10, Hortense's sojourn at Aix-en-Savoie was ruined by a catastrophic accident. She and Adèle were on a sketching expedition and decided to explore the cascade of Grésy. As Adèle tried to cross the unsteady bridge over the cascade, her foot slipped and she plunged into the swift current and drowned before she could be rescued. Both Hortense and Joséphine were shattered, for Adèle and her sister had virtually grown up in their household. "What a horrible event!" Joséphine wrote her daughter on June 16. "Since yesterday, when I heard of it, I could hardly bring myself to write. . . . I can only imagine what state you are in. I am so disturbed I am sending my chamberlain, M. de Turpin, to you so he can give me assurance of your health. I want to come myself to share your sadness."[7] Other letters followed in the same vein, but by June 29 she was again preoccupied with the children: "[They] show excellent character and great attachment to

you [Hortense]. The more I see of them, the more I love them [but] do not spoil them. . . . They follow exactly what you have ordered for their diet and studies. When they have worked hard during
the week, I allow them to lunch and dine with me on Sunday. . . . I received from Paris two small
gold chickens, which lay silver eggs by means of a spring. I gave them to [the boys] as a gift from
you, as having come from Aix."[8]

The first shots of the contest against the Coalition were fired on August 22, and Eugène was
immediately engaged against the Austrians in Italy. Besides her concern for his safety, Joséphine knew
the outcome would profoundly affect the futures of her entire family. Napoléon's father-in-law, the
Austrian emperor Francis I, had turned against him, and his former marshal, Bernadotte, had joined the
Coalition. Napoléon's German allies were about to unite with the enemy, including Eugène's father-in-
law, Maximilien-Joseph of Bavaria. Like the kings of Saxony and Württemberg, he owed his crown to
the French emperor, but they all knew Napoléon's march toward Berlin was foredoomed.

The terrible battle of Leipzig (October 16–19) was a shattering defeat for Napoléon, and the
Grande Armée was driven back across the Rhine, battle-weary and decimated by typhus. Lavalette
noticed the emperor's accustomed stamina had finally deserted him. As the allied rulers entered
Frankfurt on November 5 and 13, the princes of the Confederation, all of whom Joséphine had
entertained at the Tuileries, Mainz, and Strasbourg, hastened to salvage their thrones. Even the
grand duke of Baden (Stéphanie de Beauharnais's husband) went over to the Allies on November
20, expressing his sincere regrets to Napoléon, and the formidable Confederation of the Rhine, so
painstakingly assembled, simply shuddered . . . and fell. Joséphine tried to remain diplomatically
neutral, but on November 4 she had written a calculated letter to Napoléon: "Come home. Identify
yourself with France and all hearts will be yours."[9] What effect her letter had we do not know, but
the debilitated emperor did return to France on November 9.

Early in November the Rémusats came to dine with Joséphine at Malmaison. Augustin-Laurent de Rémusat had been among the first nobles to rally to Napoléon, a zealous functionary who
served as prefect of the palace, first chamberlain, and master of the emperor's wardrobe. Claire de
Rémusat had attended Joséphine for many years as her *dame d'honneur*, but now she was working with
Talleyrand to prepare the way for the return of the Bourbons and would be among the first to distribute
the white cockades when the enemy sovereigns reached Paris. The Rémusats brought Joséphine the
none-too-reassuring news that Louis Bonaparte had offered help to the emperor in his time of need,
knowing that Louis's presence would upset Joséphine. So she immediately wrote to Hortense: "Surely,
it is very praiseworthy and good of Louis, but his return makes me fear new torments for you. . . . Have
courage, my dear daughter; a pure soul like yours always triumphs over all."[10] Louis did return, wearing
a Dutch uniform and claiming to be the rightful king of Holland, but when Méneval saw him he was
stunned by his appearance, for "he was in a deplorable state of health, nearly crippled in all his limbs."[11]

Joseph surrendered the throne of Spain, so the emperor made him a lieutenant-general in January 1814, unwisely giving him the responsibility of defending Paris. Hortense visited him at his château at Mortefontaine and was saddened to learn that he was still betraying his wife with other women. Jérome gave up his kingdom of Westphalia on October 26 without a fight, and his wife, Catherine of Württemberg, courageously stood beside her husband despite her parents' opposition. By January 1814, therefore, Napoléon had three unemployed kings on his hands—just as Madame Mère had predicted.

In Italy Eugène was fighting his last campaign, "making his retreat in excellent order . . . the Italians show spirit," as Joséphine told Hortense.[12] Constant reported that "Prince Eugène was holding out only by dint of superior skill against a far more numerous [Austrian] army."[13] The principalities and kingdoms held by the Bonapartes and the de Beauharnais family were crumbling, one after another. Maximilian's defection probably hurt Joséphine most since it seriously affected the future of Eugène and his family. On November 22, Eugène was visited by Prince Augustus von Thurn und Taxis wearing a disguise and carrying a letter from the Allies, with a covering note from Eugène's father-in-law. Eugène realized at once that Metternich, having detached the Allies one by one from Napoléon, wanted to draw the viceroy to his side by offering him the crown of Italy, which he knew Eugène had wanted for years. Although this was no doubt the most difficult decision of his life, Eugène replied that he could sacrifice his life for his people, but not his honor. He told Prince Taxis that he could not abandon his benefactor, Napoléon, to whom he had vowed his loyalty and to whom he owed everything, although he was greatly concerned for the future of his wife and children. When Taxis returned to the Bavarian king with Eugène's answer, he was at the theater in Karlsruhe, seated in the royal box with Stéphanie de Beauharnais. Taxis handed the reply to Maximilian, who opened it. Stéphanie looked at the king and, smiling, asked, "Well?" to which the king replied: "Eugène won't do it." Stéphanie said she knew he wouldn't, for "I know him too well not to realize that it couldn't have been any other way."[14] When the king notified Metternich of the viceroy's refusal, Metternich said he suspected it all along, for he too was well aware of Eugène's exemplary character. Yet another trial came Eugène's way when the Austrians declared that they would grant an armistice on condition that Eugène abandon France. Again he refused.

The sun that rose on January 1, 1814, dawned on the epilogue of Joséphine's life. She had remarked on December 30 that she hoped for a quiet new year, but it was a futile wish. When she closed her eyes, she could see the flames of Moscow, Eugène struggling valiantly but hopelessly against the Austrians, the collapsing kingdoms of their former allies, and, for the first time in ten years, mighty armies ready to invade France. The Coalition numbered 250,000, and on January 25 the emperor would leave the Tuileries to meet them with only 80,000 conscripts, most of them very young. He was said to remark, with his usual wry humor, that it would take General Bonaparte to rescue the Emperor Napoléon from *this* predicament.

Joséphine was also concerned for Auguste, who was expecting her fifth child in war-torn Italy. Eugène was trying vainly to hold the line at the Adige, and then Mantua, but he was unable to give his stepfather a clear picture, which led to an unfortunate misunderstanding. Eugène had asked the Allies for protection when Auguste's child was born, and Napoléon misinterpreted it as a treasonable move. His mental and physical efforts were focused on the brilliant battles of the "Campaign of France," so with (unfounded) suspicions about Eugène's loyalty, the emperor once again turned to Joséphine, dispatching orders for the viceroy through her. When Napoléon's message reached her on February 9, she dashed off a brief, urgent note: "Do not lose an instant, my dear Eugène; whatever the obstacles, redouble your efforts to fulfill the orders given you by the emperor. . . . His wish is that you . . . march toward the Alps, leaving in Mantua and the Italian fortresses only troops belonging to the Kingdom of Italy. [Napoléon's] letter ends with these words: 'France before all! France has need of all her sons!' Come then, my dear son, hasten. Your zeal will never be of more use to the emperor. I can assure you every moment is precious. I know your wife was preparing to leave Milan. Tell me if I can be of service to her. Good-bye, my dear Eugène, I have no more time except to embrace you."[15]

Messages between members of the de Tascher-de Beauharnais family were passing back and forth almost daily, for on February 9—possibly before his mother's letter arrived—Eugène told Louis de Tascher to report personally about his operations to the emperor at his headquarters in France, wherever that might be. During this critical time when Napoléon was fighting for his life, it was likely that messages would be intercepted, but Joséphine and her family were privileged due to the devotion of their relative, Postmaster General Antoine Lavalette. One such letter was Joséphine's to Hortense at the Tuileries: "I am sending . . . my response to the vicereine . . . forward it by Lavalette. I told Auguste just what I thought. I am convinced that the emperor will give up Italy; but no matter what . . . our dear Eugène will leave behind his beautiful reputation; that is above everything else. . . . I cannot tell you how sad I am. I tried, in my letter, to encourage Auguste."[16]

When the report came in January 1814 that the Allies had crossed the Rhine, Hortense was dining with the emperor, Marie-Louise, and their child, the little king of Rome. After dinner, the emperor—in a surprisingly jocular mood—called in General Bertrand and, in the presence of Hortense and Marie-Louise, dictated his altogether remarkable plan for organizing the army on the plains of Chalons. On January 23, two days before he left to take command, he walked Hortense and Marie-Louise into his study and burned all the documents that might compromise them. Hortense tried to comfort the weeping Marie-Louise, who would never see her husband again after that night.

During the frightful campaign that followed, Hortense took bulletins to her mother at Malmaison. If the news was bad, however, she hid them, because Joséphine was so upset to hear of the emperor's reversals. When news came of victories, however, Joséphine's health improved visibly. In February Eugène's aide-de-camp Louis de Tascher carried a message from Eugène for Hortense to pass along to Malmaison. Murat had triumphantly entered Bologna at the end of January, and then he and Caroline, as king and queen of Naples, had signed a treaty with Austria. This meant that Eugène could no longer stay on the Adige River but had to take a position on the right bank of the Mincio, a foothold that would be advantageous for offensive action. Eugène's letter said he had just won a victory over the Austrians (no doubt the sharp defeat he gave them at the Mincio on February 8), enabling him to keep them behind the line of Mantua.

During the dark days of the battle for France, Joséphine was rolling bandages with her ladies in the salon, living on the fringes of the great storm about to lash Paris, but Hortense, who was at the Tuileries with Marie-Louise, was in the eye of the hurricane. By the last week in March, the Allies were within striking distance of the capital, and on March 28, one of Hortense's attendants announced that danger was imminent. Only the night before, Hortense had spent a deceptively quiet evening with Marie-Louise, playing whist with the minister of justice, comte Mathieu Molé, and Talleyrand.

On the evening of March 28, a council was held to decide what Marie-Louise should do. Hortense, whom Louis ordered three times to leave the city, urged her to stay in order to encourage the people, but she left anyway with Cambacérès and her son, much to the dismay of the National Guard under the ineffective Joseph Bonaparte and the contempt of Hortense, who was "revolted by such weakness."[17] The same day, Hortense sent an urgent note to her mother to leave Malmaison instantly for Navarre. This was sound advice, the Neuilly bridge having been blown up in the defense of Paris, as Hortense learned the following day. The duchesse de Reggio was among the many who fled Paris. All during the night, in a crowded inn at Versailles, she heard the passage of men, carriages, and horses, and recorded her impressions of this watershed moment in history:

> Soon, daylight revealed the most astonishing sight that human eyes perhaps had ever looked upon. We stood motionless at our windows; what we saw passing . . . was . . . the Empire! The Empire, which was departing, with all its pomp and splendor; the ministers, all in their coaches and six, taking with them portfolio, wife, children, jewels, livery; the entire Council of State; the archives; the crown diamonds; the administrations. . . . The cannon had begun to thunder at daybreak.[18]

As Joséphine prepared to join the train of refugees, she responded to her daughter's message: "My dear Hortense, I have been courageous until this moment when I received your letter. What sadness that I shall be separated from you, and God knows for how long. I am following your advice; I leave in the morning for Navarre. I have only sixteen guards, and they are all wounded; I shall keep them, but frankly I do not really need them. I am so unhappy to be separated from my children that I am indifferent to my fate. I am worried only for you. . . . Try to let me know where you are going. I will try to follow you."[19]

On the morning of March 29, wet and cold like the day she left the Tuileries, Joséphine set out with the ladies of her household, leaving her devoted botanist-gardener, Aimé Bonpland, in charge. With only a few moments to get ready, she departed from Malmaison with her jewelry cases and her finest diamonds and pearls sewn into a padded undergarment. Her party spent the night at Mantes, and on March 30, Joséphine was again in her bed at Navarre.

Louis was finally able to persuade Hortense to leave Paris when he warned her that their children might be taken hostage. Although Cossacks had been seen in the plains outside the city, Hortense, her two children, and her suite left in three carriages at 9 P.M. on March 29, headed for a friend's château of Glatigny. As they rolled out of Paris, it was strange to hear guns turned upon the city, cannon that had once signified occasions for rejoicing. Hortense did not yet know that the next morning at dawn, the emperor would be rushing to the defense of his beleaguered capital (with Armand Caulaincourt, followed by General Bertrand and Charles de Flahaut), unaware that the capitulation of his marshals rendered any further resistance futile. In Paris, as prayers were being recited at Notre Dame, Vivant Denon asked Joseph Bonaparte for authorization to pack up the precious collections at the Louvre, and the nobility of the Faubourg Saint-Germain were rejoicing.

When Hortense and her children joined her mother at Navarre, they were not cordially received by Joséphine's staff, who resented the etiquette that enveloped the queen of Holland. Mlle. Cochelet, Hortense's lady-in-waiting, left a picture of the hapless women gathering around Joséphine: "All that had been most brilliant among us at Paris was [now] at Navarre: the duchesse de Bassano, who arrived . . . with her children and . . . sisters . . . Mme. Mollien, so fondly attached to the queen [Hortense] . . . Mme. Gazzani, tearful and still beautiful. All without a man, without a notion of what to do!" But, Mlle. Cochelet added, despite Joséphine's happiness in seeing them all, she was "tortured inexpressibly about the fate of the emperor."[20]

On March 31, the allies entered Paris, but their restoration of the Bourbons under Louis XVIII was not received with unmitigated enthusiasm. An eminent Englishman, Bishop Stanley, who was in Paris that spring of 1814, witnessed it firsthand: "The king was to me a very secondary person. . . . He sat down in a fine chair of Bonaparte's . . . in a Balcony facing the Place de Carrousel, from whence he looked down on 10,000 troops. . . . The shouts here were not what they ought to have been. Comparatively few cried 'God bless him!' and I much fear the number who thought it was still less."[21] Although well-meaning, Louis XVIII was among those who "had learnt nothing and forgotten nothing," hardly the person to attempt to step into the shoes of Napoléon le Grand. Laure Junot was speaking for many of her countrymen when she remarked that the restoration "in no way evolved out of a wish of the people . . . [but rather] as the least harmful of solutions."[22]

Mme. de la Tour du Pin was invited to a dinner that the commander of the Austrian troops, Prince Schwarzenberg, had staged for his allies: "There I saw all the conquerors and was witness of all the baseness with which they were surrounded and so to speak overwhelmed. What a curious specta- cle for a philosophical mind! Everything recalled Napoléon: the furniture, the supper, the guests. . . . The thought came to me . . . that there was not one present who seemed worthy to be his conqueror. . . . As for myself, I had a feeling of shame, which was probably not shared by any one else."[23]

Joséphine's anxiety was somewhat allayed when baron de Maussion, auditor to the Coun- cil of State, arrived. She kept asking if he were certain the emperor was still alive, but upon learning he was being sent to Elba, she ran to Hortense's room at midnight and threw herself upon her daughter's bed, crying: "O . . . poor Napoléon, whom they are sending to the island of Elba! . . . If it were not for his wife, I would go and be imprisoned with him!"[24] To Eugène in Mantua she wrote of her mental suffering over the emperor's fate, the blasphemy of the newspapers, the ingratitude of people upon whom he had lavished so much. "As for you," she said, "you are free and no longer bound by any oath of loyalty; anything you might try to do now for his cause would be useless; act for your family. . . . I live in a trance and terrible anxiety."[25] Although Joséphine had all along urged Eugène to support his stepfather in every way and unconditionally approved his refusal of the Allies' offer of the Italian crown, "act for your family" was the only reasonable counsel she could give Eugène, who on April 24 consented to evacuate Italy with the French troops.

The very day that Auguste's baby was born (April 13), the despondent emperor took poi- son, which had, however, lost its potency. Thinking he was dying, he summoned Caulaincourt and asked him to send Eugène his finest dressing-case. "He had words of praise for the viceroy," wrote Caulaincourt, "and spoke of him as a prince who had always served him faithfully. 'Eugène,' he told me, 'is the only one of my family who never has given me a single cause for dissatisfaction. His mother made me very happy; those are the sweetest recollections of my life.'"[26] Then he urged the minister to support both Eugène's and Joséphine's interests, and to "tell Joséphine she has been much in my thoughts."

In his last known letter to Joséphine, Napoléon pours out his heart, telling her that the world will know what he is really like: "I shall substitute the pen for the sword. The narrative . . . will be surprising; people have only seen me in profile, and I shall show myself full-face. They have betrayed me, yes, all of them. I except only our dear Eugène, so worthy of you and of me. May he be happy under a king who can appreciate the instincts of nature and of honor! Adieu, my dear Joséphine. Resign yourself, as I am doing, and never lose the memory of one who has never forgot- ten you, and never will."[27]

In mid-April, as tulips were ready to bloom in the Malmaison gardens, Joséphine came home. But instead of the accustomed tranquility, she found a Russian guard established in her château, pieces of furniture damaged, the gardeners trying to protect their fragile plants from the horses' hooves, and an indignant Mlle. d'Avrillion, who reported that the soldiers had arrived so suddenly that no precautions could be taken.

Others were more considerate, and indeed the court that Joséphine held there in those last weeks of her life was almost as brilliant and varied in its own way as during the heyday of the Empire. Vestibule, salon, and gardens were thronged with visitors: aristocrats she had saved from execution; princes from the former Confederation of the Rhine such as Crown Prince Ludwig (Auguste's brother); reigning monarchs who formed part of the Allied Coalition; and representatives of the restored monarchy.

Among the first to visit was Joséphine's friend the marquis de Caulaincourt, who had been helping to provide for her and her family. Then came the king of Prussia with his two sons, and Stéphanie de Beauharnais' husband, the grand duke of Baden. Another was the future king of Belgium, Prince Leopold de Saxe-Cobourg, who remembered her kindness in the past and admired Joséphine's and her children's "dignified nobility" under such difficult circumstances. The burden imposed on Joséphine's staff was onerous indeed, for cuisine and decor had to meet her exacting standards. The team of gardeners under Bonpland worked overtime because everyone explored the horticultural profusion of the scented greenhouse, visited the model dairy and sheepfold, and wondered at such marvels as the female orangutan and kangaroos. The principal attraction, however, was Joséphine herself, for everyone found in her a quality sadly wanting in the Bourbon assembly at the Tuileries. Like a ballerina, Joséphine was a professional who was able to conceal from the audience the formidable efforts required to present a flawless performance.

Even members of the restored royal family sought Joséphine out. The comte d'Artois (soon to be Charles X) paid her a visit, as did his nephew, the duc de Berry, who sent Joséphine a message on the king's behalf, offering her an escort and provisions of whatever she needed. In Chevallier's opinion, this was not an innocent offer, for Louis XVIII—returning to France in the train of the victorious Allies—was not welcomed by the French people, so he tried to associate himself with the Napoleonic heritage. Napoléon's "name and glory hung over [the allied sovereigns] like giant threats, and impressed them all the more because they knew the full force of his influence with the troops."[28] The troops might be gone, but the "name and glory" were still there, and it was to Joséphine that this aura now attached. Even with the powerful Allies behind him, Louis XVIII did not dare scorn this woman so highly valued as the fallen emperor's "good star," so Joséphine suddenly "became the link between the two Frances confronting each other."[29] It was a role she knew by heart, having played it to the hilt during the golden days of the Empire, when she had been able to blend remnants of the old nobility with the so-called parvenus of her husband's régime.

Emperor Francis I of Austria wanted to visit her, too, but he feared it would pain her, and when Joséphine heard about this, she was surprised: "Why? I am not the woman he has

François Gérard (1770–1837),
Alexander I of Russia (Malmaison).
Alexander was the son of Paul I and
Maria Feodorovna, who had been
graciously received by Louis XVI and
Marie-Antoinette and took back to
Pavlovsk carriage-loads of French luxury
products. Alexandre was reared
primarily by his high-handed
grandmother, the francophile Catherine II,
and he was strongly influenced by the
mystic baroness de Krüdener, who
convinced him that his mission was to
liberate Europe. Alexander supposedly
died in 1825, but it was rumored that he
lived on as a hermit under an assumed
name for several more years in Siberia.

dethroned; it is his own daughter!"[30] Count Nesselrode hastened to assure Hortense and Joséphine that Prince Metternich would always remember the many kindnesses the empress had shown his wife and children when he was Austrian ambassador in Paris.

When Hortense returned to Malmaison on April 17 after visiting Marie-Louise at Rambouillet, she was dumbfounded to find the courtyard filled with Cossacks. Worse still was being told that her mother was promenading in the gardens with the czar of Russia! Like Charles de Flahaut, Hortense regarded Alexander as an enemy of the de Beauharnais family and of France. But there she was, the deposed empress in a white lawn dress and cashmere shawl, on the arm of the tall, handsome, courteous, impeccably dressed czar, his pale blue eyes gleaming with a mystic fervor. Joséphine introduced him, and although Hortense's cold demeanor embarrassed her mother, Alexander was undeterred. He was clearly attracted to Hortense, continued to seek her company, and wanted to serve as *chargé d'affaires* for her children. Gradually, Hortense's austerity softened, and Alexander returned again and again as his ties with the de Beauharnais family became stronger.[31] Then he brought his brothers, Grand Dukes Nicholas,

Michael, and Constantine, the last having figured prominently (along with Alexander himself) in Napoléon's most famous battle, Austerlitz, as Joséphine knew full well. No doubt the conversation turned to horticulture rather than warfare, for the gardens, punctuated with pavilions, undoubtedly reminded Alexander and his brothers of their mother's gardens at Pavlovsk.

Eugène arrived in Paris on May 9, having left Auguste and their children in Munich, and went directly to the Tuileries to pay his duty call on Louis XVIII. If he had thought it would be awkward, he was agreeably surprised, for the new court heaped embarrassingly effusive praise upon him. The king spoke to Eugène about all the good his mother had done for France; the comte d'Artois talked about his friendship with Eugène's father, Alexandre de Beauharnais; the duc de Berry expressed profound admiration for Eugène's campaigns (which he had always followed with interest); and one of the king's entourage told him that Berry was one of Prince Eugène's ardent admirers.[32] The high favor Eugène enjoyed among the Bourbons was not entirely disinterested in this case either, for his personal prestige could be eminently useful to a monarchy restored without the overwhelming support of the French people.

At the czar's request, Hortense invited him to visit Saint-Leu with Joséphine and Eugène on May 14, but Alexander felt guilty because he had foregone a Bourbon ceremony in Paris where his absence was highly conspicuous.[33] In fact, the Bourbons were so offended by the czar's absence that they sent an emissary to Hortense, saying they were shocked that she had chosen that particular day for her party and that the Empress Joséphine's popularity had given umbrage to the court. It was a cold, damp day, but they all went for a drive in the forest, and Joséphine, who rarely dressed adequately, became thoroughly chilled. She was so tired after her return that she threw herself onto her bed in all her clothing and drank the infusion of orange-flower water that Napoléon had always advised for a chill. She was also depressed, but Hortense thought the universal homage she received had momentarily lifted her spirits. When they were alone, however, Joséphine's eyes filled with tears as she talked of Napoléon on far-away Elba. She also feared that the promises for the future of her children might not be fulfilled, although the Allies had decided to treat the de Beauharnais separately from the Bonapartes.

Despite the protests of the devoted Mlle. d'Avrillion, Joséphine descended to do the honors at dinner, wearing a light, low-cut gown that displayed her still-beautiful neck and shoulders. Hortense sang her own songs for the czar after dinner, then Joséphine remained to discuss a subject of utmost concern—a settlement for Eugène. Hortense was to receive the duchy of Saint-Leu and a handsome income, and on April 20, Louis Bonaparte finally agreed to "a legal separation, entire and perfect."[34]

On May 21, Hortense and Eugène took Czar Alexander to see the waterworks at Marly, insisting that their mother remain in bed. During this visit, Alexander confided to Eugène that Hortense "seemed to be someone I have found again," and it has been claimed that he fell in love with her. He seemed to have become devoted to Eugène as well, for when the former viceroy became ill with perhaps the same virus afflicting Joséphine, the czar insisted upon remaining with him, even taking his own meals beside Eugène's bed.

The dizzying round of lunches and dinners had greatly taxed Joséphine's limited strength, but the episode that doubtless fatigued her most was the arrival of Germaine de Staël, who burst in upon her with questions the indefatigable writer "had been saving up since 1810," as someone said. She hurled them at Joséphine as they toured the art gallery, her curiosity piqued about Joséphine's feelings toward Napoléon, who had never ceased to fascinate her. The duchesse de Reggio left a vignette of Germaine's visit and Joséphine's condition:

> When the empress and Mme. de Staël appeared, the former wore an air of great . . . emotion. . . . During [their] conference, there had been shown into the drawing room . . . the Countess Walewska, the Polish woman to whom the emperor was said to have attached himself so fondly during the campaign of 1806. [Germaine bowed and left.] These two women, one had detested the emperor [Germaine], the other [he] had perhaps too well loved [Maria Walewska], drawn by the same impulse toward the repudiated consort [Joséphine], formed . . . a strange contrast.
>
> Joséphine, however, gave us no time to reflect upon this singular meeting; after responding to Mme. de Staël's farewell courtesy, she quickly came up to the hearth, where we were all standing in silence and said, without any preamble: "I have just had a painful interview. Would you believe that, among other questions Mme. de Staël was pleased to put to me, she asked if I still loved the emperor? She appeared to wish to analyze my soul in the presence of this great misfortune. I, who never ceased to love the emperor throughout his happy days . . . is it likely that today I should grow cold toward him?"
>
> The empress was already very ill. Her head was wrapped in a large English shawl; she was flushed, her breathing was oppressed. . . . One could see that she was suffering in both body and soul. She conducted almost the whole of the conversation, talking with a freedom inspired probably by the sympathy that she saw imprinted upon Mme. de Saint-Aulaire's features and mine; and when she withdrew, she made us promise to return and dine with her the next Sunday. Alas! before then she was dead![35]

This account is revealing, for as ill as she was, Joséphine still made an heroic effort to receive people who wanted to see her. It also documents her continued courtesy in welcoming Maria Walewska to Malmaison; Hortense wrote that she asked the countess to come because she had been so close to the emperor! Despite her increasing indisposition, Joséphine received the king of Prussia and his two sons on May 24, no doubt showing them the porcelain their beautiful, patriotic mother, Queen Louise, had sent her. The following day, Joséphine's condition worsened, but this did not deter the czar from bringing his younger brothers, Grand Dukes Nicolas and Michael. Hortense was impressed by their gentle manners, noble bearing, and humane sentiments, for they described to her, with tears in their eyes, the scenes of carnage they had witnessed in the ruined villages through which they had passed. Although still unwell, Eugène showed them Joséphine's art gallery and took them on a walk through the park to see the black swans and kangaroos.

Even now, Joséphine attempted to play the role of hostess, appearing for dinner in a splendid creation by Leroy. Then she danced with the czar and imprudently strolled with him through the park. Nobody seemed to realize how ill she was, for she skillfully concealed it, and the doctors assured Hortense and Eugène there was no real cause for alarm. The flow of visitors continued, Grand Duke Constantine coming several more times, telling Hortense he had heard nothing but praise for her and her mother wherever he traveled in France.

When Alexander returned on May 27, there was a large number of guests, including, according to tradition, the mysterious "Englishman" who had known Yeyette (Joséphine) in Martinique forty years earlier. Hortense officiated, and although the others had left early, the czar stayed and insisted on sending his personal physician for a second opinion. On May 28, Joséphine took a turn for the worse, so Hortense insisted upon calling her doctor, but her mother forbade it on the grounds that it might hurt her own doctor's feelings. When Hortense was persuaded to rest, a maid stayed with Joséphine and later reported that her mistress was calm, repeating from time to time: "Bonaparte. . . . l'Ile d'Elbe . . . le Roi de Rome."[36] These were among her last audible words.

The next morning, May 29, Hortense and Eugène went early into Joséphine's room, accompanied by Aimé Bonpland, her friend since 1804. She reached out her arms to her children but could barely speak, and Hortense found her mother so changed in appearance that she knew death was near. Since Joséphine's own chaplain, Monseigneur Barral, was away, Abbé Bertrand (tutor of Hortense's children) was asked to administer the last rites of the Catholic Church at 11 A.M., which Joséphine received, "submitting herself completely to the will of God."[37] Fully conscious until the end, she talked calmly about her approaching death and appeared to be perfectly resigned to her fate. As the bells rang the noon hour in the village church in Rueil that Pentecost Sunday of 1814, Empress Joséphine breathed her last, only a few days before her fifty-first birthday.

Joséphine's bedroom at Malmaison was the place she would have chosen to die, for, like the tented chamber where she and Bonaparte began their married life on rue de la Victoire, it too was in tent form, hung with imperial crimson, appropriate cerements for an empress. On the cloth-draped walls were displayed Redouté's flower images she loved so much. Another strange fact of her implausible story is that the setting for the emperor's death, although far more modest, would be so similar to her own, for only seven years later, Napoléon's own life would end in his simply draped iron campaign bed in the damp house on St. Helena. Hanging on the walls were pictures of flowers, too, the ones he had cut from his own copy of the *Description de l'Egypte* by Joséphine's old friend, Dominique-Vivant Denon.

After Joséphine's death, Mlle. Cochelet cut off the empress's abundant chestnut hair and

Auguste Garneray (1785–1824). The Park at Malmaison. *The principal attraction of Malmaison for Joséphine was the large terrain that she could transform into her ideal garden. Here some of her guests have embarked upon the ornamental lake in a small canopied barque, for an excursion through her wondrous gardens. The black swans with coral beaks floating on the lake are native to Australia but were acclimatized at Malmaison.*

gave it to Hortense, and the sorrowing daughter and son left for the château of Saint-Leu at 2 P.M. According to imperial decorum, they were not allowed to remain on the premises, a rule of etiquette that no doubt derived from ancient royal protocol forbidding a king or queen to remain in a dwelling with a corpse or to attend funerals. Joséphine's body also lay in state in accordance with royal tradition: the room was hung with black crape, lighted with candles. She held her final reception on June 2, when crowds came from Paris to pay their last respects. Twenty thousand mourners filed past her bier, and those who could not squeeze into the village church at Rueil for the funeral lined the roads all the way back to the château of Malmaison. In death as in life, Joséphine was escorted by the military. On May 29 her Dragoons of the Imperial Guard had come to pay homage at her tomb, the local National Guards formed an honor guard all along her funeral route, and military honors were provided by a detachment of Russian Imperial Guards in full-dress uniform.

For the funeral service, the Archbishop of Tours invoked an encomium to Joséphine—"Blessed are the merciful, for they shall obtain mercy"—and as Msgr. Barral began to speak, a long rolling of drums was accompanied by the peal of bells from the churches of neighboring towns.

Crowded into the village church were foreign ambassadors, generals, marshals, aides-de-camp, peers of France, scholars, artists, representatives of the czar and of the king of Prussia, people of all nationalities, and the inhabitants of Rueil, who had considered Joséphine an angel of mercy. Eugène and Hortense were represented by Hortense's two sons Napoléon-Louis and Louis-Napoléon, along with other members of the de Tascher and de Beauharnais families.

News soon spread throughout the country that the Empress Joséphine was no more, and the nation figuratively draped itself with crape and felt itself orphaned. In her own way, she had been all things to all people: some said she had been "the guardian angel of France;" the émigrés honored her as the one who had restored them to their families and country; the unfortunate called her "our mother"; and thousands considered her Napoléon's lucky star. What they meant was that Joséphine had personified the emperor's great good fortune, mere superstitions, of course, but surprisingly widespread. What is certain, though, is that Joséphine lived during one of the most fecund periods in history, and that she moved at its very center. "Many lives were broken or snuffed out, destinies out of the common realm traversed history like meteors," Bernard Chevallier wrote. "Joséphine knew all of them—their most dramatic situations and their most intense joys. Her life was a résumé of the passions of her times."[38]

Not only the French, but foreigners as well were affected by Joséphine's death. One was Bishop Stanley, who hastened to Malmaison just after she died and wrote home to London on July 10, 1814:

> The French all speak highly of her, and it is impossible, on seeing Malmaison and hearing of [Joséphine's] virtues, not to join in their opinion. To be sure, as a Frenchman told me in running through a list of virtues, "Elle avait été un peu libertine, mais ce n'est rien çela, [She was a little free, but that was nothing]," and indeed, I could almost have added, "That is quite true," but every allowance should be made. Consider the situation in which she was placed, her education, her temptations; many a saint might have fallen from the eminence on which she stood; I never . . . felt more inclined to coincide in that benevolent verdict of the best of judges of human nature and human frailty, "Neither do I condemn thee, go and sin no more," than in criticizing the character of Joséphine.[39]

Attributed to Pierre-Paul Prud'hon (1758–1823), Napoléon During the Hundred Days (private collection). It is fitting that Joséphine's favorite artist, one of the most original of his day, should have painted this poignant last portrait of her husband at the time of his final visit to Malmaison. Prudhon's image captures the pathos of the moment: the former master of Europe is about to be exiled for life to a rocky island off the African coast, where he would try to recapture the joys of Malmaison by planting some of the flowers that had adorned Joséphine's garden.

Strange as it may seem, neither Hortense nor Eugène thought to inform the emperor of her death immediately. Although it has usually been said he learned of it by chance through a newspaper, Fanny Bertrand (wife of Marshal Bertrand) insists that she told him. When he heard the news, he "appeared profoundly afflicted; he shut himself up within, and would see no one but his grand marshal."[40] During the Hundred Days between his escape from Elba on March 1, 1815, and the Battle of Waterloo on June 18, Napoléon went to Malmaison with Hortense. Although she found it almost too painful to revisit the scene of her mother's death, she arranged a small luncheon for her stepfather on April 12 and the guests included, besides General Bertrand, Mathieu Molé, to whom Napoléon had offered the highest posts in government upon his return. The other was, not surprisingly, one of their oldest friends, Dominique-Vivant Denon, who had immediately offered his services. When the emperor arrived, Hortense did the honors, writing that he was overcome with emotion: "He walked everywhere with me and kept saying each moment: 'How all of these places remind me of her! I cannot believe she is not still here.'"[41] Before leaving, he told Hortense he wanted to go alone to see the room where Joséphine had died, and afterwards, he slowly walked out into the courtyard.

Napoléon's last visit took place on June 24, just before he left France on July 15 for his final exile. During the few days left him as a free man, he asked Hortense to go with him to spend five of them at Malmaison. As they walked through the house, he mused upon the early days of the Consulate, when he and Joséphine, Eugène, and Hortense had lived in that pleasant country retreat like a bourgeois family. He dwelt especially upon Joséphine who, as he liked to say, had adorned fifteen years of his life.

Then he and Hortense walked out into the gardens, and she recorded that the paradise her mother had created there elicited another flood of memories from her stepfather. They strolled past the cedar of Marengo, the meandering stream with the little barque they had launched one bright summer day with Vivant Denon, the Temple of Love with its floating bouquet of rhododendrons. Then the emperor suddenly stopped before a bank of roses, the flower that has come to be so intimately associated with Joséphine. Here in the Malmaison gardens with Hortense beside him, Napoléon was overwhelmed with sorrow as he paid his final tribute to his wife: "Poor Joséphine! I cannot accustom myself to living here without her. I seem always to see her coming along the path, gathering one of these flowers which she loved so well. Truly she was the most graceful woman I have ever seen."[42]

NOTES

INTRODUCTION

1. Quoted by Imbert de Saint-Amand, p. 74.

2. Quoted by Mansel, p. 121.

3. Ibid.

4. It is possible that Knapton meant that she was not a complex personality, which might be valid.

5. Chevallier 1996, p. viii.

6. Chastenay, p. 414.

7. This information was received by oral and written communication.

8. Dowd, p. 59.

9. Written communication from Gary Tinterow, May 25, 2000.

10. Ibid.

11. Chevallier 1988, p. iii.

12. Quoted by Herold 1963, p. 379.

CHAPTER 1

1. Janssens, p. 210.

2. These predictions have generally been considered to be authentic by many scholars, including Denys Sutton (*Apollo*, July 1977, p. 2). For a discussion of the matter see Hanoteau 1935, pp. 2–5.

3. Janssens, p. 37. Hanoteau does not attach any value to such stories, claiming that Joséphine did not show these qualities until she had been some time in France (Hanoteau 1935, p. 72).

4. Ibid., p. 38.

5. "Between 1787 and 1791, I saw M. de Beauharnais daily ... in fashionable society. He and his wife moved in different circles from ours, but M. de Beauharnais was accepted everywhere, for during the war he became acquainted with the highest in the land. Handsomely built, he was the finest dancer in Paris." (Bennett, p. 15).

6. Kircheisen, p. 68.

7. Hanoteau 1935, p. 76.

CHAPTER 2

1. Hanoteau 1935, p. 92. The details of the relationship described here come from this source.

2. Ibid., p. 85.

3. Quoted by Chevallier 1988, p. 49.

4. Quoted by Chevallier 1988, pp. 57–58.

5. Hanoteau 1927, vol. I, p. 5.

6. Janssens, p. 78.

7. Ibid., p. 112.

8. Ibid., p. 94.

9. Ibid., p. 87.

10. Ibid., p. 215.

11. Knapton, p. 89.

12. Bernard Chevallier and Ernest Knapton.

CHAPTER 3

1. Sollers, p. 216.

2. Laing, p. 51.

3. Quoted by Janssens, pp. 150–51.

4. The Goncourt brothers' phrase, quoted by Janssens, p. 152.

5. Chevallier 1988, p. 107.

6. Janssens, p. 151.

7. Adelbert de Bavière, p. 17.

8. Godechot, p. 250.

9. Desirée kept Bonaparte's letters to the end of her life and could never abide Joséphine. She married Napoleon's marshal, Bernadotte, and they became king and queen of Sweden.

10. Janssens, p. 188.

11. Hanoteau 1927, vol. I, p. 44.

12. Janssens, p. 201.

13. This letter is usually thought to be his first love letter to Joséphine, and although undated, it was most likely written in December 1795.

14. Janssens, p. 208.

CHAPTER 4

1. Hanoteau 1927, vol. I, p. 46.

2. Tomiche, p. 164.

3. d'Houville, p. 100.

4. Andoche Junot, duc d'Abrantès, fought with distinction at Milesimo, Lonato, and Venice. He was among the first Bonaparte told of the Egyptian Campaign, and he performed valiantly. His wife, Laure Permon Junot, wrote her memoirs as the duchesse d'Abrantès.

5. Bourgeat, pp. 33–34.

6. Imbert de Saint-Amand, p. 16.

7. Laing, p. 101.

8. Chevallier 1988, p. 136.

9. Imbert de Saint-Amand, p. 106.

10. Quoted by Chevallier 1988, p. 141.

11. Ibid., p. 142.

12. d'Houville, p. 120.

13. Knapton, p. 141.

14. Aubenas, vol. I, pp. 348–49.

15. Mauguin, p. 21.

16. Imbert de Saint-Amand, p. 189.

17. Sollers, p. 46. Stendhal said that Denon's discretion was legendary.

CHAPTER 5

1. In 1787 Volney had published his *Voyage en Syrie et en Egypte pendant les années 1783, 1784, et 1785.* He and Bonaparte had met in February 1792, and he was a frequent guest at Malmaison.

2. Junot, p. 121.

3. Sollers, p. 220.

4. Eugène's memoirs report 35,000 troops, almost 400 transports, and 13 ships of the line.

5. Masson 1920, p. 131.

6. Ibid., p. 132.

7. Chevallier 1988, p. 183.

8. Adalbert de Bavière, p. 23.

9. Ibid., p. 24.

10. Ibid.

11. Quoted by Imbert de Saint-Amand, p. 74. Although Claire de Rémusat's memoirs must be used with caution, she was nevertheless a well-informed and intelligent observer, and her opinion in this case is entirely valid.

12. Chevallier 1988, p. 124.

13. Kircheisen, p. 187.

14. Marshal Jean Lannes, later duc de Montebello, was called the "Roland of the army."

15. Adalbert de Bavière, p. 30.

16. If Roustam was stunned by his first glimpse of Paris, the Parisians were equally amazed by their first sight of him. Mounted on a superbly caparisoned horse, attired in a resplendent costume with a saber flashing at his side, Roustam became a fascinating complement to Joséphine's entourage and a favorite with the crowds. He was painted by Carle Vernet and one of Joséphine's favorite artists, Jean-Baptiste Isabey (probably at her suggestion), and Roustam's white turban lights up almost every battle scene, for he was never far from his master. Mameluke costumes would provide an exciting alien note in French culture and make an indelible impression on art, literature, music, theater, and even fashion.

17. Adalbert de Bavière, p. 31.

18. Ibid., p. 32.

19. Constant Wairy served Eugène for only a few months and then briefly became Joséphine's *valet de chambre.* Napoleon took him on as his *premier valet de chambre* from the time he left for Marengo in 1800 until April 1814. Constant's copious memoirs (see Jones) contain some errors as to places and dates and must be used with care.

20. Imbert de Saint-Amand, p. 267.

21. Hanoteau 1927, vol. I, p. 63.

22. Imbert de Saint-Amand, p. 299.

Chapter 6

1. Chevallier 1988, p. 261.

2. What Bonaparte accomplished during his first five months as first consul was amazing: he brought a long civil war to an end; he created an administrative system that essentially survives in France to this day; and he rescued the state from chaos and almost certain bankruptcy.

3. Chastenay, p. 297.

4. Tour du Pin, p. 313.

5. Greer, p. 94.

6. Jones, p. 165.

7. Bourgeat, p. 77.

8. Laborde, p. 65. The Jardin des Plantes in Paris, founded in 1626 by Louis XIII, was one of the first botanical gardens.

9. In his thirty-eight-year career, Talma participated in more than seventy presentations, and during the Paris season, he acted every other night. Talma was forever in debt in spite of imperial largesse. He entertained his friends lavishly and spent unstintingly to attain perfection in every aspect of his art, from costumes to props.

10. Tour du Pin, p. 1.

11. Fox's death in 1806 would be an irreparable loss to Bonaparte, who said sadly, "If he had lived, we would have had peace." One of the provisions of the Treaty of Amiens was that the English relinquish Malta to the Knights, but they kept stalling, never really intending to do so.

12. Chastenay, p. 9.

13. Ibid., p. 308.

14. Masson 1920, pp. 367–68.

15. The German historian Kircheisen supported Napoléon, stating that Enghien deserved his fate by all the rules of war, but the Enghien affair became a *cause célèbre* and cleaved an irreparable breach between the Bonapartes and the Bourbons.

16. Adalbert de Bavière, p. 42.

17. Chastenay, p. 347.

18. Pauline, the sister most devoted to Napoléon, lost her first husband, General Leclerc, in November 1802. She married Prince Camille Borghese of the ancient Roman family on August 31, 1803, at Joseph Bonaparte's château of Mortefontaine. Elisa had married the Corsican officer Pascal-Felix Bacciochi in May 1797. Lucien was excluded because after his first wife, Christine Boyer, died in 1800, he remarried the widow Alexandrine Jouberthon instead of Napoléon's choice, the queen of Etruria. Jérôme had disqualified himself by marrying Betsy Patterson of Baltimore on December 1803. Although she was the daughter of a rich merchant, she was not of royal European blood and therefore unable to fulfill Napoléon's dynastic vision. As the emperor fumed about the marriage, however, the new city of Washington rejoiced. At a large reception held in the capital for leaders of the young republic, Aaron Burr remarked that he could put everything that Mme. Bonaparte wore into his vest pocket. The diaphanous dress that was now out of style in France was now all the rage in America.

19. *Lettres de Napoléon à Joséphine . . .* (hereafter LNJ), vol. II, p. 222.

20. Gérard Hubert, in Tulard 1989.

Chapter 7

1. Quoted by Chevallier 1989, pp. 133–34.

2. The Ossianic legend in both painting and music was doubtless an effort to provide a secular form of heavenly immortality for soldiers of the new imperial "republic."

3. The Invalides had been a Temple of Mars during the Revolution, but Napoléon restored it to Catholic worship. This ceremony began with a religious office celebrated by Cardinal Caprara and concluded with a *Te Deum*.

4. Quoted by Oman, p. 157.

5. d'Houville, p. 16.

6. Eugénie was the wife of Hortense's third son, Louis-Napoléon, who became Napoléon III. She presented the reliquary to the cathedral of Rheims after the war of 1914, an appropriate gesture since it was at Rheims where the kings of France were traditionally crowned. It is often, and erroneously, said that Napoléon took the emblem of the bee from the Barberini family.

7. Hortense's intimacy with Flahaut is accepted by almost every reliable historian despite the impression Hortense gives in her memoirs (Hanoteau 1927). His mother's first husband was Marshal Flahaut, who was nearly forty years her senior and was guillotined. In 1802, she married José-Maria de Souza, a Portuguese diplomat. It is believed by most historians, however, that Charles's real father was Talleyrand, although the British diplomat William Windham has also been suggested.

8. Roederer, p. 214.

9 Marie de Médicis had been anointed and crowned but was only a queen.

10. Knapton, p. 282.

11. Laure Junot reported that the *chérusque* (a tulle ruff with long points, embroidered with gold or silver) had already been introduced in Joséphine's salon at the Tuileries (p. 250).

12. Ibid., p. 264.

13. Hanoteau 1927, vol. I, p. 165.

14. There would later be many points of conflict between Napoléon and the pope, such as the latter's refusal to annul Jérôme's marriage to Betsy Patterson in 1805, the military occupation of Rome in 1808, the annexation of the pontifical estates to the Empire in 1809, and others.

15. Hanoteau 1927, vol. I, p. 199.

16. Junot, p. 264.

17. Quoted by Guerrini, p. 146.

CHAPTER 8

1. Canova owed much of his success to the Bonapartes. One his first important works was a statue of *Perseus with the Head of Medusa*, which was inspired by the Apollo Belvedere, an antique work Napoléon had brought to Paris from Italy. In 1801 Pope Pius VII bought Canova's Perseus and placed it on the Apollo's pedestal in the Vatican (it was subsequently returned). In 1802 Canova was commissioned to make a colossal nude portrait of Napoléon in marble (finished in 1806) in which the conqueror is shown as an ancient ruler dressed like a classical deity. And his elegant portrait of Napoléon's sister Pauline Borghese as a reclining Venus (1808) is an obvious precursor to Ingres's *Odalisque*.

2. Hanoteau 1927, vol. I, p. 206.

3. Adelbert de Bavière, p. 47.

4. After announcing Eugène's promotion, Napoléon added: "Among all the acts of our sovereignty there is none dearer to our heart. Brought up by us, and under our eyes since his childhood, he is worthy to imitate and—with the help of God—to one day surpass the examples and lessons we have given him.... Our paternal benediction will go with this young prince in all his career...." (Adelbert de Bavière, p. 47).

5. Napoléon once remarked to Roederer, his secretary of state, that his wife had only "diamonds and debts" (Adelbert de Bavière, p. 45).

6. Claire le Corbellier, in Le Bourhis, p. 133.

7. It is true that Joséphine died leaving debts of almost 3 million francs. However, when her assets were sold for 11 million and her debts paid, there still remained 8 million for Eugène and Hortense.

8. Kirstein, p. 14.

9. Boime, p. 25.

10. Quoted by Chevallier 1988, p. 307.

11. *Le Moniteur* announced with satisfaction that "the Italians combined what to the ancients was most spectacular and what to modern science was most daring, in the presence of a hero who surpasses both the ancients and the moderns." (Quoted in Imbert de Saint-Amand, p. 176).

12. Guerrini, p. 155.

13. When news of the victory at Austerlitz was received in December, Spontini was so carried away that he produced in 1806 the flattering cantata *L'Eccelsa gara*.

14. Bourgeat, p. 97.

15. Ibid., p. 105. Even during the hazardous campaign of Ulm, Napoléon had written faithfully to his wife, and he would write her three letters from the field during the coming terrible battle of Austerlitz, under unimaginable conditions.

16. The fame of the "sun of Austerlitz" was perpetuated in literature and films. It was reported that after Napoléon's body was being returned from St. Helena to Paris in 1840, the sun broke out as the funeral cortege passed under the Arc de Triomphe, causing veterans along the route to cry out "Vive le soleil d'Austerlitz!"

17. Bourgeat, p. 105.

18. Quoted by Oman, p. 194.

CHAPTER 9

1. Hanoteau 1936, p. 166.

2. Adelbert de Bavière, p. 73.

3. In her memoirs, Hortense wrote that foreign sovereigns all sought an alliance with the emperor, and even if the proposed spouse was only adopted by Napoléon, it was sufficient grounds for a marriage (Hanoteau 1927, vol. I, p. 235).

4. Quoted by Adelbert de Bavière, pp. 45–46.

5. The latter would be particularly appropriate since Joséphine had just received a generous gift of Prussian porcelain the summer before from Maximillian I's niece, the beautiful Queen Louise of Prussia (and Napoléon's avowed enemy). The following year, Queen Louise would again try to push her husband, the uncertain Frederick William III, into war against Napoléon, but such political tensions had no effect upon Louise's relationship with Joséphine, for the porcelain that Queen Louise sent to the empress of France was accompanied by a warm letter calling her "ma soeur," and Joséphine thoughtfully accorded it a place of honor in the salon of her conservatory.

6. Adelbert de Bavière, p. 76.

7. Ibid., p. 78.

8. Junot succeeded Murat, who gave up this post when the duc d'Enghien was executed.

9. Adelbert de Bavière, p. 84.

10. It was Lewis Goldsmith. See Jacques Jourquin in Tulard 1989, p. 1481.

11. Victor Richards, M.D. (Jones, p. 425).

12. Adelbert de Bavière, p. 87.

13. Ibid., p. 88.

14. Most of what strikes the attentive visitor was built by Napoléon in just a little over a decade, and John Russell reminds us that this grand scheme is composed of works that "impose from a distance; the unit of communication between them is not the conversational voice … but the bugle call and the far glint of a helmet" (Russell, p. 168), which is just what the emperor intended.

15. Fontaine added that the emperor overruled Josephine's order and told the architect to put them in the room used by the Institut in the Louvre, next to the gallery of Apollo (vol. I, p. l39).

16. Guerrini, p. l94.

17. Hanoteau 1927, vol. I, p. 253.

18. Napoléon wrote Eugène that he was to be commander in chief of the Army of Italy, his cherished dream for a long time, but it seemed that the Army of Italy might for the moment be only an army of observation.

19. Massin, p. 203. Napoléon was to accommodate the beautiful queen in two ways, for he would give her the spectacle of not one battle, but two.

20. Massin, p. 205.

21. Bourgeat, p. 112.

22. Ibid., pp. 125–26.

23. Jones, p. 213.

CHAPTER 10

1. Guerrini, p. 208.

2. *LNJ*, CXIII, dated March 35, 1833. She preferred the smaller, more informal theaters, but he discouraged her from attending, for he wanted her to be constantly on view.

3. Bourgeat, p. 128. The letter was dated January 23.

4. *LNJ*, XCIII.

5. Ibid., XCIV.

6. Ibid., XCV. Tascher was the second son of comte de Tascher, who enjoyed a high position as senator and chancellor under the Empire. The letter is dated February 9.

7. Ibid., XCVI.

8. Massin, p. 214. Napoléon was so upset over the suffering at Eylau that he would not even permit a *Te Deum* to be chanted for the victory.

9. Guerrini, p. 211.

10. Junot, p. 299.

11. Joséphine understood that Junot did everything in excess. He was so fanatically devoted to Napoléon that on one occasion, his enthusiasm led him into a duel in which he was almost killed. During the Russian campaign, however, his apathy probably prevented Napoléon from gaining a decisive victory at Valoutina; he was relieved on his command, became increasingly depressed and disoriented, and on July 29, 1813, at the age of forty-four, he died from injuries sustained when he hurled himself from a window.

12. Arjuzon, p. 89.

13. Junot, p. 307.

14. Tomiche, p. 168.

15. Bourgeat, p. 138. The letter is dated May 10, 1807.

16. Ibid., p. 145.

17. *LNJ*, CXV.

18. Adelbert de Bavière, p. 97.

19. Ibid.

20. Quoted by Fisher, p. 91.

21. *LNJ*, CXXVI.

22. Junot, p. 310.

23. *LNJ*, CXXXIX.

24. *LNJ*, Vol. II, XXVII.

25. *LNJ*, CXL.

26. Adelbert de Bavière, p. 99.

27. However much the nineteen-year-old Jérôme may have loved his first wife, Betsy Patterson, he was obliged to obey his brother, who had not allowed the marriage to be recognized in France. Because they were both minors at the time and because he had not given his permission to the marriage, Napoléon declared the marriage void, although the pope refused to sever the religious bond. Jérôme was recalled to France by Napoléon in April 1805, and Betsy reluctantly resigned herself to the annulment. The emperor offered to protect their son if she would send him to France, but Betsy declined and chose to rear the boy as a Bonaparte in Baltimore.

28. Junot, p. 346.

29. Hanoteau 1927, vol. I, p. 328.

30. Ibid., p. 310. Laure also mentions Hortense's unique collection of drawings and her numerous musical compositions.

31. Junot, p. 330.

32. Ibid., p. 331.

33. Ibid., p. 333.

34. Chevallier l988, p. 335.

35. Adelbert de Bavière, p. 101.

36. Guerrini, p. 239.

37. Quoted in Jones, p. 168.

38. Junot, p. 276.

CHAPTER 11

1. Junot, p. 335.

2. Cole, p. 87.

3. Fontaine, p. 328. The theater was not sufficiently heated, a problem that the architect struggled with for some time, for he did not want to spoil the pristine decor. Finally large stoves were installed, which made the theater more bearable.

4. Ibid., p. 187.

5. Kirchheisen, p. 421.

6. Jean-René Aymes in Tulard 1989, p. 808.

7. Herold 1963, p. 184.

8. Quoted by Chevallier 1988, p. 336.

9. Ibid.

10. Hanoteau 1927, vol. I, p. 341.

11. Jones, p. 255.

12. Hanoteau 1927, vol. II, p. 6.

13. Quoted in Jones, p. 257.

14. It is curious that Ferdinand, however undeservedly, had the support and confidence of the Spanish people. It may have been that they expected him to lead a resistance against the invaders.

15. Brinton, p. 146.

16. Hanoteau 1936, p. 53.

17. Tour du Pin, p. 327. Lucie was distantly related to Joséphine.

18. Ibid., p. 332.

19. Ibid., p. 333. Lucie de la Tour du Pin must be confused, however, about the dates they were in Bordeaux, for she indicated that it was before Joséphine's visit to Bayonne.

20. Fontaine, p. 214.

21. Jones, p. 168.

22. William Smith in Tulard 1989, p. 894.

23. Tour du Pin, p. 343.

24. Adelbert de Bavière, p. 105.

25. Jones, p. 257.

26. Hanoteau 1927, vol. II, p. 19.

27. Maurois, p. 99.

28. Quoted by Chevallier 1988, p. 337.

29. Wilson-Smith, p. 262.

30. Guerrini, p. 269.

31. Hanoteau 1927, vol. II, p. 22.

32. *LNJ*, CLV.

33. Ibid., CLVIII.

34. Fontaine, p. 218.

35. *LNJ*, CLXIV.

CHAPTER 12

1. The other two were Antoine Thibaudeau and Regnault de Saint-Jean d'Angély.

2. Hanoteau 1927, vol. II, p. 32.

3. *LNJ*, CIX.

4. Quoted in Cole, p. 111.

5. Hanoteau 1936, p. 58.

6. Quoted by Guerrini, p. 276. Bausset's *Mémoires* appeared in 1827–29 and in some respects should be used with prudence, according to Jean Tulard.

7. Fontaine, p. 222.

8. Massin, p. 243. Massin agrees with Felix Markham (p. 310) that Talleyrand had taken this stance, but Crane Brinton does not (p. 147).

9. Napoléon reportedly said to Talleyrand: "Vous êtes de la merde dans un bas de soie!" (You are excrement in a silk stocking!)

10. Cited by Guerrini, p. 278.

11. Hanoteau l936, p. 59.

12. Caulaincourt, p. 338.

13. Adelbert de Bavière, p. 106.

14. Hanoteau l936, p. 62.

15. According to Hortense's letter of April 30 (Hanoteau 1927, vol. II, p. 234).

16. Hanoteau 1936, p. 64.

17. *LNJ*, CLXVI.

18. Jones, p. 267.

19. Hanoteau 1936, p. 66. The comte de Lavalette was one of Joséphine's principal sources of information. He was

director of the postal service, which he put at the disposal of Napoléon and his family, as evidenced by Joséphine's letter. Lavalette was married to Joséphine's niece, Émilie de Beauharnais, mistress of Joséphine's wardrobe. Sometimes Napoléon would dispatch an officer directly to his wife, as he did May 12, when he wrote her from Schönbrunn that he was sending the duchess of Montebello's brother to tell her he was master of Vienna (*LNJ*, CLXVIII).

20. Adelbert de Bavière, p. 111.

21. *LNJ*, CLXIX.

22. Hanoteau 1927, vol. II, pp. 32–37.

23. Ibid., p. 40.

24. Caulaincourt, p. 355.

25. *LNJ*, CLXXIV.

26. Massin, p. 250.

27. Jacques Garnier in Tulard 1989, p. 1739.

28. Eugène said that he and Duroc dined on July 27 with Bessières, who must have recovered sufficiently to come to Vienna. Brown, however, states that he was not in Vienna on August 15, having been sent to Paris to rest and recover (p. 167).

29. *LNJ*, CLXXXV.

30. Constant, quoted in Jones, pp. 279–80.

31. Kircheisen, p. 494.

32. Hanoteau 1927, vol. II, p. 43.

33. Ibid., p. 45.

34. Ibid., p. 50.

35. Sergeant, pp. 506–7. Several accounts of this scene exist, but Sergeant's seems most authentic, being based upon Masson. For Constant's version, see Jones, pp. 280–8l. For Bausset's see his *Memoires*, vol. II, pp. 2–8.

36. Adelbert de Bavière, p. 130.

37. Sergeant, p. 282.

38. Ibid.

39. Guerrini, p. 292.

40. Constant, quoted by Jones, p. 282.

41. Guerrini, pp. 293–95.

42. Constant erroneously gave it as December 16. Jones, p. 284.

43. Sergeant, p. 517.

44. Masson 1900, p. 80.

45. Jones, p. 285.

46. Quoted in Hanoteau 1927, vol. II, p. 56.

47. *LNJ*, CXC, p. 105.

48. Ibid., CXCV, p. 116.

49. Quoted by Oman, pp. 306–7. Although there are some exaggerations (the importance of her family), one may accept the description of the court since it is corroborated by other witnesses, and the passages concerning the clothing worn by people in court circles are invaluable.

50. Quoted by Sergeant, p. 642.

CHAPTER 13

1. *LNJ*, CC, p. 125. Sèvres had become the Imperial Manufactory in 1804. The extra 100,000 francs for Malmaison may have been for operating expenses, but on January 23, 1810, Joséphine added two canvases by Isaac Van Ostade to her collection, likely *The Rustic Interior* and *The Postman Stopping Before an Inn*.

2. Sergeant, vol. II, p. 529.

3. One was Archduke Ferdinand, one of the emperor's five brothers. Joséphine had also helped bring about the Peace of Campo Fornio between Emperor Francis II (later Francis I) and Bonaparte in 1797, for which Francis had sent her a splendid team of horses from the imperial stables.

4. Sergeant, vol. II, p. 531. She must have taken up residence on February 3, according to the king of Bavaria's letter to his son, which read: "The Empress Joséphine leaves Malmaison today for her new palace, the Elysée, and Eugène is living there with her" (Adelbert de Bavière, p. 136). Eugène returned briefly to Milan on February 28 and returned in mid-March, bringing Auguste with him.

5. Quoted by Mansel, p. 121.

6. Adelbert de Bavière, p. 134.

7. Letter dated November 19, 1810 (Hanoteau 1936, pp. 80–81).

8. While Eugène was in Paris, his friend Marshal Duroc brought him a marvelous offer from the emperor, that he become the prince presumptive of Sweden, for Gustav IV had been deposed and banished. Eugène refused, for he had not yet given up hopes of retaining something in Italy. Later, Bernadotte accepted the position. This meant that Eugène would eventually rule not only the territory of Frankfurt but also the adjoining principalities, a total of 300,000 inhabitants. Karl Theodor von Dalberg abdicated his position in 1813 in favor of Eugène.

9. Adelbert de Bavière, p. 136.

10. Schwarzenberg was one of Napoléon's few rivals in the art of warfare. He would assume supreme command of the allied armies that France would have to face in 1814.

11. Sergeant, vol. II, p. 544. Of course, she had not yet seen it during those months, but the inhabitants apparently told her that these were the best for the gardens.

12. Tour du Pin, p. 365. By "policy" she meant that Louis let in English contraband goods for the welfare of his Dutch subjects, thus incurring Napoléon's wrath.

13. *LNJ*, XLI, pp. 315-17.

14. *LNJ*, CCXVIII, p. 18.

15. Hanoteau 1927, vol. II, p. 94. Jacques Jourquin, in Tulard 1989, p. 736, states that Flahaut and Hortense met in June 1810 in Plombières, but we have chosen to believe Hortense on this point.

16. Ibid., p. 98.

17. Ibid.

18. Tour du Pin, p. 357.

19. Boigne, p. 246.

20. Hanoteau 1927, vol. II, pp. 96-97.

21. Brinton, pp. 27-28.

22. Josephine's letter dated November 19, 1810 (Hanoteau 1936, pp. 80-82).

23. Ibid., p. 554.

24. Chevallier 1988, p. 367.

25. Adelbert de Bavière, p. 151.

26. Kircheisen, p. 552.

27. Malmaison, p. 20.

28. *LNJ*, L, pp. 345-47.

29. Hanoteau 1927, vol. II, p. 119.

30. Duc Louis de La Rochefoucauld had been Alexandre de Beauharnais's patron, and the old comtesse de La Rochefoucauld, we recall, was Joséphine's principal lady-of-honor.

31. Sergeant, vol. II, p. 578.

32. Hanoteau 1927, vol. II, p. 131. Joséphine even wanted a portrait of the child, so she engaged Mme. Thibault to have a copy made of one in the emperor's possession.

33. Adelbert de Bavière, p. 156.

34. Quoted by Guerrini, p. 360.

35. Ibid.

36. Eugène's plans changed, and he was able to see her after all.

37. Hanoteau 1936, pp. 100-1.

38. Ibid.

39. Quoted in Jones, p. 345.

40. Hanoteau 1927, vol. II, p. 149.

41. Bourgeat, p. 215.

42. *LNJ*, LI, pp. 348-58.

43. Ibid., LIII, pp. 354-58.

44. *LNJ*, LIX, p. 370.

45. Hanoteau 1936, p. 110.

46. Kircheisen, p. 576.

47. Quoted in Adelbert de Bavière, p. 172.

48. *LNJ*, L, p. 342.

49. Flauhaut especially singled out Eugène's performance, and Mme. de Souza certainly shared her son's letter with her friend Joséphine, who would have passed it along to Hortense. She knew that her daughter was as anxious for news of Charles de Flahaut as she was for the latest tidings of her brother and the emperor.

50. Hanoteau 1936, p. 113.

51. Guerrini, pp. 381-82.

52. Adelbert de Bavière, p. 174.

53. Ney had to sacrifice his artillery, spending the night on thin ice, so he asked Eugène's help. Although in danger himself, the viceroy returned immediately. In order to deceive the enemy about the strength of his forces, he had fires lighted at different points and fired cannons to indicate the direction to his comrades. After three days between life and death, Ney and Eugène were reunited. Everyone had given up Ney for lost, but he reappeared with 1,500 utterly spent men. Eugène had saved them.

54. Hanoteau 1927, vol. II, p. 151.

55. Ibid., p. 159.

56. Ibid.

Chapter 14

1. Sergeant, vol. II, p. 587.

2. Ibid., pp. 588-89.

3. Chastenay, p. 404.

4. Hanoteau 1927, vol. II, p. 162.

5. *LNJ*, LXL, pp. 374-76.

6. Hanoteau 1936, pp. 115-16.

7. *LNJ*, LXII, pp. 377-79.

8. Ibid., pp. 385-87.

9. Chevallier 1988, p. 403.

10. *LNJ*, LXVII, pp. 388-90.

11. Jones, p. 406.

12. *LNJ*, pp. 391–92.

13. Jones, p. 400.

14. Adelbert de Bavière, p. 204; du Casse, vol. IX, pp. 200–206.

15. Sergeant, p. 594.

16. *LNJ*, pp. 393–94.

17. Hanoteau 1927, vol. II, p. 185.

18. Oudinot, p. 255.

19. *LNJ*, LXIX, pp. 395–96.

20. Sergeant, p. 601.

21. Stanley, p. 139.

22. Junot, p. 378.

23. Tour du Pin, pp. 391–92.

24. Hanoteau 1927, vol. II, p. 200.

25. Hanoteau 1936, pp. 118–19.

26. Caulaincourt, pp. 243–44.

27. Masson 1920, p. 317.

28. Chevallier 1988, p. 419.

29. Ibid.

30. Kircheisen, p. 495.

31. Adelbert de Bavière, p. 236.

32. Hanoteau 1927, vol. II, p. 227.

33. Ibid., p. 232.

34. Ibid., p. 230.

35. Oudinot, pp. 269–71.

36. Hanoteau 1927, vol. II, p. 249.

37. Adelbert de Bavière, p. 237.

38. Chevallier 1996.

39. Stanley, pp. 130–31.

40. Masson 1920, p. 371.

41. Hanoteau 1927, vol. II, p. 358.

42. Ibid.

BIBLIOGRAPHY

Adelbert de Bavière. *Eugène de Beauharnais, Beau-fils de Napoléon*. Paris, n.d. For English translation, see Oman, Carola.

Archives Nationales. *Napoléon, Tel qu'en lui-même*. Exh. cat. Paris, 1969.

Aubenas, Joseph. *Histoire de l'impératrice Joséphine*. 2 vols. Paris, 1857.

Baillio, Joseph. "Jean-Baptiste Isabey (1767-1855), Chroniqueur de la Naissance du Roi de Rome," *L'Oeil* (June 1995), pp. 38-45.

Barret, André. *Sautecoeur*. Paris, 1998.

Bausset, Louis. *Mémoires anecdotiques sur l'intérieur du Palais et sur quelques événements de l'Empire depuis 1805 jusqu'au 1er mai 1814 pour servir à l'histoire de Napoléon*. Paris, 1827-29.

Bechtel, Edwin De Turck. *Our Rose Varieties and their Malmaison Heritage*. New York, 1949.

Bennett, Anne, trans. *Roses for an Empress: Joséphine and Redouté*. Milan, 1983.

Billington, James H. *The Icon and the Axe: an Interpretive History of Russian Culture*. New York, 1966.

Bogaert-Damin, Anne-Marie. *Images de Jardins du XVI au XX Siècle*. Namur, Belgium, 1996.

Boigne, comtesse de. *Mémoires de la Comtesse de Boigne*. New York, 1907.

Boime, Albert. *Art in an Age of Bonapartism: 1800—1815*. Chicago, 1990.

Botanical Library, Carnegie Institute of Technology. *A Catalogue of Redouteana*. Exh. cat. Pittsburgh, Pa., 1963.

Bourgeat, Jacques. *Napoléon: Lettres à Joséphine*. Paris, 1941.

Brier, *Napoléon in Egypt*. Brooksville, New York, 1990.

Brinton, Crane. *Lives of Talleyrand*. New York, 1936.

Brookner, Anita. "Prud'hon: Master Decorator of the Empire," *Apollo* (September 1964), pp. 192-95.

Brown, Anne S. K., adaption from the French of Henry Lachouque, *Anatomy of Glory. Napoleon and his Guard*. Providence, R.I., 1962.

Carlson, Victor I. and John W. Ittman, *Regency to Empire: French Printmaking 1715–1814*. Exhibition, Baltimore Museum of Art, c. 1984.

Caulaincourt, Armand-Augustin, marquis de, duc de Vicence. *No Peace with Napoléon!* New York, 1936.

Chastenay, Madame de. *Mémoires de Madame de Chastenay*. Paris, n.d.

Chevallier, Bernard. *l'Impératrice Joséphine*. Paris, 1988.

—. *Malmaison: Château et Domaine des Origines à 1904*. Paris, 1989.

—. *Napoléon*. Exh. cat. Memphis, Tennese, 1993.

—. *Impératrice Joséphine, Correspondance, 1782–1814*. Annotations by Bernard Chevallier, Maurice Catinat, and Christophe Pincemaille. Paris, 1996.

—. *Les Sèvres de Fontainebleau*. Paris, 1996.

—. *L'Art de Vivre au temps de Joséphine*. Paris, 1998.

Clement, Charles. *Prud'hon*. Paris 1872.

Cohen, Sarah R. *Art, Dance and the Body in the French Culture of the Ancien Régime*. New York, 2000.

Cole, Hubert. *The Betrayers: Joaquim and Caroline Murat*. New York, 1972.

Council of Europe, *The Age of Neo-Classicism*. Exh. cat. London, 1972.

Crick, Clare. "Wallpapers by Dufour et Cie," *Connoisseur* (December 1976), pp. 310-16.

Crow, Thomas E. *Painters and Public Life in Eighteenth-Century Paris*. New Haven, 1985.

—. *Emulation*. New Haven, c. 1995.

Currie, Laurence. *The Baton in the Knapsack*. London, 1934.

Dard, Emilie. *Napoléon et Talleyrand*. Paris, 1935.

Delacroix, Eugène. *Journal de Eugène Delacroix.* André Joubin, ed. 3 vols. Paris, 1932.

Delécluze, E. J. *Louis David: Son école et son temps: souvenirs de M. E. J. Delécluze.* Paris, 1855.

DeLorme, Eleanor. *Garden Pavilions at the Eighteenth-Century French Court* Woodbridge, England, 1996.

Demoriane, Hélène. "Splendeur Retrouvée à l'Hôtel de Beauharnais," *Connaissance des Arts* (June 1968), pp. 72-79.

Dowd, David Lloyd. *Pageant-Master of the Republic: Jacques-Louis David and the French Revolution.* Lincoln, Neb., 1948.

du Casse, A., ed. *Mémoires et correspondance politique et militaire du prince Eugène.* 10 vols. Paris, 1858-60.

Duval, Marguerite. *The King's Garden.* Charlottesville, Va., 1982.

Escholier, Raymond. *Gros.* Paris, 1936.

Fisher, H. A. L., *Bonapartism.* Oxford, 1914.

Fontaine, Pierre-François Léonard. *Journal, 1799– 1853.* Paris, 1986.

French Painting 1774–1830: The Age of Revolution. Exh. cat. Paris, Detroit, New York, 1974-75.

Godechot, Jacques. *Napoléon.* Paris, 1969.

Gosuderstvennyi, Ermitzh. *Western European Paintings in the Hermitage.* New York, 1978.

Grandjean, Serge. *Inventaire après le decès de l'Imperatrice Joséphine.* Paris, 1964.

—. "Le service de l'Empereur." *Art de France* 11 (Paris, 1962), p. 70.

—. "Trois Objets en Tôle," *Revue du Louvre* (1977), pp. 322-31.

Greer, Walter. *Napoléon and Joséphine.* New York, 1924.

Guerrini, Maurice. *Napoléon et Paris.* Paris, 1967.

Guth, Paul. *L'Impératrice Joséphine.* Paris, 1979.

Hanoteau, Jean, ed. *Mémoires de la Reine Hortense.* 2 vols. Paris, 1927.

—. *Le Ménage Beauharnais: Joséphine avant Napoléon.* Paris, 1935.

Hanoteau, Jean, ed. *Les Beauharnais et l'Empereur. Lettres de l'Impératrice Joséphine et de la Reine Hortense au Prince Eugène.* Paris, 1936.

Hardouin-Fugier, Elisabeth. *French Flower Painters of the Nineteenth Century.* London, 1989.

Harris, Ann Sutherland. *Women Artists, 1550—1950.* New York, 1976.

Herold, J. Christopher. *The Age of Napoléon.* New York, 1963.

—. *Mistress to an Age.* New York, 1958.

Hillairet, Jacques. *Dictionnaire des rues historiques de Paris.* 2 vols. Paris, c. 1985.

Holtman, Robert B. *The Napoleonic Revolution.* Philadelphia, 1967.

Horne, Alistair. *How Far From Austerlitz?* New York, 1996.

Houville, Gerard d'. *La Vie amoureuse de l'impératrice Joséphine.* Paris, c. 1925.

Hubert, Gerard. *Napoléon.* Paris, 1999.

Humbert, Jean-Michael. *Egyptomania.* Exh. cat. Paris, Ottawa, 1994.

Imbert de Saint-Amand, Arthur Leon, baron. *Citizeness Bonaparte.* New York, 1897.

Irwin, David G. *Neoclassicism.* London, 1997.

Jabarti. *Napoléon in Egypt.* New York, 1993.

Janssens, Jacques. *Joséphine de Beauharnais et son Temps.* Paris, 1963.

Johns, Christopher M. S. *Canova and the Politics of Patronage in Revolutionary and Napoléonic Europe.* Berkeley, Calif., 1998.

Jones, Proctor Patterson, ed. *Napoleon: An Intimate Account of the Years of Supremacy (1800–1814).* Based on the journals of Claude-François de Méneval (1778-1850) and Constant Wairy (1778-1845). San Francisco, 1992.

Jouanin, Christian. "Joséphine and the Natural Sciences," *Apollo* (July–September 1977), pp. 50-59.

Junot, Laure, duchesse d'Abrantès. *At the Court of Napoleon. Memoires of the Duchesse d'Abrantès.* New York, 1989.

Kircheisen, F. M. *Napoleon.* New York, 1932.

Kirstein, Lincoln. "The Taste of Napoléon," *Nelson Gallery Bulletin* 9-12 (1969-70).

Knapton, Ernest. *Empress Josephine.* Cambridge, Mass.: 1963.

Laborde, Alexandre de. *Nouveaux Jardins de la France et ses Anciens Châteaux.* Paris, 1808.

Laing, Margaret. *Joséphine and Napoléon.* New York, 1973.

Laveissière, Sylvain. *Pierre-Paul Prud'hon.* New York, 1998.

Le Bourhis, Katell, ed. *The Age of Napoléon: Costume from Revolution to Empire, 1789–1815.* Exh. cat. New York, 1989.

Ledoux-Lebard, Denise. "The Furnishing of the Tuileries under the Consulate," *Apollo* (September 1964), pp. 199-205.

—."Les Vases de Mars et de Minerve," *Gazette des Beaux-Arts* (January 1974), pp. 49–52.

—."Joséphine and Interior Decoration." *Apollo* (July-September 1977), pp. 16–24.

—."La campagne de 1805 vue par la Manufacture impériale de Sèvres," *Revue du Louvre et des Musées de France* 3 (1978), pp. 178–85.

Lettres de Napoléon à Joséphine . . . et lettres de Joséphine à Napoléon et à sa fille. 2 vols. Paris, 1833.

Lévi-Strauss, Monique. *The Cashmere Shawl.* New York, 1988.

Licht, Fred. *Canova.* New York, 1983.

Lindsay, Jack. *Death of the Hero: French Painting from David to Delacroix.* London, 1960.

Malmaison, *Eugène de Beauharnais, honneur et fidelité.* Exh. cat. Paris, 2000.

Mansel, Philip. *The Eagle in Splendour.* London, 1987.

Markham, Felix. *Napoléon.* New York, c. 1963.

Massin, Jean. *Almanach du Premier Empire du Neuf Thermidor à Waterloo.* Paris, 1965.

Masson, Frédéric. *Souvenirs et mémoires, recueil mensuel de documents . . .* Paris, 1898–99.

—. *Madame Bonaparte, 1763–1804.* Paris, 1920.

—. *Joséphine Repudiée, 1809–1814.* Paris, 1900.

Mauguin, G. *L'Imperatrice Joséphine: anecdotes et curiosités.* Paris, 1954.

Maurois, Andre. *Napoléon.* New York, c. 1963.

Moulin, Jean-Marie. *Le Château de Compiègne.* Paris, 1987.

Nicoullaud, M. Charles, ed. *Memoirs of the comtesse de Boigne (1781–1814).* 3 vols. New York, 1907.

Nora, Pierre, ed. *Lieux de Mémoire.* 3 vols. Paris, 1992.

Oman, Carola. *Napoleon's Viceroy: Eugène de Beauharnais.* Imprecise translation of Adelbert de Bavière, *Eugène de Beauharnais.* New York, c. 1966.

Oppenheimer, Margaret A. "Four Davids, a Regnault, and a 'Girodet' Reattributed." *Apollo* (June 1997), pp. 38–44.

Ostergard, Derek E., ed. *Sèvres Porcelain Manufactory: Alexandre Brongniart and the Triumph of Art and Industry, 1800–1847.* New Haven, 1997.

Oudinot, Eugénie de Courcy, duchesse de Reggio. *Memoirs of Marshal Oudinot, duc de Reggio.* Gaston Stiegler, ed. Alexander Teixeira de Mattos, trans. London, 1896.

Palmer, Alan. *An Encyclopaedia of Napoleon's Europe.* New York, 1984.

Peltre, Christine. *Les Orientalistes.* Paris, c. 1997.

Pincemaille, Christophe. *Il y a 200 ans, Joséphine achetait Malmaison.* Malmaison, 1999.

Prendergast, Christopher. *Napoléon and History Painting.* Oxford, 1997.

Quynn, Dorothy Mackay. "The Art Confiscations of the Napoléonic Wars," *American Historical Review* 50, no. 3 (April, 1945).

La Reine Hortense, Une Femme Artiste. Exh. cat. Malmaison, 1993.

Réunion des Musées Nationaux, *David.* Exh. cat. Paris, 1989.

—. *Les Etrusques et l'Europe.* Exh. cat. Paris, 1992.

Ribeiro, Aileen. *Ingres in Fashion.* New Haven, 1999.

Robriquet, Jean. *La Vie Quotidienne: Au Temps de Napoléon.* Paris, 1942.

Roederer, P. L. *Journal.* Paris, 1909.

Russell, John. *Paris.* New York, 1983.

Samoyault, Jean-Pierre. "Les remplois de sculptures et d'objets d'art dans la décoration et l'ameublement du palais de Saint-Cloud sous le Consulat et au debut de l'Empire," *Bulletin de la Société de l'histoire de l'art français* (1971), pp. 153–91.

—. "Furniture and objects designed by Percier for the château of Saint Cloud." *Burlington Magazine* (1975), pp. 457–65.

—. "Chefs-d'oeuvre en tôle vernie de l'époque consulaire et impériale (1801–1806)," *Revue du Louvre* (1977), pp. 322–33.

—. *Musée national du château de Fontainebleau: Catalogue des collection de mobilier, vol. I: Pendules et bronzes d'ameublement entres sous le Premier Empire.* Paris, 1989.

Sergeant, Philip W. *The Empress Josephine,* vol. II. New York, 1909.

Seton-Watson, Hugh. *The Russian Empire 1801–1917.* Oxford, 1967.

Sollers, Philippe. *Le Cavalier du Louvre (Vivant Denon).* Paris, 1997.

Stanley, Edward, Bishop of Norwich. *Before and After Waterloo.* New York, 1908.

Sutton, Denys. "A Palace for a Paragon: The Hôtel de Beauharnais," *Apollo* (June 1976), pp. 502–7.

Taigny, Edmond. *Jean-Baptiste Isabey.* Paris, 1859.

Tarle, Eugene. *Bonaparte.* John Cournos, trans. New York, 1937.

Tascher, Maurice de. *Journal de Campagne d'un Cousin de l'Impératrice (1806–1813).* Paris, 1933.

Tomiche, N. *Napoléon Ecrivain.* Paris, 1952.

Tour du Pin, la marquise de la (Henriette-Lucie Dillon). *Recollections of the Revolution and the Empire.* Walter Geer, trans. and ed. New York, 1920.

Tscherny, Nadia and Guy Stair Sainty. *Romance and Chivalry.* Hong Kong, 1996.

Tulard, Jean. *Nouvelle Histoire de Paris, le Consulat et l'Empire.* Paris, 1970.

Tulard, Jean, ed. *Dictionnaire Napoléon.* Paris, 1989.

Veyrier, Henri. *Le Grand dictionnaire de Cuisine.* Torino, 1978.

West, Alison. *From Pigalle to Préault.* New York, 1998.

Wildenstein and Co. *Catalogue of the Exhibition of Italian Nineteenth-Century Paintings.* New York, 1949.

Wilson-Smith, Timothy. *Napoléon and His Artists.* London, 1996.

Wright, Constance. *Hortense de Beauharnais.* Paris, 1961.

INDEX

Page numbers in italics refer to illustrations.
Endnotes in parentheses refer to chapter and note number, respectively.

PHOTO CREDITS